"There Are No Slaves in France"

"There Are No Slaves in France"

*The Political Culture of Race and Slavery
in the Ancien Régime*

SUE PEABODY

OXFORD
UNIVERSITY PRESS

OXFORD
UNIVERSITY PRESS

Oxford   New York
Auckland   Bangkok   Buenos Aires   Cape Town   Chennai
Dar es Salaam   Delhi   Hong Kong   Istanbul   Harachi   Kolkata
Kuala Lumpur   Madrid   Melbourne   Mexico City   Mumbai   Nairobi
São Paulo   Shanghai   Singapore   Taipei   Tokyo   Toronto

Copyright © 1996 by Oxford University Press, Inc.

Published by Oxford University Press, Inc.
198 Madison Avenue, New York, New York 10016

www.oup.com

First issued as an Oxford University Press paperback, 2002

Oxford is a registered trademark of Oxford University Press

Library of Congress Cataloging-in-Publication Data
Peabody, Sue.
"There are no slaves in France" : the political culture of race and slavery in the Ancien Régime
/ Sue Peabody
p. cm.
Includes bibliographical references and index.
ISBN 0-19 510198-7; 0-19-515866-0 (pbk.)
1. France—Race relations—History—18th century.   2. Racism—France—History—18th century.
3. Blacks—Legal status, laws, etc.—France—History—18th century.   4. Political culture—France—
History—18th century.   I. Title.
DC133.4.P43   1996
305.896'044'09033—dc20   95–39056

9 8 7 6 5 4 3 2

Printed in the United States of America
on acid-free paper

To Scott

Contents

Acknowledgments

I am grateful to the American Historical Association, the Stanley Foundation, the University of Iowa Department of History, and the University of Iowa Student Association, all of which generously helped to fund research for this project. Program committees of the Society for French Historical Studies, American Historical Association, and the French Colonial Historical Society gave me a forum to explore early versions of this work. I am grateful to Peter Iverson for permission to include material that was originally presented in an earlier form in the pages of *The Historian*. Chris Africa, Philip Boucher, Jeff Cox, Richard Hewitt, Paul Greenough, Claire Moses, and Rebecca Rogers all offered valuable criticisms of early drafts. I am particularly grateful to Sarah Hanley for her support and encouragement as I prepared my thesis on the Freedom Principle. I also want to thank Seymour Drescher, whose careful and insightful reading of the manuscript dramatically strenghthened its final argument. Pierre Boulle has been the very essence of generosity and collegiality as he shared with me documents and insights pertaining to the topic. Michel Antoine guided me to some important documents in the Archives Nationales and the Bibliothèque Nationale. David Avrom Bell also provided me with informaton on Parisian lawyers that would have been extremely difficult to locate without his expertise. Elaine Kruse opened her home and her kitchen to me in Paris during crucial stages of the research. I am also grateful to Bernard Barbiche, Robert Forster, John Garrigus, Albert Hamscher, Kathleen Higgins, Shanti

Marie Singham, Bailey Stone, and Dale Van Kley, all of whom helped me to journey through the daunting mazes of French legal and colonial history. David Wills and Albert Raboteau, editors of *Afro-American Religion: A Documentary History,* were especially generous in supporting my post-doctoral research on the religion of slaves in French Colonies as I brought this volume to press. My editor, Nancy Lane, and the rest of the staff at Oxford University Press are to be commended for bringing the book out quickly and ably. Needless to say, any errors or inconsistancies in the work are entirely my own.

Many others helped me to think this project through and supported me in ways too numerous to mention. I want especially to acknowledge Martina Kemphausen and Ruth Dickens, who assisted me in the Archives Nationales, and Donna Wahlgren, who helped prepare the index. Thanks, too, to Richard Hewitt, whose initial enthusiasm persuaded me that this was a topic worth pursuing. Last, but certainly not least, I wish to thank Scott Hewitt for editorial insight, boundless good humor, patience, and crucial support in all things earthly and intangible.

"There Are No Slaves in France"

Introduction

"There are no slaves in France." This maxim is such a potent element of French national ideology that on a recent trip to Paris to do research on "French slaves" I was informed by the indignant owner of a boarding house that I must be mistaken because slavery had never existed in France. The maxim is a very old one, thriving at least two hundred years before the phrase "Liberté, egalité, fraternité" echoed in the streets of Paris.

In this work I set out to discover the origins, manifestations, and consequences of France's "Freedom Principle"—the notion that any slave who sets foot on French soil becomes free—during a period when France was, on one hand, becoming thoroughly entangled in the Atlantic slave system and, on the other, developing a radical new political discourse based on notions of freedom, equality, and citizenship. By the late 1780s, France's Caribbean colonies produced more than two-fifths of the Western world's sugar and coffee, and the French government was increasingly dependent on colonial commerce as a source of revenue. The tension between France's economic dependence on colonial slavery and its celebration of liberty is manifest in hundreds of court cases in which slaves who were brought to France as servants by their colonial masters sought to escape slavery in the final century of the Ancien Régime. On the basis of the Freedom Principle, nearly all of them obtained their freedom, particularly in the jurisdiction of the Parlement of Paris.

Exactly how many blacks, free or enslaved, resided in France at this time is difficult to know with certainty.[1] One lawyer estimated the number at 4,000 in 1738.[2] Modern historians have not improved much on this figure. Shelby McCloy noted that eighteenth-century police put the number at 5,000 but calls this figure "preposterous" based on a 1777–1778 census that counted no more than 1,000 blacks in all of France.[3] Pierre Boulle, using the same census records, has counted 765 blacks in Paris alone from 1777 to 1790 but has not yet published his conclusions on the nationwide black population.[4] Meanwhile, Léo Elisabeth, using the Admiralty records of Bordeaux, counted 3,242 slaves and 358 free people of color passing through that city over the course of the eighteenth century.[5] It seems, then, that an upper limit of 4,000 to 5,000 is the highest acceptable figure if we take into account the fact that blacks were constantly entering and leaving the realm throughout the century. Until a thorough study of French Admiralty records and of the census generated by the *Police des Noirs* is complete, the exact quantification of French blacks will remain elusive. It is nevertheless apparent that France's black population was disproportionately small compared to that of England, estimated by contemporaries to be between 3,000 and 30,000 with the figure of 10,000 generally accepted by most historians.[6] The total population of England at mid-century was about nine million compared with approximately twenty million in France. Hence, blacks comprised no more than .025 percent of the French population compared with .11 percent in England.

Yet although there were relatively few blacks in France, their symbolic presence loomed large—both for eighteenth-century French administrators and for our present understanding of the origins of modern notions of freedom and race in the larger Atlantic world. The presence of black slaves in northern Europe provoked an ideological crisis that has had repercussions to the present day. It is therefore important to examine the situation in a comparative context. France, for instance, was by no means the only nation to develop a version of the Freedom Principle, whereby slaves attained their freedom upon entering a free territory. Although slavery had been commonplace on the Iberian peninsula since the Muslim Conquest and the subsequent Reconquista, English popular and legal culture celebrated the idea that "England was too pure an Air for Slaves to breathe in."[7] Lawyers for the American slave Dred Scott made a similar argument, arguing that Scott had won his freedom by setting foot in the free territories of Illinois and Missouri. A similar principle seems to have been a part of Dutch culture since the sixteenth century, although abrogated by legislation in 1776.[8]

There are important differences, however, between the invocation of the Freedom Principle in the American context and those of England and France. The American case is considerably more complex, involving a much larger enslaved population, more constant and immediate intercourse between slave and free territories, and questions of federalism versus state's sovereignty. In 1857 the U.S. Supreme Court negated the validity of the Freedom Principle when it ruled that Dred Scott, as a slave not a citizen, had no right to bring suit. Slavery, the balance of economic and political power between North and South, and related crises would ultimately lead the United States into its bloodiest war.

The French, Dutch, and English invocations of the Freedom Principle have more in common. None of these countries had agricultural slavery within its borders, yet each entered the slave trade at about the same time to supply labor to new American colonies. All came to depend on the sugar, cotton, cocoa, coffee, indigo, and other tropical products produced by slave labor. And, in the case of England and France, both were developing liberal political discourses that celebrated the notion that their nation bore a special relationship to the principle of liberty.

One important difference between France and England was the French courts' unwavering commitment to the Freedom Principle from as early as 1571. The Parlement of Paris, whose jurisdiction comprised one-third of the realm, and its appellate Admiralty courts consistently ruled in favor of blacks seeking their freedom right up until the Revolution. By contrast, English courts wavered in their application of the Freedom Principle, avoiding a definitive ruling on slaves who entered the realm until Lord Mansfield's celebrated 1772 decision in the Somerset case.[9] Further research remains to be done on the status of black slaves in the Dutch courts.

The most striking difference between the continental and the English cases, however, is the advent of French, and later Dutch, legislation on the status of slaves who entered the kingdom as compared with England's complete absence of positive law on slavery. Indeed, an English judge writing in the early eighteenth century noted that "the law takes no notice of the Negro [slave]."[10] This would remain true until the slave trade was abolished by Parliament in 1808. Instead, English judges ruling over the status of slaves in the metropole made piecemeal and often contradictory decisions, leaving slaves and their masters to rely on guile, force, and community networks to resolve disputes among them.[11] Judge Mansfield lamented the lack of positive law that made his decision so difficult in 1772.[12]

The situation in France was quite different.[13] As more and more slaveowners began to travel to France with their enslaved domestic servants in the late seventeenth century, the king, through his minister of the marine, was called upon to set policy regarding slaves who reached French shores. Louis XIV's first response was to uphold the Freedom Principle by fiat, granting freedom to individual slaves who petitioned for the recognition of their new free status upon arrival in France. By the early eighteenth century, however, French provincial courts, notably that of Nantes, were demanding legislation that would unambiguously resolve the status of slaves in France. The result was the royal Edict of October 1716 that stated that colonial property owners and military officers could temporarily bring their slaves to France to learn a trade or to receive instruction in the Catholic faith without fear of losing their property rights under the condition that they gain permission from colonial governor before departure and that they register the slaves with the clerk of the Admiralty upon arrival in France. If an owner should fail to meet the requirements of the law, however, the slaves would be recognized as free, thus preserving the Freedom Principle as a kind of default status. Later royal legislation undermined the Freedom Principle in an effort to restrict the flow of blacks entering France. The Declaration of December 15, 1738, reiterated the provisions of the 1716 edict requiring colonial governor's permission and registration with French admiralty clerks. In addition, it set a limit of three years on the slaves' stay in France and, more important, stipulated that slaves held in violation of these conditions would no longer be freed to live in France, but confiscated in the name of the king and returned to the colonies.

The Declaration of 1738 would seem to have abrogated the Freedom Principle in its entirety. However, neither the 1716 edict nor the 1738 declaration was registered by France's most powerful court, the Parlement of Paris. This put the laws' status in a state of legal limbo for the high court's jurisdiction. Technically according to the law of the land, the two acts could be overlooked by the courts as not having been ratified. In fact, in a flurry of lawsuits beginning in the 1750s, over 150 slaves won their freedom in Paris's Admiralty Court, their lawyers arguing that the unregistered laws were not valid and that the Freedom

Principle, a fundamental maxim of the kingdom, guaranteed freedom to all slaves who set foot on French soil.

In a landmark 1759 case, the Parlement of Paris recognized the freedom of Francisque, a slave who had been brought to France by his master Sieur Brignon. This opened the gates for a flood of lawsuits before the Admiralty Court of France in Paris in the 1760s and 1770s, all of which resulted in the slaves' freedom and sometimes back wages for services rendered.[14] These lawsuits in turn spurred the king's administrators to develop new legislation that would halt the flow of blacks to the nation's capital.

Royal efforts to draft new legislation culminated in the August 9, 1777, *Declaration pour la police des Noirs,* a wide-ranging law that prohibited the entry of all "blacks, mulattoes, and other people of color" into the kingdom. So that colonists would still be able to make use of their enslaved domestic servants during the ocean voyage, the new law established depots at each of France's ports where the slaves would be detained until they could be sent back to the colonies on the next available ship. What was most important in the eyes of Sartine, France's new Minister of the Marine, was that the Parlement of Paris could not fail to register the law because the law substituted racial categories for the word *slave.* The *Declaration pour la Police des Noirs* has the dubious distinction of being France's first royal legislation based entirely on skin color.[15]

Seymour Drescher has argued that the reason that the French developed legislation on the status of slaves who traveled to France and the English did not is that the legislative branch of the French government, that is, the monarch and his council of ministers, was able to unilaterally draft legislation without consulting a wide body of public opinion. The English parliament, on the other hand, had to be responsive to a wider range of interests and was consequently unable to reach consensus on the issue.[16] This is plausible, as far as it goes. What has not adequately been addressed is why French legislation shifted from the acceptance of metropolitan slavery during the first half of the eighteenth century to the exclusion of blacks in the latter half of the eighteenth century. I would argue that it was precisely because France lacked a constituent body for the expression of public opinion (such as the moribund Estates General), that the French courts had such a strong role in shaping later legislation. The Paris Parlement's refusal to register legislation containing the word *esclave* forced the monarchy to adopt racial terminology to police its boundaries against colonial slavery.

From the perspective of the late twentieth century, the notion of using racial sanctions to preserve France's commitment to the abstract principle of freedom strikes us as contradictory, if not downright hypocritical. However, our reaction anachronistically conflates the principles of freedom and social equality that, after all, were only beginning to be addressed at the end of the eighteenth century. Modern consciousness, shaped by struggles over imperialism, apartheid, and civil and human rights, tends to see freedom and equality as inextricably bound, two sides of the same coin. At the end of the Ancien Regime, French lawyers and magistrates celebrated themselves as the champions of the public's freedom over despotic tyranny, yet this in no way implied for them universal social equality or access to equal rights. Indeed, some of the most vociferous defenders of slaves' rights in the Paris Admiralty court were also the most patronizing and racist when it came to their black clients and their Jewish owners.

One of the main themes of this work, in fact, is that France's commitment to the Freedom Principle, the notion that "There are no slaves in France," when faced with the crisis of colonial slaves imported to the metropole, yielded two distinct responses, both characteristic of modern thought. One of these is the liberal notion of individual or human rights that over the course of the nineteenth and twentieth centuries has extended the category of what is "human" from a limited class of elite, white, male property owners, to include the poor, women, nonwhites, and now animals. The second reponse to the crisis of slaves in the land of liberty is the formulation of conservative ideologies that justify hierarchy and the status quo—here racism—but ultimately all of the "-isms" now challenged by modern liberals. In other words, the problem of social hierarchies in a world where all people are to be considered "free" (i.e., not subject to others' domination) has yielded, on one hand, a commitment to an ideology of absolute social equality and, on the other, a system of justification for why some classes of individuals are entitled to more privileges than others. It is therefore not surprising that the age of liberalism, with its attendant movements of antislavery, socialism, feminism, and so on coincides precisely with the development of "scientific" racism in France, England, and the United States.[17] Both are responses to ambiguities inherent in the notion of freedom.

Robert Darnton, citing Lévi-Strauss, has argued that cats are "good for thinking''[18] because cats, being at once members of the domestic family and animals from the wild, cross the essential boundary between interior and exterior, civilization and nature. Belonging to neither world entirely, cats are taboo, imbued with symbolic importance.

Similarly, I would argue that eighteenth-century slaves who came to France and England, and perhaps other northern European countries, are ''good for thinking,'' too. Their presence as slaves in nations with abstract commitments to liberty, as human chattel in a developing discourse on property rights, as brothers of a different color, placed them on the threshhold, as it were, of new notions of citizenship, property, and identity. As cultural critic Paul Gilroy has observed, blacks in the Atlantic world are essential to our understanding the constitution of modernity.[19]

This study is methodologically indebted to Robert Darnton and other cultural historians in yet another way. Although the larger narrative concerns France's institutional and attitudinal responses to the presence of blacks in France, I have tried to be attentive to the lives and experiences of individual blacks and their communities in the French realm. At the heart of many of these chapters is a microhistory, that is, a study of how particular blacks, lawyers, and government officials made their way in French Atlantic society.[20] I use ''thick description'' to situate those individuals—Jean Boucaux, Catherine Morgan, Francisque, Guillaume Poncet de la Grave, Henrion de Pensey, and Antoine de Sartine—within their cultural, social, and legal contexts.[21] In so doing, I have tried to render an account that is both personal and institutional, emphasizing the ways in which people act within the possibilities and constraints of their historical milieus.

This brings me to another concept essential to my analysis: the notion of political culture. Keith Baker, building in part on the anthropological theories of Marshall Sahlins, has done much to show how individuals and groups use language and other symbolic forms already present in society to make new claims, thereby fashioning new political discourses.[22] In the 1760s and 1770s, several prominent writers, including Rousseau, Voltaire, Raynal, and Diderot, used the symbol of the African slave to criticize the perceived tyranny of the French crown. At the same time, Louis XV's conflicts with the parlements escalated to new heights, culminating in Maupeou's complete overhaul of the French courts. A prominent lawyer, Henrion de Pansey, found a way to criticize Maupeou's reforms by pleading a slave's case before Paris's Admiralty

Court. In the third quarter of the eighteenth century, then, members of France's intellectual and judicial elite appropriated the symbol of the slave to criticize perceived excesses of royal authority.

The work ends deliberately in 1789, prior to the fall of the Old Regime. This is a natural stopping place for several reasons. First, the Admiralty Court, where so many slaves successfully sued for their freedom, was an early casualty of the Revolution. Second, the political culture of race and slavery during the Revolution itself is so complex as to merit its own treatment and has recently received the attention of some excellent scholars.[23] What has been lacking until now is an understanding of how the categories of race and slavery functioned in the century before the Revolution. I hope that the present work will ground future analysis of the Revolution in a better sense of the cultural and institutional past.

1

Slavery in France
*The Problem
and Early Responses*

In the early seventeenth century the French Caribbean colonies of Martinique, Guadeloupe, and Saint Christophe imported indentured servants from France to raise crops like tobacco, which could be farmed in small plots by only a few fieldworkers. Some colonists did well by these and other ventures, increased their landholdings, and began to invest in a labor-intensive but potentially more lucrative product: sugar.[1] To meet the increased demand for labor that accompanied sugar production in the West Indies, Louis XIV's minister Colbert granted the Compagnie des Indes Occidentales (1664) and its successors, the Compagnie du Sénégal (1674), and the Compagnie de Guinée (1683), exclusive permission to transport slaves from Africa to the French colonies.[2] By 1685, the French government had found it necessary to establish rules that would regulate the relationship between masters and slaves for all the French colonies. These were set out in 1685 in an elaborate royal decree known as the Code Noir.[3]

None of the laws regulating slavery or the slave trade, however, specified what should happen if a colonial slave made his or her way to France. When the king and his ministers granted slave-trading privileges to the Senegal and Guinea Companies, they were thinking of the financial revenues that would cross the Atlantic, not the transportation of institution of slavery into the nation's bosom. The Code Noir, subtitled "the police of the islands of America," was designed to bring Catholicism to the heathen and curb the abuses of cruel masters across the sea.

French policymakers acknowledged slavery as a necessary evil "over there," not a problem for the French at home.

In France, where the financial benefits of the institution were not immediately felt, the attitude toward slavery was quite different. In 1571, a Norman slave merchant arrived in Bordeaux with a cargo of slaves. When he attempted to sell them, he was arrested and the slaves were freed.[4] The tradition of freeing slaves upon arrival in a French city extends back to a time prior to the transatlantic slave trade. For example, in 1402 four slaves escaped from Perpignan to Toulouse. Their masters followed them there and attempted to reclaim them, but the city's *syndic* intervened, ruling that by the privilege of that city, any slave who set foot within its suburbs (*banlieue*) was free.[5]

Yet these cases of slaves arriving in France or in particular urban centers were quite isolated and infrequent until the late seventeenth century, when French commerce with Africa and the Caribbean increased both the incidence of slavery and the opportunities for slaves to travel to France. The growing numbers of slaves within the kingdom of France (which was viewed as territorially distinct from the French colonies) created a dilemma for royal administrators and the courts. Slavery could be accepted and even encouraged in the colonies, where it was seen as a necessary solution to the labor problem and justified by the Christian missionary imperative. But in the early years of French colonial slavery, at least, the king, his ministers, and the *parlementaires* all cooperated to uphold the tradition of France as a land free of slaves.[6]

The problem of slaves on metropolitan soil was brought to the attention of Pontchartrain, secretary of state for the marine, in 1691 when a pair of stowaways made it safely to France. In his instructions to M. d'Esragny, the secretary outlined the situation and Louis XIV's response:

> The king has been informed that two negroes from Martinique crossed on the ship *l'Oiseau*. His Majesty, to punish Sir Chevalier de Hère, who commanded the ship, for not having paid enough attention to prevent them from embarking, gives order to Sir Ceberet to withhold the price of them from his salary, at the cost of 300 *livres* for each one, and to remit it to the writer of the ship *le Vaillant* to pay, following your orders, the owners of the negroes. He has not judged it apropos to return them to the isles, their liberty being acquired by the laws of the kingdom concerning slaves, as soon as they touch the soil.[7]

The king's response was unequivocal: because the slaves had reached France, they were free. Their owner would be reimbursed at the expense of the ship captain who was unwary enough to allow them to sneak aboard. A letter from D. de Goimpy of the following year complained, however, that the reimbursement was not enough. One of the two blacks was a skilled tradesman, worth more than 1000 *écus* and capable of bringing in more than 400 *francs* annually. The reimbursement of 100 *écus* would hardly be enough to purchase a young, unskilled farm laborer.[8] In 1694 the government formalized the penalty at "400 *livres* for each negro, whatever age and strength he may be" if a captain wittingly or unwittingly transported them to France.[9]

Once the problem of stowaways was settled, a new permutation emerged: that of colonists who wished to bring their slaves to France as domestic servants. In response to a letter to the intendant of Martinique, Pontchartrain wrote in 1696: "I have not found any ordinance which permits colonists to keep their negro slaves in France when they [the slaves] want to serve themselves of the liberty acquired by all who touch its soil."[10] In other words, colonists might bring their domestic slaves with them to France, but if these slaves availed themselves of the Freedom Principle, there was nothing the king's ministers could do.[11] A second ministerial letter to the intendant confirmed not only that slaves gained their freedom automatically upon arrival, but also that the government could not force them to return to the colonies against their will.[12]

The grounds for Louis XIV's position are not entirely clear. As discussed in the next chapter, the principle that all slaves who set foot on French soil were free upon baptism had been known to constitutional theorists since the sixteenth century. It appears that at this early date colonial slave owners did not have enough clout to rattle the king's commitment to this precept.

Yet the government was not entirely consistent in its application of the Freedom Principle. Slaves who returned to France in 1699 from the expedition to Cartagena, were manumitted only on the condition that their owners were paid for them. Otherwise they were to be returned to their masters in the colonies.[13]

In 1704 Mithon, *Conseilleur* of Martinique, wrote to the minister of the marine to seek advice regarding slaves who traveled to France and then returned to the colonies with their masters. He acknowledged the king's decision of 1696 whereby slaves setting foot on French soil were free and under no obligation to accompany their masters back to the island. In practice, however, Mithon noted that the former slaves who returned to Martinique were treated as freedmen (*affranchis*), rather than men of free birth, and consequently owed a lifetime of service to their former masters.[14] At least one such former slave, a young man named Louis, after having spent thirteen or fourteen years in France, resisted all attempts to return him to submission.[15] Mithon urged the minister to accept a compromise measure whereby slaves who returned from France would be recognized as freedmen, fed and paid a small amount for their labors ("up to ten or twelve *livres*" per year), but required to serve their former masters until death. Currently, lamented Mithon, those former slaves returning from France "fill the island with libertines who are rarely up to any good, and who only occupy themselves with theft or receiving stolen goods, and hold to the negroes' cabarets where they always commit disorders and a frightful libertinage."[16] By requiring former slaves to serve their masters for the rest of their lives, argued Mithon, the government could reduce the wanton debauchery "without disturbing the privileges of the kingdom." There is no record of the minister's response to Mithon's proposal, and it seems unlikely that the suggestion was taken up.

As time passed, the problem of colonial slavery in the French metropolis became even more complex. For example, what was to be done about a slave woman who traveled to France in 1677 but never claimed her freedom, returning soon thereafter to the colonies and raising her family in slavery? Thirty years later her children and grandchildren demanded their freedom, based upon the French tradition that children followed the status of their mother. According to the minister this was stretching the principle a bit far: "The intention of His Majesty is that the negroes who had been brought into the kingdom by the planters of the islands, who refuse to return there, could not be forced to do so. However, if by their own free will they follow them back to America, they cannot claim the privilege of the soil of France, since they seem to have renounced it by their voluntary return to the place of slavery."[17] The intent of bestowing freedom on those who traveled to France was to prevent slavery from entering the metropolis, not to increase the numbers of freedmen in the colonies. During the early stages of French colonial slavery, the government tried hard to preserve the spatial and legal distinctions between the colonies, where slavery was permitted as a necessity, and France, the land of liberty. They were supported in this effort by the French courts.

The French Courts and the Edict of 1716

At the beginning of the eighteenth century, France's legal system was a complex patchwork of overlapping jurisdictions and systems of appeal. At the highest level were the twelve *parlements* and two sovereign courts that presided over specific regional districts. The most important of these was the Parlement of Paris, whose jurisdiction included approximately one-third of the territory of France, including the capital city of Paris and the court of Versailles.

France's admiralty court system had been developing since the fourteenth century, following the expansion of maritime commerce and the navy.[18] Disputes arising from trade or warfare at sea could be brought to the nearest of fifty *sièges particuliers* (local seats) of the Admiralty. The sentences of the *sièges particuliers* could be appealed to a higher court, occasionally a regional court, known as a *Table de Marbre,* or more usually, directly to a regional Parlement, depending on the jurisdication. The city of Nantes, which, like Bordeaux, experienced a tremendous commercial boom during the seventeenth and eighteenth centuries as a result of its colonial business, had its own *siège particulier* whose decisions could be appealed to the Parlement of Rennes, which presided over Brittany.

As seen, some French courts, such as the Parlement of Bordeaux, had granted freedom to slaves who made their way to France. Until the eighteenth century, these cases were relatively rare. But as slavery became the primary source of labor within the colonies, the number of slaves who traveled to France also increased. During the eighteenth century many of these slaves employed the French courts to demand freedom from their masters.

In 1715 a young female slave was brought to France from the colonies and placed with the nuns of Calvary in Nantes while her mistress made a trip to Paris. On the mistress's return, the nuns refused to release the girl.[19] The matter was taken to the Admiralty Court of Nantes and sharply debated, culminating in a decision of liberty for the slave on the grounds that the owner had failed to declare her as a slave when entering France.[20] According to Gérard Mellier, the mayor of Nantes, the lawyers who argued the case had searched diligently for some positive regulation on the issue, but had found none. The judges in the case relied on "common usage" to decide that the woman should be recognized as free. Mellier urged the king's ministers to draw up definitive legislation to which judges could turn when deciding such cases.[21]

Mellier's request came at a highly unstable period for the French monarchy. In 1715 Louis XIV had reigned for seventy-two years and his death was imminent. Only a few years earlier his line of succession had appeared sturdy, but during the intervening time disease and misfortune had eliminated all legitimate successors except his great-grandson, a mere boy of five years. In the hope of giving his illegitimate sons, the Duke of Maine and the Count of Toulouse, some influence in state policy, Louis XIV named a regency council to rule the kingdom until the child reached maturity.[22] The council was to be led by Louis XIV's nephew, the Duke of Orléans, assisted by the Duke of Maine and the Count of Toulouse, the Duke of Bourbon-Condé, the chancellor Voisin, the marshals of Villeroi, Villars, Uxelles, Tallard, and Harcourt, the four secretaries of state, and the comptroller general. Yet on September 2, 1715, the day after Louis XIV's death, the Parlement of Paris, in collusion with Orléans, annulled the dead king's will and named Orléans the boy-king's sole regent, making him the effective ruler of France. The parlement's action was contestable given the regency pattern that had been established over the previous two centuries. For this reason Orléans was beholden to the parlement for his power.

During this political and constitutional crisis, a new law was drafted to address the problem of colonial slave owners who wanted to bring their slaves to France. This statute proved inordinately important. Known as the Edict of October 1716, this new law set conditions whereby slave owners could bring their slaves to France without fear of losing them once they set foot on French soil.

According to the edict, there were two legitimate purposes for bringing slaves to France: to give them religious instruction or to teach them a trade. The edict underlined the principle set out in the Code Noir of 1685, that all enslaved fieldworkers "be taught and instructed with all possible attention, in the principles and the practice of the Catholic, Roman and Apostolic religion."[23] But, if some colonists or colonial officials wanted to bring some of their slaves "of either sex, in the quality of domestic servant, or otherwise" for further religious instruction or to learn a trade that would be useful to the colonies upon their return, the edict permitted them to do so if they complied with certain formalities.[24] First, slave owners were required to obtain written permission to transport their slaves to France from the colonial governor. Second, the permit had to contain the name of the owner and the slaves' names, ages, and descriptions. Third, the slave owners were required to register their slaves at the *greffe* (office of the clerk of the court) both in the French colonial district where they resided and in that of the Admiralty where they disembarked in France.

Slave status in France depended on observing these regulations. If the slave owners or their designates complied with these formalities, slaves would remain the property of their owners and would be required to return to the colonies "when their masters judge appropriate." But, continued the edict, "If the masters fail to observe the formalities proscribed by the preceding articles, the negroes will be free and will not be able to be reclaimed."[25]

It is significant that the penalty for failing to fulfill the formalities of the edict was the slaves' freedom. Presumably the government felt that the loss of such valuable property was enough to compel the owners' compliance. At the same time, however, the law also formalized slaves' legal right to challenge masters in court. For the first time the Edict of 1716 gave slaves a statutory, in addition to a customary, basis for claiming their freedom in France.

Within this new legal framework masters could keep their slaves in France for an indefinite period of time, unless or until they lost their connection to the colonies. For example, once a military officer was relieved of his commission, he was required to return his slave to the colonies within a year. Colonists who sold their plantations were similarly prevented from retaining their slaves for more than a year in France.[26] Yet these rules were for the most part lax, as an absentee landowner in the colonies could retain enslaved domestic servants in France indefinitely as a symbol of wealth and status.

Other articles in the Edict of 1716 established penalties for anyone who might steal slaves from their master, assigned the master responsibility for feeding and supporting slaves while in France, permitted the inheritance of slaves should the master die, gave the slaves' savings to the master if the slaves should die in France, prohibited the sale or trade of slaves in France, and prohibited creditors from seizing slaves against a debt. One additional article equated slaves' marriage with tacit manumission.[27]

In sum, the Edict of October 1716 created an intermediate slave status

for the kingdom that restricted the master's rights over a slave more than
in the colonies, yet was not so lenient as to equate a French slave's status
with that of a free servant in the kingdom. For example, in the colonies,
a person could own slaves regardless of whether he or she owned land or
held a military commission. Owning an enslaved domestic servant or a
skilled laborer was not especially uncommon, particularly in urban
areas. In France, as a result of the Edict of October 1716, the privilege of
owning a slave was limited to an elite. On the other hand, the new law
opened an avenue whereby slaves could legitimately challenge their
masters' power over them through the French courts. In the colonies the
Code Noir had specifically prohibited slaves from being a party in a civil
suit.[28]

In early modern France a piece of royal legislation such as the Edict
of October 1716, once issued, was sent to the Parlement of Paris and
other regional parlements to be registered. Specifically, the king or one
of his ministers sent the ordinance to the parlement's *parquet,* whose
senior officers would review the law to see whether it was sound and
consistent with prior legislation.[29] If so, they would write up their conclusions and urge the parlement to register the law. If the officers objected to aspects of the law, they might recommend changes or refuse
outright to register it. Formal objections, known as *remonstrances,* were
sometimes published and circulated by the court to influence public
opinion. If the monarch felt strongly about the law's registration, he
could use various methods to coerce the parlement to comply. In the
eighteenth century the *Lit de Justice* assembly, formerly a consultive
constitutional ceremony, was increasingly used to urge parlementary
cooperation. If the magistrates still refused and went on strike, the king
could exile or imprison individual magistrates or the entire court with
lettres de cachet. Wielding such weapons, the king generally had the
upper hand.[30]

During the regency for Louis XV a struggle broke out between the
Parlement of Paris and the king's regent, Orléans, over fiscal and religious matters. One of the most important ways in which the monarchy
and the parlements battled for authority was through the legislative
registration. When the Parlement of Paris refused to register certain acts
of which it disapproved, the regent insisted that the laws remained valid
nonetheless. Without parlementary registration, however, a law did not
receive adequate publicity and the court might refuse to prosecute cases
involving the law. Consequently an unregistered law was of dubious

legitimacy. Technically part of France's legal code, an unregistered law might go unenforced.[31]

Though the parlements of Dijon and Rennes, and possibly other high courts of France, registered the Edict of October 1716, the Parlement of Paris did not.[32] The reason why the Parlement of Paris neglected to register the new law is difficult to pin down with certainty. What follows is the only available documented account to explain why the Edict of 1716 remained unregistered by the Parlement of Paris. It is based on the recollections of Guillaume François Joly de Fleury, as recorded by his son in 1756.

When the king's council issued the edict on October 28, 1716, it was sent to the elder Joly de Fleury, the *avocat général* of the parlement's *parquet* chambre who was responsible for offering his opinion on legislation before it was registered by the court.[33] As he remembered it nearly forty years later, Joly de Fleury felt that because the edict concerned "a subject which has been regarded for several centuries as concerning religion," he should solicit the opinion of an ecclesiastical lawyer.[34] He consulted with Pierre Lemerre the younger, barrister of the clergy at the Parlement of Paris, for his opinion.[35]

What did Joly de Fleury mean when he said that the Edict of 1716 was concerned with "a subject which has been regarded for several centuries as concerning religion"? There are at least three ways in which Joly de Fleury might have linked Christianity to slavery. The first concerns some general precepts of Christian doctrine. The second involves missionary justifications for slavery. The third and, I argue, most important has to do with the highly charged atmosphere concerning Jansenism in 1716, when the edict was issued.

Many historians have commented on the ambiguous relationship between slavery and Christian doctrine.[36] On one hand, slavery was acknowledged in both scripture and canonical law.[37] At the same time, certain Christian teachings seem to oppose slavery and would later be used by abolitionists to justify their cause. For example, the idea that all humans are equal in the eyes of God was taken up by Quakers and other Protestant sects in their eighteenth- and nineteenth-century crusades against slavery.[38]

Presumably, however, when Joly de Fleury linked slavery with religion he had French legal precedents in mind. The Code Noir (1685), France's most comprehensive legislation on slavery, was entangled in complicated ways with the Roman Catholic faith. Supported by the

Jesuits, this law rested on the Christian justification of slavery as a means to spread the gospel. The law's second article, for example, required slave owners to baptize all slaves and instruct them in the Catholic religion. By this means, it was thought, the "true faith" would be brought to Africans and their descendants in the colonies.

Issued during the same year as the revocation of the Edict of Nantes and the promulgation of the Edict of Fontainbleau, the Code Noir also manifested Louis XIV's policy of religious intolerance, extending it to the colonies. The code's first and third articles enjoined colonial officers to "chase all the Jews who have established residences from our isles" and prohibited the public practice of any non-Catholic religion by either masters or slaves. Another article invalidated all marriages but Catholic ones.[39]

Although the Edict of 1716 specifically mentioned the Code Noir in its preamble, there is reason to believe that Joly de Fleury was not thinking of the older law when he linked slavery with the Church in his decision not to register the Edict of 1716. Or rather, to his mind, the Code Noir was merely a symptom of a much larger problem. To understand how he and others saw the relationship between slavery and the Church in the eighteenth century, we must be aware of the more general conflicts between the Parlement of Paris and the regent Orléans during this period. The most important of these was the struggle over the registration of the papal bull known as *Unigenitus*.[40]

Unigenitus was part of a prolonged attack on Jansenism, a dissenting creed that had gained a large following among French elites during the seventeenth and eighteenth centuries.[41] Jansenists, following St. Augustine, emphasized the absolute power of God over human free will, closely paralleling the doctrine of predestination favored by Calvinists. The Jesuit order, whose members followed the Molinist doctrine of free will and human agency in the betterment of the world, opposed the Jansenist teachings and lobbied for papal condemnation, which they received in the form of two papal bulls. The first, *In eminenti*, was proclaimed in 1643. The second bull, *Unigenitus,* issued by Clement XI on September 8, 1713, condemned Quesnel's *Nouveau Testament avec des réflexions morales,* a tract that laid out many of the Jansenist precepts.[42]

The bull *Unigenitus* was controversial in France from the very beginning, and not only because of the popularity of Jansenism among the elite. Also at stake were the relative powers of Rome and the French

Church. Since the struggles of Philip the Fair with Pope Boniface VIII in the late thirteenth century, the doctrine of the Gallican liberties held that the French general councils were superior to the pope and that the king and clergy in France could unite to limit papal intervention within the kingdom. Six months after the publication of *Unigenitus,* four French bishops appealed the bull to a future general council and were supported by the faculties of theology in Paris, Rheims, and Nantes. They opposed parlementary registration of the bull because recognizing the law would circumvent the general council's traditional authority over the pope.

In October 1716, when Joly de Fleury consulted Pierre Lemerre the younger regarding the new edict, Lemerre's father was preparing to publish a treatise that supported the bishops and the faculties of theology who challenged the bull *Unigenitus.* In 1718 the elder Lemerre would publish a second work criticizing the regent Orléans for his stand on *Unigenitus.*[43] We know that the Lemerres, father and son, worked closely together on many writings.[44] It is therefore not unlikely that both Lemerres were Jansenist sympathizers, if not Jansenists themselves. Could it be that Joly de Fleury, whom historian François Bluche has described as a "friend of the Jansenists," deliberately sought a Jansenist position on the Edict of October 1716?[45]

Lemerre obliged by presenting Joly de Fleury with a lengthy report establishing the legal traditions that underlay the maxim that all slaves are free upon arrival in France. Beginning with ancient Hebrew slave laws, Lemerre surveyed the church's teaching on slavery and manumission, concluding that "one can not have recourse to Roman civil law nor to canonical constitutions to establish French liberty."[46] Rather, according to Lemerre, the long-standing association between France and freedom was based on three elements: (1) Henry II's edict, which enfranchised all serfs in the Dauphiné in 1556 on the grounds that earlier kings could not tolerate their subjects to be in a servile condition; (2) natural law, which recognized all men as equal; and (3) Christianity, which held that man was created in God's image and could not be treated as a beast under the domination of other men.

The principle that this French freedom should be extended to all those who set foot in the kingdom, as stated by Antoine Loisel in his collection of French legal maxims, seemed to be based, according to Lemerre, on the customary practices of several French cities, including Toulouse, Bourges, and St. Malo. But he cited several authors who questioned whether this tradition was valid for the city of Paris.

Perhaps because the customary basis of the Freedom Principle in Paris was tenuous, Lemerre quoted at length from the seventeenth-century Parisian lawyer Antoine Le Maistre, who claimed that France's traditional affiliation with freedom was inextricably linked to its role as a Christian nation: "'The God of the Christians,' said this celebrated lawyer [Le Maistre], 'is the God of liberty. By taking the form of servant, he lifted us from servitude; he broke our chains; he made us to walk with our head held high. . . . This kingdom is not that of France but that of Jesus Christ.'"[47] Le Maistre was, perhaps not coincidentally, author of a pamphlet defending Jean du Vergier de Hauranne, the abbé of Saint-Cyran, from accusations of Jansenism. The vision of France as a Christain nation with a special link to the principle of freedom is thus consonant with Jansenist teachings, if not inspired by them.[48]

Lemerre's emphasis on French customary law and his celebration of France's supposed tradition of liberty as a Christian nation is thus consistent with both Gallican and Jansenist positions. Though Roman civil and Catholic canonical precedents could be seen to support the introduction of slavery to France, Gallican and Jansenist sympathizers apparently decided to resist these traditions as external to an indigenous French celebration of the principle of liberty.[49]

Conclusion

Based on Lemerre's report, Joly de Fleury and de Chauvelin, the keeper of the seals, decided that the Parlement of Paris should not register the Edict of October 1716. They informed the count of Toulouse, who had drafted the legislation, of their opinion, and he did not insist on its registration, perhaps because he did not think that the presence of slaves in the landlocked region around Paris would ever amount to very much and, in any event, was not worth a public controversy.[50]

The fact that the Edict of 1716 was never registered by the Parlement of Paris created a legal limbo for slaves who came to Paris or other cities within the parlement's jurisdiction. The matter of the law's legitimacy would remain unresolved for several decades, but for the present the ambiguity was ignored.

2

The Case of *Jean Boucaux v. Verdelin*
Fashioning the National Myth of Liberty

For more than two decades after the Edict of 1716 established conditions whereby slaves might legally be retained in France, no slaves petitioned for their freedom before the Admiralty Court of France in Paris. During this period two of the Admiralty's actions did involve slaves. In August 1734 the court permitted a colonist from Saint Domingue who had duly fulfilled the requirements of the 1716 edict to seize his runaway slave, then under the protection of a French noblewoman.[1] In 1736 the Admiralty clerk accepted the declaration of a Parisian woman who stated that a female slave from Madagascar had been sent to her by a colonist from Ile de Bourbon for training in religion and a trade.[2] Neither action could have been based strictly on the Edict of 1716 because it did not contain provisions regarding runaway slaves or require slave owners to register their slaves in Paris.[3] Still, it is interesting that both actions tended to favor the property rights of slave owners over the human rights of their slaves. Two years later this trend would be permanently reversed.

In June of 1738 the Paris Admiralty Court heard its first two petitions for freedom by slaves. It was through these cases that the 1716 edict's lack of registration was first discussed by the court. One of these cases, brought by Jean Boucaux, a slave from Saint Domingue, against his master Sieur Verdelin, is significant for several reasons. First, it was extremely well documented. In addition to Boucaux's petition and the sentences of the court that can be found in the court's archives, there are two published sources outlining the arguments used by the lawyers on

both sides of the case. Boucaux's lawyer, Mallet, summarized the arguments for the plaintiff's freedom in a *mémoire* that circulated at the time
of the trial.[4] An abridged version of this brief, along with the arguments
of the defense and the concluding statements by the *procureur du roi,*
were also reproduced in the 1747 collection *Causes célèbres et intéressantes.*[5]

Second, this case presented the arguments and authorities against
slavery in France that would be the basis of all such future cases. In
order to argue that Boucaux was free, it was necessary for his lawyers to
resurrect and justify the national maxim that held that any slave who set
foot on French soil was free. This was no easy matter because, like the
so-called Salic law that prevented women from ascending to the French
crown, the maxim equating France with freedom seems to have been
invented by legal scholars in the fifteenth and sixteenth centuries by
bending ancient statutes and precedents to present needs.[6] To win their
case on the basis of the maxim, the lawyers for Boucaux had to manu-
facture a particular account of French history that justified the principle
that any slave setting foot in France was free.

Third, the case of *Boucaux v. Verdelin* set an important precedent for
future decisions in the Admiralty Court of France by deciding in favor of
the former slave. Finally, the case stimulated the king's council to draft
more stringent legislation in the form of the *Déclaration concernant les
nègres esclaves des colonies* of December 15, 1738.[7]

Jean Boucaux v. Bernard Verdelin

Jean Boucaux was the son of two slaves owned by the Governor of Saint
Domingue, Sr. de Beau-manoir. After the governor died, his widow
married Bernard Verdelin, a sergeant in the King's army, in January
1724, apparently in France.[8] Two years later Verdelin and his wife went
to Saint Domingue to make arrangements regarding the estate with the
children of Mme Verdelin's first marriage.

Upon returning to France in December 1728 (or January 1729), Verdelin brought with him two slaves; one of them was Jean Boucaux.
Boucaux served as Verdelin's cook for over nine years. Near the end of
this period Boucaux married a French woman (her race is not mentioned), apparently without Verdelin's consent. According to Boucaux's
lawyer, "From this moment on, [Boucaux] became the object of
Sr. Verdelin's hatred. He suffered indisputably cruel treatment."[9]

The Edict of 1716 specifically required a slave to obtain his master's consent to marry in France. The edict also stated that upon marrying, a slave should be recognized as free. Though the records do not explicitly state why Boucaux's master began to abuse him at the time of the wedding, it is possible that Boucaux began to behave differently, perhaps believing himself to be free.

In June 1738, Verdelin had Boucaux arrested "because he suspected Boucaux of planning an escape and he was afraid to lose him."[10] Boucaux was imprisoned in the dungeon of Paris' Châtelet prison, and from there he initiated his petition for freedom.[11] On June 25 the judges of the Admiralty Court ruled that Boucaux should be removed from the dungeon but held under the king's protection in the Châtelet prison until both parties could be heard.[12]

During his stay at the Châtelet, Boucaux sent two more petitions to the Court of the Admiralty with the help of his lawyer, Mallet. The first, of July 29, 1738, demanded that the Verdelins pay him 4,200 *livres* in back wages for the nine years that he had served them in France, that he be freed from prison, and that his imprisonment be stricken from the record. The second petition of August 21 requested that Sieur and Dame Verdelin be condemned to pay damages and interest for "unjust and torturous imprisonment."[13]

In late summer, the lawyers for Boucaux and Verdelin presented their cases in a hearing before the Admiralty Court of France. Because the arguments in this case formed the basis of future legal challenges to slavery, it is important to examine them in some detail. The arguments in favor of Boucaux, stating that he had been free ever since he arrived in France, were articulated in the brief written by Boucaux's lawyer, Mallet. Further arguments on Boucaux's behalf were supplied by the king's representative in the Admiralty court (the *procureur du roi*), Le Clerc du Brillet. The crux of their case was that Boucaux should be recognized as free because slavery did not exist in France; upon setting foot on French soil, Boucaux became a free man. If, however, the Code Noir of 1685 and the Edict of 1716 could be construed to permit colonial slaves to reside temporarily in France, the lawyers argued that Boucaux should nevertheless be recognized as free because his master, Verdelin, neglected to fulfill the prescribed formalities of the Edict of 1716.

Mallet and Le Clerc du Brillet each opened their arguments with a history of the legal status of slavery in France since the time of the Romans. The history they recounted was designed to show how slavery had arisen in France, how it had been abolished, and whence came the maxim that a slave who sets foot in France is automatically free. As we shall see, the lawyers' interpretation required a slight misreading of historical evidence.

According to natural law, argued Mallet and Le Clerc du Brillet, all men are born free. But man's ambition prevents this condition from lasting very long. When men go to war, the winners enslave their enemies. This, Mallet says ironically, is called charity by "the Philosophers," because the winners condescend to spare the lives of their opponents.[14]

In this account of the origins of slavery, the eighteenth-century lawyers were echoing sixteenth-century legal philosopher Jean Bodin's critique of Aristotle.[15] Bodin had summarized Aristotle's justifications for slavery in the following way: Slavery is evidently agreeable to nature because it has endured so long and so many commonwealths have benefited by it; second, when faced with killing a captive or a criminal or enslaving him, enslavement is the more charitable act. Bodin answered the longevity argument as follows:

> True it is in things merely natural, which according to their natural propriety follow the immutable ordinance of God: but having given unto man the choice of good & evil, it chanceth oftentimes to the contrary; him to choose the worse, contrary to the law of both God and nature: in whom his corrupt opinion hath so great a power, that it passeth in force of a law, of greater power than nature itself.[16]

In other words, man by his free will sometimes chooses to do the wrong thing. If this error is made by those in power, the evil can endure for a long time, despite its opposition to nature. Bodin offered the example of human sacrifice as an evil practice that had endured for centuries in many cultures yet was contrary to both God and nature. In response to the idea that it is more humane to enslave one's captives than to kill them, Bodin pointed to the case of the unjust war, wherein "it is the thieves and pirates who brag themselves to have given life unto them who they have not deprived of life."[17]

From the presumed origins of slavery in the distant past, Boucaux's lawyers passed to its practice in Greek and Roman times. Mallet explained that the Romans conquered and enslaved the Gauls, bringing slavery to France. The Council held at Mâcon in 581 ruled that no Christian could be held as the slave of a Jew.[18] The uprising under Louis le Gros was proof, according to Mallet, that slavery existed in France in 1108.[19]

Mallet, Le Clerc du Brillet, and many later writers on the history of slavery credited Christianity with the abolition of slavery in early medieval France.[20] According to Mallet, a truly Christian spirit of charity caused the French to release their slaves through several methods of manumission. Because this interpretation of the disappearance of Roman slavery in Europe would later be supplanted by a more secular version of history, Mallet's assertion merits some attention.

Historian Marc Bloch observed that Christian charity was cited almost universally in the preambles to manumission charters during the early Middle Ages. Although he cautions against taking these formulae literally, pointing out that the practice of manumitting slaves by testament was prevalent in the Roman world, "there is no doubt," he argues, "that Christianity had contributed greatly to its spread."[21] Furthermore, the laws that prohibited enslaving Christians meant that Christian Europe needed to go farther afield to find captives or find other solutions to its labor problems.

The role of Christianity in the abolition of Roman slavery during the Middle Ages was an object of passionate debate by professional historians of the nineteenth century. In 1884, for example, it was asserted that because the Catholic Church opposed all carryovers from the pagan Roman era, it sought to stamp out slavery and to ameliorate the conditions of the serf.[22] That notion was challenged by arguing that the Church had little to do with increasing manumission during the Middle Ages, historians citing secular social motives instead.[23]

More recently, the influence of Christianity has been overshadowed by economic or sociopolitical analyses of the problem. Marxist historians have sought to show either that slavery gave way to the more productive and efficient feudalism through technical advances or that slave revolts brought the slave system to its knees.[24] Legally oriented historians have argued that the two predominant medieval forms of unfree labor, serfs and villeins, though similar in appearance, arose from distinct Roman legal statuses, including slaves, farmers, and freedmen.[25] A recent work, influenced in part by Marxist thought, suggests that the transition from slavery to feudalism was abrupt and brutal, rather than gradual, at least in Spain and southern France.[26] In none of these works is the Church seen as a very significant factor in the transformation of the institution of slavery.

Yet in the minds of the French judicial elite a decade before the publication of Montesquieu's *Esprit des lois,* the self-evident assumption was that Christianity contributed to the gradual disappearance of slavery after the Roman era. In the lawyer Mallet's interpretation, various forms of serfdom arose as former slaves still owed their former masters certain obligations, such as the *droit de corvée* and the *droit de mainmorte.*[27] In 1141, according to Mallet, a charter published by Father Suger, regent of the kingdom, freed all the *mainmortes* in France.[28]

An important linchpin in Mallet and Le Clerc du Brillet's argument was an ordinance issued by Louis X on July 3, 1315. This is the only known royal statute to link the freeing (*affranchisement*) of French subjects with the name of France.[29] Le Clerc du Brillet quoted from the king's ordinance: "We, considering that our Kingdom is called and named the Kingdom of Francs, and wishing that the thing be in truth according with its name, . . . have ordained and do ordain that generally, throughout our kingdom, as much as it can be shared by us and our successors, such servitude will be restored to freedom, . . . at good and suitable conditions."[30] Yet, even though the linguistic relationship between France and freedom is explicit in this passage, a close examination of the ordinance reveals just how tenuous it is when connected to the eighteenth-century maxim of freeing slaves in France.

Two aspects of the law lessen its relevance for the case of Boucaux and all slaves who sought their freedom on this basis. First, the law refers specifically to certain types of serfdom, such as *formariage* and *mainmortes,* rather than slavery per se.[31] Second, the law abolished servitude "at good and suitable conditions," that is, for a price. Serfs who could afford the master's price might achieve their freedom, but serfdom was hardly abolished universally or unconditionally. Thus, no matter how suggestive the linguistic similarity between *France* and *affranchissement,* the fact remains that the practice of freeing slaves upon arrival in France had no basis in Louis X's 1315 ordinance.

From statutory law Mallet and Le Clerc du Brillet turned toward judicial precedents of the principle that arrival on French soil sets one free. By invoking previous incidents of extending freedom to slaves, Boucaux's lawyers were justifying the maxim based on customary law. In early modern French courts ancient customs were held to be just as valid, if not more so, as the Roman or Canon Law codes, because of their indigenous origins.

A number of legal cases dating from the sixteenth century held that certain aspects of slavery would not be tolerated in France and that slaves brought from abroad would be freed upon arrival. For example, Mallet recalled the 1558 case involving the Lord of Rocheblanche in Gascony who went beyond the privileges of *mainmorte* and ordered that shackles be placed on those of his subjects who left his land without permission. The Parlement of Toulouse refused to allow this abuse as contrary to natural liberty.[32] To this, Le Clerc du Brillet added several examples. One involved a Norman slave merchant who, in 1571, landed with a shipload of slaves in Bordeaux. When he attempted to sell some of them, the Parlement of Guyenne intervened and freed them all because, "France, the mother of liberty, doesn't permit any slaves."[33]

Le Clerc du Brillet also furnished several extrajudicial historical examples to prove that slavery had been contrary to French custom for centuries. According to François de Belleforest's *L'Histoire universelle du monde* (1570), "the custom is such that not only the French, but foreigners arriving in French ports and crying *'France et liberté,'* are beyond the power of those who possess them; [their owners] lose the price of the sale, and the service of the slave, if the slave refuses to serve them."[34] The same text contains a lengthy description of an incident that took place under the reign of Henry III (1574–1589). The main galley of the Spanish army ran aground on a sand bar outside the port of Calais. The governor of the city sent all of the galley slaves to the king who was staying at the time in Chartres with the Duke of Guise. The Spanish ambassador went to the duke to request the return of the slaves, as the two countries were then at peace. The duke appealed to the king, but the king said that he had to consult with his royal council first. Quoting the *Histoire universelle,* Le Clerc du Brillet wrote: "The two or three hundred galley slaves lined themselves up along the steps of the church by which his majesty had to pass on his way to mass. The slaves, as soon as they saw him, they threw themselves on their knees, . . . and being naked as when they pulled the oar, they set themselves to crying, *'Misericordia, Misericordia.'* "[35] The king was moved by the slaves' appeal and, after meeting with his council, ruled that: "Seeing that the Turcs, Moors and Barbarians [of the Barbary Coast] were taken as slaves by Spain by the hazard of war, and by the same chance they arrived in France, where only criminals are used as galley slaves, it was held that they acquired their liberty."[36] The French government sent the slaves back to Constantinople by way of Marseille, with an *écu* apiece.

Mallet added to this another anecdote involving Spanish slaves. During the siege of Metz in 1552, Dom Louis Davila, general of the Spanish Cavalry, wrote to the Duke of Guise to request that a slave who had been taken be returned to him. The duke responded that "according to the ancient and good custom of France," he could not return the slave who acquired his freedom in the city of Metz.[37]

Thus, by citing statutory and circumstantial precedents, Mallet and Le Clerc du Brillet justified the maxim that a slave became free upon entering the kingdom of France. The principle, they argued, was "so imprinted in the hearts of Frenchmen that they regard it as the first, the greatest, privilege of the kingdom."[38]

Let us pause for a moment here to examine the notion of the "maxim" and its force in early modern French law. Not until 1787 did France have a written constitution in the sense of a formal document defining the institutions of the state and their respective powers. Instead, French governmental institutions developed historically; that is, over the centuries certain practices became encrusted with tradition, such as the inheritance of the crown, the practices of the parlement, and the formation of the estates general. In the early sixteenth century numerous legal theorists sought to justify these practices based upon what they knew of the historical record.[39]

Legal scholars were aided by the explosion of knowledge that accompanied Renaissance humanism, making it possible to compare the practices of a wide variety of states from different historical periods. Jean Bodin, for example, made extensive use of the comparative method. Yet by the end of the sixteenth century, most French theorists placed the highest value on those elements of law that were derived from French custom. A maxim of the realm needed no greater justification than being the way it had "always" been done. The force of tradition was so strong that, according to Bodin, French customary law could only be changed in consultation with France's three estates, although the king, as sovereign, could go against their advice if so influenced by "natural reason and the justice of his wishes."[40]

Given the high regard with which customary law was held, Antoine Loisel's *Institutes coutumières,* first published in 1608, must have been attractive to lawyers. This manual summarized in pithy proverbs the essential traditions of French custom. For example, Loisel's *"Qui veut le Roy, si veut la loy"* underscored Bodin's conception of indivisible legislative sovereignty.[41] It was here that Boucaux's lawyers found additional support for the fundamental maxim that recognized the freedom of any slave who arrived in France.

The original 1608 edition of Loisel's manual of French customs stated: "All persons are free in this kingdom; and as soon as a slave has arrived at the borders of this place, being baptized, is freed."[42] Loisel himself provided no commentary on his maxims. Thus we do not know what Loisel considered to be the origins or practices of this custom. It is noteworthy that in Loisel's original formulation of the maxim, a slave needed to be baptized as a Christian before being manumitted.

Later editors of Loisel's *Institutes coutumières* attempted to explicate the sources of French customary law. In the 1657 and 1665 editions, Paul Challine, an *avocat* in the Parlement of Paris, cited Thomas Aquinas's *Summa Theologica* as a source for the principle that baptism confers freedom on slaves.[43] François de Launay's commentary in the 1688 edition dispensed with Aquinas, preferring a historical dimension to the discussion of slavery: "Servitude, which was introduced by the law of men among the French, as among all peoples of the earth, was entirely removed from them in the time of the third generation of our kings."[44] Drawing heavily on Bodin, De Launay cited the example of Toulouse, which extended freedom to slaves who sought refuge there. Significantly, though the condition of baptism remained in Loisel's maxim, it was virtually ignored by De Launay.

Finally, in 1710, Eusèbe de Laurière published a new edition of Loisel's *Institutes coutumières* with extensive additional commentary. Eusèbe broke the maxim down into its constituent parts, reasoning that the first premise of the maxim, *"toutes personnes sont franches"* [all persons are free], must posit freedom in opposition to slavery rather than serfdom considering "there are still serfs in France, who are neither free persons [*personnes franches*] nor slaves in any way."[45] As for the second proposition, "as soon as a slave has arrived at the borders of this place, being baptized, [he] is free," Eusèbe quoted from a variety of Church sources that showed that Christians could not be held as slaves by Jews.[46] "As for those who had Catholic masters," wrote Eusèbe, "they did not become free outright by conversion to the faith; but the masters almost always manumitted them upon baptism."[47] Finally, Eusèbe noted that "today every slave is free from the moment he sets foot in the kingdom." Nevertheless, Eusèbe qualified this statement with a peculiar caveat: "It is necessary, however, to remark that this law is not in effect with regard to the negro slaves of our isles of America who come with their masters."[48] Thus even before the formulation of the Edict of 1716, Eusèbe de Laurière had excluded the application of this maxim to black slaves brought to France by their masters.

The successive editions of Loisel's *Institutes coutumières* show how historical myth gradually built up over the original customary maxim granting freedom to slaves who entered France. By the time lawyers trotted out the proverb for Boucaux, it had lost its baptismal qualification and acquired additional historical citations linking it to Louis X's ordinance and several court decisions. Like a seashell tossed by the tides, the maxim's barnaclelike accretions and collisions with opposing forces eventually distorted its original form.

In sum, Boucaux's lawyer, Mallet, and the *procureur du roi,* Le Clerc du Brillet, were crafting the maxim, or legal principle based on custom, from a variety of sources, none of which alone was precisely pertinent to the situation at hand. First, the supposed statutory basis for the maxim, Louis X's 1315 ordinance, *did* equate freedom with the name of France, but in its own historical context it applied to the freeing of serfs, not slaves, and only under certain conditions. A second, canonical, precedent, documented by Eusèbe de Laurière, granted freedom to Catholic slaves owned by non-Catholics, but noted that freedom from Catholic masters depended on their own good graces. Eusèbe de Laurière explicitly denied the privilege to black slaves arriving in France from the American colonies. A third precedent, first documented in Toulouse in the early fifteenth century, granted freedom to slaves who escaped their masters in other cities and made their way to the protection of that city. A fourth precedent was the freeing of an enemy's slaves—the Spaniards' in particular—when they sought refuge during wartime on French soil. Yet despite the divergent origins of this rather vague notion equating France with freedom, eighteenth-century lawyers were able to wrestle all of these threads into a single inviolable skein: the "maxim" that as soon as a slave set foot upon French soil, he or she was free.

In this process of historical myth making, the various prior conditions on that freedom were eliminated. The slave owner need not be foreign or non-Catholic. The slave need not be baptized. The region conferring freedom was extended from the free cities (e.g., Toulouse and Bordeaux) to the entire kingdom (but not, conveniently, to the French colonies). In this way, lawyers justified present beliefs or principles by presenting their version of French custom built on history from time immemorial.

It is significant that the slave owner's lawyer, Tribard, did not challenge the uncodified maxim that France offers freedom to those who step on its shores. On the contrary, he affirmed the principle no fewer than four times, despite the fact that, as he put it, "it is not possible to discover the primitive source of this concept."[49] The mythic character of customary law was so strong that the lawyer who stood most to gain by challenging the principle did not attempt to critique it.

Instead, Tribard rested his case on the two pieces of French legislation that did acknowledge colonial slavery: the Code Noir of 1685 and the Edict of 1716. Tribard argued that the Code Noir defined the conditions of Boucaux's slavery in the colonies and that the 1716 edict permitted slavery to extend to the French kingdom. Tribard's main line of argument against Boucaux was that his mere geographical relocation was insufficient to change his status as a slave: "Slave by the law of the state, [Boucaux] has not become a new man by approaching the source of the law which fixed his destiny."[50] Rather, Boucaux's identity as a slave was recognized by the French Code Noir and was extended to France by the Edict of 1716.

Because Tribard was not interested in justifying or discrediting the maxim that gave freedom to those who came to France, his historical account accentuated different periods and aspects of the French past. Like Mallet and Le Clerc du Brillet, Tribard affirmed the notion that in their original state, humans were free, but that greed caused them to wage war and take the losers as slaves. He reviewed Roman slave law in more detail using Justinian's code to show that one of France's legal traditions did accept slavery. When it came to the abolition of Roman slavery, Tribard shared the opposing lawyers' view that Christianity was responsible, evidence of the pervasiveness of this second historical myth.[51]

To emphasize the fact that unfree relations were a persistent feature of French life and law, Tribard dwelt heavily on the varieties of serfdom still active in France. He pointed to the continuing existence of the institution of *mainmorte* in several provinces until the eighteenth century, among them Nivernois, Bourgogne, Vitry, and Auvergne. He showed how the institution of *formariage,* which penalized serfs who married outside of their masters' domain, paralleled the Code Noir's prohibition of marriage without the master's consent. "All of these laws," wrote Tribard, "which subject the weakest to . . . the strongest and the most rich, reveal the entire illusion of this flattering name of liberty, by which we often take appearances for the reality, and for which the name holds the place of effects."[52] The lawyers for Boucaux emphasized a gradual, linear progression from past slavery to a universally free future, but Tribard painted a spottier portrait of past laws and institutions responding to the vicissitudes of historical circumstance.

In his conclusion, Tribard called the court's attention to the four thousand blacks who were already resident in France, studying religion or a trade, and to the many more enslaved in the French colonies. He warned darkly of the dangerous results that might follow from a decision in Boucaux's favor: "The worship of Religion, the tree of the Cross which our Kings have planted on this horizon would soon be sacrificed to the return of idolatry; our Temples, our Altars, abandoned or destroyed; the help, the infinite riches that the King and the Nation take from these fertile regions would become the price of the disorder and of the revolt."[53] In so doing, he underscored the relationship between slavery and Christianity, between the rule of law and maintenance of the social order.

The *procureur du roi,* whose role was to represent the interests of the state in each case, challenged many of Tribard's points in the second half of his brief. Regarding the persistence of slavelike conditions in the institution of serfdom, Le Clerc du Brillet observed that the law's purpose was to reduce the conditions of serfdom to obligations regarding the use of land:

> If several of our customs still preserve dispositions which speak of *gens de mainmorte,* our jurisprudence brings every object of this pretended servitude back, little by little, to certain duties and to certain rights which are discharged in recognition of the superiority of the Seigniory, by those who hold his real property in the extent of his fiefs and titled lands; but corporal serfdom no longer exists.[54]

He emphasized that the outright ownership of a person by another person had been totally eradicated in France.

To challenge Tribard's central thesis, that the Code Noir and the Edict of 1716 authorized slavery under certain conditions, Le Clerc du Brillet charged that neither law was registered by the Parlement of Paris and consequently had no standing in the Admiralty Court of the same jurisdiction.[55] By introducing the laws' lack of registration, Le Clerc du Brillet raised some thorny legal issues. The judges might decide, as he hoped, that if the laws were unregistered, they could have no bearing on the case, leaving the undisputed maxim as the basis of the judges' decision to free Boucaux. On the other hand, the judges might feel that, though unregistered, the law remained valid, setting conditions whereby slavery might be extended to France. Yet its lack of registration and therefore publication might be seen as sufficient reason for Verdelin, the slave owner, to be unaware of its provisions (though the law was published in Saint Domingue). The law's lack of registration might prove just the excuse that Verdelin needed for not having adequately fulfilled its formalities.

Having already supported the basis of the maxim, Le Clerc du Brillet proceeded to tackle the registration of the Code Noir and the Edict of 1716.[56] If the judges determined that the two unregistered laws were pertinent to this case, argued Le Clerc du Brillet, they should take note that the Code Noir applied only to the colonies and said nothing about slaves who might travel in the kingdom. And even though the Edict of 1716 did permit colonists to bring their slaves with them to France, Verdelin had violated both the spirit and the letter of the law, according to the two lawyers, and thus must forfeit Boucaux's unwilling service.

In a lengthy argument, Le Clerc du Brillet sought to prove that Verdelin had violated nearly every aspect of the Edict of 1716. First, the law provided only two legitimate purposes for bringing a slave to France: for religious education or training in a trade. Verdelin had brought Boucaux merely to serve him as a cook with no intention of returning him with his newfound skills to the colonies. Moreover, the Edict of 1716 was meant to apply only to property holders and military officers of the colonies. Verdelin, having married the widow of a colonist, was neither. To prevent abuse, the edict established certain formalities: before transporting their slaves to the colonies, slave owners had to obtain permission from the colonial governor and register that permission in the colonies and upon arrival in France. "If the masters fail to observe these formalities," argued the *procureur du roi,* "the slaves are free and cannot be reclaimed."[57] Verdelin did receive permission from the governor to bring two "negroes" to France, but this permission omitted the names, ages, and descriptions required by law.[58] The governor's permission was registered in both Cap Français and La Rochelle, but there was significant confusion about whether the latter registration of January 28, 1729, took place within the eight days of Verdelin's arrival in France.[59]

In his concluding remarks, the *procureur du roi* called attention to the Verdelins' remaining black servants, "a *nègre,* named Colin, and a *négresse,* called Bibiane, who have served their masters in their houses for nine years in the quality of slaves."[60] Le Clerc du Brillet asked that the court look into the status of these people as well.

It is significant that the case for Boucaux was argued entirely on the basis of Boucaux's status as a slave. Neither Mallet nor Le Clerc du Brillet found his race relevant to the case. Nor was the race of the French woman who became Boucaux's wife ever mentioned (perhaps it was taken for granted that because she was French, she was white). The *procureur du roi* portrayed Boucaux as a Frenchman, a man "equal to us," and a citizen: "French, because he was born the subject of our monarch; our equal, as much by humanity as by the religion which he professes; and citizen because he lives with us and among us."[61] There is no trace of antiblack sentiment in these lawyers' briefs.

Verdelin's lawyer, Tribard, did, on the other hand, try to argue that Boucaux's race was relevant to the case. He argued that the general principle, "whoever sets foot in this kingdom is free," was true for "any slave other than a negro slave." For example, Tribard continued, "If a foreigner or a French merchant arrives in this kingdom with some American Indians [*sauvages*] that he claims as his slaves; or a Spaniard or an Englishman comes to this kingdom with negro slaves from the colonies of his nation,"[62] then the principle that "once in France a slave was free" would hold true and these slaves would be freed. However, in the case of "negro slaves" brought to France by a Frenchman, Tribard insisted that the general principle ceased to be valid, because French law—notably the Code Noir of 1685—recognizes slavery in its own colonies as "necessary and authorized."[63] The fact that Boucaux was a negro slave from the French colonies meant that merely stepping on French soil was not enough to free him. Given Le Clerc du Brillet's devastating account of Verdelin's lapses with regard to the provisions of the 1716 edict, it seems likely that the issue of Boucaux's race was not seen as a serious challenge. Two decades later, however, a slave's racial identity would take center place in a legal contest.[64]

After hearing the arguments by Boucaux's lawyer, Mallet, Verdelin's lawyer, Tribard, and the king's representative, the *procureur du roi* Le Clerc du Brillet, the Admiralty Court of France issued its judgment in favor of Boucaux in two sentences rendered on August 29 and September 10, 1738. By these sentences, Boucaux was freed and his imprisonment struck from the record. Verdelin and his wife were sentenced to pay Boucaux 4,200 *livres* for nine and a half years of wages, including interest and damages plus court costs. The court also found the attorney general's remarks about the slaves Colin and Bibiane troubling and planned to look further into their case.[65]

In keeping with a long tradition that sees judges as mere instruments, rather than interpreters, of the law, eighteenth-century French legal decisions do not normally reveal the grounds on which a case was decided. We therefore do not know the basis for the judges' decision to free Boucaux. It is possible that they acknowledged the validity of the Edict of 1716, despite its lack of registration, and ruled that because Verdelin was not a colonist himself, and because he had not properly registered Boucaux upon arrival in France, that the slave should be freed. On the other hand, the judges may have discounted the edict entirely because of its lack of registration and ruled for Boucaux's freedom on the basis of the accepted maxim that "any slave arriving in France is free."

The Declaration of 1738

Three months after the Admiralty Court rendered Boucaux his freedom, the king issued a declaration "concerning the enslaved negroes of the colonies."[66] This new law, the Declaration of December 15, 1738, followed the general provisions of the Edict of October 1716 but attempted to eliminate many of the loopholes that favored the proliferation of black slaves in France. The preamble to this new act explained why it was necessary to reinforce the provisions of the Edict of 1716:

> We have been informed that since . . . [1716] a large number [of slaves] have arrived [in France]; that the colonists who have left the colonies, and have come to establish themselves in the kingdom, keep their negro slaves here, in violation of Article 15 of the same edict; that the greater part of the negroes contract a spirit of independence here which may have troublesome results; that, moreover, their masters neglect to teach them a useful trade so that few of those who are brought to France are returned to the colonies, and that those who are, are often useless and even dangerous.[67]

Although the declaration does not mention the case of *Boucaux v. Verdelin* specifically, the fact that it was issued so soon after the case and that it mentions some of Verdelin's abuses (such as neglecting to teach Boucaux a useful trade), suggests that the case may have prodded the king's ministers to act on the problem.

The new declaration reiterated the provisions of the Edict of 1716, which required colonists who brought their slaves to France for religious or technical instruction to obtain permission from the colonial governor and to register the slaves in the colonies and in the French port of arrival: A new provision required the *greffiers* (clerks) at these ports to record the date that the slaves arrived in France. This new requirement stemmed, no doubt, from the confusion in the Boucaux case regarding the exact date of Verdelin's arrival.

The third article required colonists who brought their slaves to Paris to register them at the Table de Marbre of the Palace in Paris (that is, the Admiralty of France) and the *greffes* of the admiralty to register them in other parts of the kingdom. The *greffes* in each case were charged with recording the trade that the slave would learn and the master in charge of the slave's instruction.

One significant change, from the perspective of the slaves themselves, was that if their owners neglected to comply with the formalities of the law, the slaves were no longer freed but confiscated *au profit du roi* and returned to the colonies "there to be employed at such work as we ordain."[68] This provision was aimed at reducing the number of free blacks in the metropolis. Colonial officers were still permitted to use slaves as domestic servants during their leaves in France, but if the slaves were not returned to the colonies at the end of the leave, they, too, would be confiscated *au profit du roi.*

In another important change, the Declaration of 1738 put a limit of three years on the amount of time a slave could remain in France to learn a trade. Under the Edict of 1716, there had been no time limit on a slave's residence in France. The French government likely hoped that this measure would prevent masters such as Verdelin from retaining their slaves in France with no intention of returning them to the colonies. Slave owners who expected to keep their slaves in France longer than the prescribed period were now required to pay 1,000 *livres* before obtaining the governor's permission.[69]

Article 9 of the Declaration of 1738 required anyone who currently had slaves in France to declare them at the nearest seat of the Admiralty within three months of the act's publication. The penalty for noncompliance was confiscation of the slaves *au profit du roi.*

Final articles of the declaration forbade slaves from marrying in France with or without their masters' consent (thus overturning article 7 of the Edict of 1716, which allowed marriage if the master permitted it); prohibited masters from freeing their slaves in France, except by testament; and enjoined slave owners to raise their slaves in the Roman Catholic faith.[70]

The Declaration of 1738 was registered by every sovereign court of France except that of Paris.[71] By refusing to register the declarations, like the Edict of October 1716 before it, the Parlement of Paris set the stage for a series of lawsuits that began in the 1750s and continued until the Revolution.

Despite the fact that the Parlement of Paris, and consequently the Court of the Admiralty for the same jurisdiction, did not register the Declaration of 1738, the Admiralty clerk did begin to keep records of slaves who were brought to the capital as required by the declaration.[72] These records were incomplete and were the exception rather than the rule.

Conclusion

In their successful pleas for Jean Boucaux, the slave's lawyer Mallet and the *procureur du roi* Le Clerc du Brillet set the stage for many of the events that would unfold in the Paris courts during the remainder of the century. First, their published briefs articulated and justified the maxim that any slave who sets foot on French soil is free. This justification was primarily historical, relying on statutes and precedents to support what was essentially a mythical relationship between France and freedom. In keeping with the prevalent assumptions of their era, these lawyers credited Christianity with the elimination of Roman slavery and its transformation into serfdom.

Second, the case called the government's attention to slave owners' abuses of the Edict of 1716, prompting new, more stringent legislation in the Declaration of December 15, 1738. Like the earlier edict, the new declaration was not registered by the Parlement of Paris, nor consequently by the lower Admiralty Court of France. Yet, for the moment, the Admiralty office in Paris began to fulfill some of the requirements specified by the new law, keeping track of some of the slave owners who brought their slaves to Paris.

Boucaux's story does not end with the sentence of September 1738. Verdelin and his wife decided to appeal over the decision of the Admiralty Court directly to the king. They offered to free Boucaux outright and asked that the court's decision be overturned. Louis XV's initial response, dated September 12, 1738, approved of their request.[73] The following April, the king issued orders concerning the former slave:

The king, having regard for the very humble demand made to His Majesty by Sir and Dame Verdelin, to free . . . Jean Boucaux, their negro slave, the which they would have sent back to their plantation in Saint Domingue in France, His Majesty has ordained and does ordain that the said Jean Boucaux be held and deemed free; [but] wishes, however, that he leaves the city of Paris within eight days, without being able to return there for any reason or under any pretext that there could be; similarly prohibits him from returning to the island of Saint Domingue, nor to any other of the French islands of America under the pain of disobedience.[74]

The king's minister sent the orders to Le Clerc du Brillet, the Admiralty's *procureur du roi,* with additional orders to free Boucaux from the the prisons of Porte L'Évêque, where he had apparently been detained. "I pray of you," wrote the minister:

to put this latter order into execution and to remit the other to this *nègre*; but before everything, you would be agreeable to get from [Boucaux] a general and absolute desistance of all presentations against Mr. and Mrs. Verdelin, in a manner that they cannot ever be disturbed. It has appeared proper to so terminate this affair which, as you know, has already made too much uproar.[75]

One likely conjecture, based on the evidence, is that Boucaux never received his 4,200 *livres* in back wages and pressed the Verdelins for justice. They sought to escape the penalty by pleading directly to the king, agreeing to free Boucaux outright.

The stipulation that Boucaux not return to the colonies is intriguing. Could it be that by affirming Boucaux's rights against his former master, the Admiralty Court of France strengthened his resolve for justice and contributed to the formation of the "disorder and revolt" that Verdelin's lawyer Tribard had warned of? However the case, the officers of the Admiralty Court may have been reluctant to dabble again in such affairs. They would not hear another petition for freedom for more than a decade. Meanwhile, in Brittany, one of the provinces that had registered the Declaration of 1738, a slave named Catherine attempted to sue for her freedom. We turn now to her case.

3

The Impact of the Declaration of 1738:
Nantes, La Rochelle, and Paris

The Declaration of December 15, 1738, held that when masters neglected to complete the necessary formalities, such as registration of their slaves with the nearest clerk of the Admiralty, the slaves would be confiscated *au profit du roi* and returned as slaves to the colonies whence they came. As we shall see, the Parlement of Paris and the Admiralty Court of France refused to confiscate slaves and instead freed them unconditionally. However, the case of Catherine Morgan, who was brought to Nantes by her master in 1746, illustrates how the courts of Brittany enforced the Declaration of 1738 to the letter.

The Case of Catherine Morgan

In August of 1747, the Count of Maurepas, minister of the marine, received a rather peculiar letter. It purported to be from a black woman named Catin. Evidentally, she did not know how to write because the letter had been drafted for her by someone named "Sapotin." The letter's style was clumsy and irregular, full of gushing, endless sentences and inconsistent spelling. The story that spilled out was even stranger:

> As I don't know who to plead to, someone has told me that I might turn to you to render me justice[.] I must tell you that when Terrien the lawyer took me away from my Master, making me believe that he would make me free

within eight days of this life I agreed to leave my Master and without his knowledge gathered my things . . . money containing nine hundred *livres* in pieces of six *livres* that a second captain had given me to help me get my freedom. This [is] the captain with whom I had traveled to France, with whom I had commerce during the entire passage and also in France, and by whom I am now pregnant. As soon as I left my Master I found the said Terrien and gave him the sum of nine hundred *livres*.[1]

Maurepas paused to underline the last sentence, which seemed to be the crux of the dispute, and continued reading:[2]

He promised that he would take me the next day to the Good Shepherd which is the place where he led me during the night accompanied by his wife so as to hide my escape from my master who was most distressed with me. Since this time *Mr. le Commissaire ordonnateur de la Marine* made me leave the Good Shepherd and go to the hospital of this city of Nantes, I had a letter written to Sr. Terrien to ask for my money. He gave me word that he never had more than the sum of 650 *livres* from me and that he brought it to the Good Shepherd something which I haven't any knowledge of. . . . Is it fair, sir, that after having lured me away with promises of freedom from my master where I was happy that he should keep my money?[3]

This was messy indeed. The remainder of the letter castigated the lawyer Terrien for interfering between the woman and her master and accused him of wanting her as a servant for his child so that he could say that his daughter had a negress for a servant. There were witnesses who could testify that he had stolen her money. She closed with a plea: "Your Grace, render me justice so that the said Terrien returns my money into the hands of my Master Morgan or those of *M. le Commissaire ordonnateur*."[4] The letter was signed "Sapotin, writing for the negress named Catin Morgan held at the hospital of Nantes by the orders of his Grace, the Count of Maurepas." There was a postscript that identified the captain who had given her the money as "Pierre Rambaud," living in Painboeuf, River of Nantes.

Maurepas scrawled in the margin, "To M. Millain, to verify and speak to these affairs." Perhaps the commandant of the marine at Nantes would be able to get to the bottom of this. Maurepas drafted a letter to Millain asking him to look into the situation.[5] Millain received the minister's missive within a few days. He knew of Terrien, a prominent lawyer in Nantes, and perhaps more than he wished to of the whole sordid affair. Obediently, he contacted Terrien who agreed to write a report on his part in the controversy.

Terrien's report brought a completely new perspective to the case. The lawyer claimed that the letter to Maurepas was not written by "Sapotin" or "Catin" at all, but was written by the negress's master, Morgan. Terrien's account of the woman's flight from her master was different and somewhat more plausible. He called her "Catherine."

According to Terrien, Morgan returned to Nantes from Saint Domingue with Catherine and their eighteen-month-old child in September 1746. Lemesle, another colonist who had recently arrived from Saint Domingue, put the family up in his home. The baby was baptized in November in Ste. Croix. Then Morgan, Catherine, and the child retired to Lemesle's house near Nantes. Terrien claimed that Morgan began to mistreat Catherine and that she went to Lemesle for protection. Terrien heard her complaints while visiting Lemesle. Lemesle brought Catherine back to Morgan and admonished him for treating her so harshly. But to no effect: the same thing occurred two more times. Finally, during a visit to Lemesle, Terrien heard Catherine shouting in the kitchen, and "having contracted a spiritual affinity with her" felt obliged to intervene on her behalf with Morgan, saying that "one doesn't treat blacks that way in France."[6]

Lemesle returned Catherine to Morgan for a fourth time but, when Morgan hit her with a fireplace shovel on Ash Wednesday, Catherine remembered Terrien's advice and went to him directly. Terrien counseled her to hide at the home of another negress who lived in a suburb of Nantes. She came back to Terrien several times at night to ask whether he couldn't obtain her freedom. Terrien said he would try, but warned her that it was more likely that she would be placed under the "protection" of the king and returned to the colonies.[7] Catherine replied that she would prefer that to remaining in the hands of Morgan. Terrien remembered her stating in front of witnesses that she would prefer to die rather than to return to Morgan's possession. Terrien unsuccessfully attempted to secure Catherine's freedom by purchasing her from Morgan through Lemesle. Then he proceeded to petition the judges of the Admiralty of Nantes.

Meanwhile, Catherine was taken to the convent of the Good Shepherd by the widow Jan François (a free negress). The widow Jan François had posted a deposit with Terrien of 648 *livres* and came from time to time to retrieve the money. Terrien claimed that he gave her 210 *livres* on several occasions. Terrien knew that Jan François was feeding and caring for Catherine at Good Shepherd. The mother superior of the convent was also aware of the situation.

Morgan, Catherine's master, was enraged by Terrien's interference. He sought out Terrien in the public square of Puits Lory and told him that he would kill him. He waited for Terrien at Carquefou, a village ten kilometers northeast of central Nantes (presumably for a duel—illegal but still practiced in France), but Terrien never showed up, going instead to the criminal judge of Nantes to complain of this threat against his life. He was presented by the Seneschal of Nantes to Louis Jean Marie de Bourbon, duc de Penthièvre, to demand justice against Morgan.[8] As a result, M. Demenou, king's lieutenant in Nantes, gave Morgan a reprimand. Terrien was satisfied, but Morgan continued to pursue him, saying that if he should ever meet him in America, he would kill him with a pistol shot, and that perhaps he would do it in Nantes before returning to America. Terrien reported that these threats alarmed both himself and his family as he believed Morgan capable of such a deed.[9]

Terrien pleaded his case before the public audience of the Admiralty, but Morgan never bothered to appear. Morgan's friend Lemesle came to explain but didn't deny the charges. It was from Lemesle that Terrien learned that Morgan had been sentenced in Saint Domingue for excessive beating and torturing of blacks and that he had lost his fortune there.

The judges of the Admiralty Court of Nantes ruled that Catherine should be confiscated from Morgan *au profit du roi* and returned to Saint Domingue. Despite the fact that Morgan's lawyer opposed this sentence, Terrien wrote a *mémoire* on her behalf and sent it to the count of Maurepas and Delaporte, the bishop of Nantes, requesting that Catherine be transfered to the hospital (*hôtel dieu*) of Nantes.

According to Terrien, this is when Morgan discovered Catherine's "secret" (the lawyer's account was a bit vague here) and forged a letter in her name, signing it "Sapotin." The fact that the letter was a fraud could easily be deduced by comparing its handwriting to Morgan's.

Terrien concluded his report by charging that everything in the original letter was "false and slanderous." First, it was the widow Jan François who gave him the deposit, not Catherine. Second, the amount was only 648 *livres,* not 910 *livres.* Terrien kept 146 *livres* to cover the costs of the case, fees, and "the pains without number that this unhappy affair cost him by being embraced by a spirit of charity." The remainder was returned to the widow. Third, Terrien had not "sought to profit by the negress . . . [nor did he] dream of retaining her at his house in the service of his child; on the contrary, he advised her to hide herself where she could." Finally, Terrien protested the slander against his good reputation as a lawyer.[10]

Certainly Terrien's story was easier to understand than the stream-of-consciousness complaint signed by "Sapotin." And the lawyer's story had strong explanations for everyone's motives. But Terrien was hardly an unbiased observer. He was defending his reputation. It was only one person's word against another's. Millain decided to go to a nonpartisan witness for a better perspective on the case. He sent notaries to take the testimony of the widow Jan François.

The document containing the widow's testimony is rare because it is one of the few cases where a black woman speaks directly from an eighteenth-century text. Her voice is no doubt mediated by the formalities imposed by the notary, but the substance of the text is the woman's own framing of the events. It reveals a perspective quite different from the lawyer Terrien's or the forged letter by Morgan from a supposed "Catin." Terrien's account is plausible, but that of the widow Jan François reveals certain details that may bring us closer to Catherine's own perspective.

In the notarized statement, the widow is named as "Charlotte Bourbouin, free negress, widow of Jan François Coffy, also negro." The notaries recorded that Madame Bourbouin lived in the parish of St. Nicolas in one of the suburbs of Nantes. She confirmed Terrien's story that Catherine (here specified as *"fille négresse de nation sengalle"*) ran away from her master Morgan on Ash Wednesday of the same year after he had beaten her so hard that she feared for her life. Whereas Terrien claimed that Catherine had come directly to him for aid, Bourbouin noted that she had first sought refuge with another black woman named Henriette.[11]

Bourbouin refers to Terrien as "the godfather of one of [Catherine's] children," which explains his knowledge of the baby's baptism, a year earlier. It also implies that Catherine had more than one child. According to Bourbouin, Terrien counseled Catherine to go into hiding to prevent herself from being beaten again "by such a hard master whose most recent marks she still bore."[12] Bourbouin says that she and Henriette went to Terrien to try to persuade him to purchase Catherine from her master. To this end they gave him 648 *livres* in pieces of six *livres* that Terrien counted in Bourbouin's presence. But Terrien was unsuccessful in arranging the sale. Bourbouin and Terrien accompanied Catherine to the Convent of the Good Shepherd with the convent administrators' permission. While she was there, Catherine discovered that she was pregnant since before arrival there (the "secret" to which Terrien had delicately alluded). Bourbouin secured money from Terrien several times to buy "all sorts of food for Catherine, such as bread, wine, meat and other necessities."[13]

Meanwhile Terrien attempted to secure Catherine's freedom through the Admiralty Court of Nantes. On May 17, 1747, the court ruled that because Morgan had failed to fulfill the requirements of the Declaration of December 15, 1738, Catherine should be confiscated *au profit du roi* and returned to the colonies.[14] After the case was judged, Terrien remitted to Bourbouin the sum of 252 *livres*. Terrien said that he retained the surplus to reimburse himself for his advances and to pay himself for his pains, cares, and services. Bourbouin assured the notaries that he didn't take more than he was due. After having received the money from Terrien, she turned it over to Pierre Raimbaud, a ship captain, because he had originally furnished this amount to Catherine a little while after she left Morgan, in the presence of Bourbouin, "Lopy" (another black woman), and several others.

In Bourbouin's account, the story takes on a different shape. Catherine is not portrayed as a helpless victim seeking the lawyer's "charity," but as a young woman—a girl—who nevertheless has a history: she is Senegalese. Fearing for her life, she turns to a free black woman for assistance. Only then do they turn to the lawyer Terrien.

Perhaps the most remarkable fact that Bourbouin's testimony uncovers is the network of black women who supported Catherine through her difficulties in Nantes. When beaten by Morgan, Catherine turned to Henriette. It is not clear how Bourbouin was drawn into the affair; perhaps she was the *négresse* that Terrien directed Catherine to the night that she was beaten. Or it is possible that Henriette sent for Bourbouin as an older, more experienced woman who would know what to do. Bourbouin's own account suggests that the idea to purchase Catherine from her master originated with herself and Henriette. These women approached the mysterious "Captain Raimbaud" (in the presence of "Lopy, another negress"), who provided the money with which to buy her. There were apparently a number of black women involved in the network.

The white women at the Convent of the Good Shepherd were also apparently sympathetic to Catherine's plight and sheltered her just as the nuns of Calgary had protected a young girl from her mistress in 1715.[15]

Having gathered the various pieces of evidence, Commandant Millain sent them to Minister Maurepas in Paris with two cover letters on September 12, 1747. The first letter mentioned that Catherine had been confiscated *au profit du roi* and had already embarked for Saint Domingue. He felt that Terrien's report was amply supported by the widow Bourbouin's testimony. Furthermore, as a result of his own inquiries, Millain was inclined to believe that, "the complaints leveled by the negress Catherine in her plea were suggested to her by Morgan, and appear to be beyond respect."[16] In other words, Millain did not embrace the notion that "Catin's" letter was literally forged by Morgan, but he acknowledged that Morgan had had a hand in composing the complaints.

Millain's second letter contained a significant postscript to Catherine's story: "The negress Catherine, that I had the honor of mentioning to you in my letter of [August] 31, to be embarked on the *St. Alexis,* wasn't taken there until the ninth of this month [September], finding herself *en mal d'enfant* with the baby which she bore."[17] Apparently Catherine successfully bore another child whom she took with her back to Saint Domingue.

The birth of this child may explain a few loose ends. If Catherine bore the child in September, she probably became pregnant early in 1747. If the mysterious Captain Pierre Raimbaud was indeed the father of the child, as "Sapotin" claimed in the letter, this might explain why he was willing to front the money for Catherine's escape. Furthermore, if Morgan became aware that Catherine was pregnant and had reason to believe that he was not the father, it might explain the severe beating of Ash Wednesday. On the other hand, it is also possible that Morgan was the father of this second child.

When Catherine and her children arrived in Saint Domingue, the intendant Maillart was waiting with the king's orders for them: "His Majesty . . . wishes that the said negress Catherine and her children . . . be employed in public works [*travaux publiques*] in the said colonies; or, supposing that they cannot fulfill this intention, be sold to the highest bidder and the price of their sale be put to use for the cost of these [public] works."[18] Maurepas interpreted some aspects of the king's order for the intendant: "You know that such confiscated slaves must be put to use at public works. It is up to you to dispose of her in the manner which seems to you most appropriate. But you must make sure that she does not fall back into the hands of Morgan, supposing that he returns to the colony."[19] By confiscating Catherine and her children, sending them back to Saint Domingue, ordering them to labor at public works or to be sold to any but Morgan, the Admiralty Court of Nantes and the king's administration were enforcing the Declaration of 1738 to the letter. Though Catherine Morgan attempted to win her freedom with the attorney Terrien's help, the court decided that Catherine should be confiscated and returned to the colony, as provided by law. This contrasts sharply with the decisions of the Admiralty Court of Paris, as we shall see later. We may safely presume, however, that the decision in Catherine's case was the norm, rather than the exception, for courts within the jurisdiction of the Parlement of Rennes, that is, Britanny (including Nantes, Lorient, Brest, Quimper, and Saint Malo), where a significant portion of French slaves would have disembarked.

Catherine Morgan's case offers a rare insight into the social connections between blacks and whites in the port city of Nantes. It is unique among all the cases examined in that it reveals how a slave was able to make contact with a lawyer and to pay for the lawyer's services. Through informal networks, Catherine sought the assistance of Terrien, a prominent lawyer who was friends with her master's friend, Lemesle. At the same time, she made contact with free black women who attempted to purchase her freedom by borrowing money from a sympathetic ship captain. When the sale could not be arranged, the lawyer Terrien deducted his fees. It is unclear whether or how Captain Raimbaud was repaid the money he loaned.

At the same time, the case illustrates a popular notion of justice that operated independently of statutes. Catherine sought her freedom only after she had been beaten quite severely. This pattern appears frequently in other lawsuits for freedom. It seems that popular belief held that a slave, like a servant, might be beaten to a certain degree without fear of reprisal. However, if a subordinate feared for his or her life, the community accepted this as a justifiable basis for flight.[20]

In another sense, the case demonstrates how some customs regarding slavery in the colonies had already begun to be imported to France. For example, the widow Bourbouin, Terrien, and Raimbaud all conspired to purchase Catherine from Morgan although the sale of slaves was specifically prohibited by Article 11 of the Edict of 1716. In other cases, as we shall see, the act of baptism was also popularly connected with manumission.

La Rochelle and Paris

La Rochelle, on France's Atlantic Coast, was one of a handful of port cities whose appeals from the Admiralty Court were made to the *Siège*

général de L'Amirauté à la Table de Marbre, known as the Admiralty
Court of France, in Paris.[21] As has been suggested, the decisions in
lawsuits for freedom in the Admiralty Court of France differed from
those of other juridictions because the Parlement of Paris and the Admiralty Court of France never registered the Edict of 1716 or the Declaration of December 15, 1738. One immediate consequence of the lack of
registration was that the control of black slaves within the jurisdiction of
the Parlement of Paris and the Admiralty Court of France was main-
tained through the king's administrative apparatus, headed by the minister of the marine, rather than through the judicial branch of the government.

An example of the confusion caused by the lack of registration is
apparent in the records of the minister of the marine, the count of
Maurepas. On August 31, 1741, nearly three years after the declaration
had gone into effect, the minister wrote to Barentin, the *intendant* of La
Rochelle, with the king's orders that all persons with negroes (*nègres*)[22]
in their service were required to send them back to the colonies within
six months.[23] It is likely that an identical letter was sent to each of the
ports within the jurisdiction of the Admiralty of France and possible that
such a letter was sent to other major ports, such as Marseille and Bordeaux, as a followup to the Declaration of 1738.

Barentin responded to the minister by querying whether freeing the
nègres in question would exempt them from expulsion.[24] He counted 58
nègres (33 men, 7 women, and 18 boys) in his city, noting that in
addition to these, there was a black man, his wife and son who worked at
the mint, and three mulatto women who worked as laundresses. "Since
these two latter types of *nègres* have been free for a long time, I don't
believe that the King's orders concern them," he wrote.[25] Barentin also
pointed out that the Declaration of 1738 was never sent to him nor
registered by the Admiralty of La Rochelle and requested a copy of it.

Barentin's later correspondence notes several other exceptions to the
king's order to return all *nègres* to the colonies within six months. Naval
officers were generally exempted from the order. Specific exemptions
were granted for Messieurs Girandeau and White, for unclear reasons.[26]
Finally, an abbot claimed that the servant living with him had been freed
by testament in 1730 and so should not be expelled from France.[27]

Barentin's letters assured the minister of the marine that all of the
remaining blacks would be returned to the colonies within six months,
but it is not apparent whether the mission was ever fully accomplished.
In 1747, the year Catherine's case was tried in Nantes, the minister of

the marine was still nagging the officials of La Rochelle to confiscate any slaves whose masters had not complied with the requirements of the Declaration of 1738.[28]

During the early 1750s there is further evidence that the Declaration of 1738 was not being properly enforced—both within and outside the jurisdictions of the Admiralty Court of France in Paris. A letter from the minister to the colonial officials dated May 11, 1752, states: "I have been informed that despite the precautions taken by the King's Declaration of December 15, 1738 concerning the enslaved negroes who are brought from the islands to France, they multiply more and more every day in nearly every city of the kingdom."[29] The minister ordered Dubois de la Motte to send him a list of the blacks who had left the islands for France, including the names of their masters and the vessels by which they traveled. The list was to be updated every six months. Meanwhile, the minister continued, "I will take measures to have [the Declaration of 1738] executed in France."[30]

A similar letter was apparently sent to the governors of the other Caribbean colonies on the same date.[31] In their response, the administrators of Saint Domingue dutifully reported the names of blacks who had left for France, but warned the minister against returning blacks to the colonies *en masse* after they had lived in France:

> Almost always the leaders of revolts and the worst subjects among the blacks and mulattoes are those who have been in France; and the usefulness that the colonists can extract from them by the skills that they have learned there or the trades that they have learned there cannot compare with the harm they can do, or that they actually do, in this land.[32]

Thus a tension arose between the king's administration in France and the colonial administrators of the islands. The royal government wanted to demarcate clear boundaries between the slavery practiced in the colonies and the freedom traditionally accorded to French subjects. The colonists were sympathetic to the government's goals in principle but wanted to preserve the colonists' right to domestic service during the ocean voyage and to prevent the return of blacks to the colonies who had profited by the higher prestige and practices of resistance that they had been exposed to in France.

Though the Parlement of Paris and the Admiralty of France did not register the Declaration of 1738, the Admiralty of France behaved during the 1740s and 1750s as though the declaration was in effect in certain ways. For example, it began to keep records of the slave masters who registered their slaves upon arrival in Paris, as required by article 3 of the declaration.[33] Also, though one might have expected a flood of lawsuits for freedom because of the law's lack of registration, no slave used the Admiralty Court of France between December 15, 1738, and November 1752 to sue for freedom. To understand why this occurred, we must explore the obstacles in the way of any slave who might consider using the court.

First, the enslaved person would have had to have been unhappy in his or her circumstances. Typically, a slave in France was a domestic servant, provided with food, clothing, and lodging in exchange for the services rendered by the slave. Slaves did not receive a wage, but free domestic servants were not necessarily paid in cash either. A slave could be beaten, but so could a servant or a recalcitrant child. To challenge one's slave status and its perquisites, a person would have to determine that the risks of leaving the master's service (unemployment, starvation, arrest, and imprisonment) were worth the gains (liberty in the abstract and possible physical safety in the case of extreme abuse). Many slaves must have determined that the hardships of their condition were offset by the benefits.

Second, a slave would have to have access to legal representation and the means to afford it. Catherine's case illustrates that access to legal professionals was possible, but we may guess that finding a sympathetic lawyer could be difficult. For a slave to be able to afford a lawyer's fees was more difficult still. Lack of access to legal representation was thus a major impediment to seeking freedom through the Admiralty Court of France.

Finally, until the first successful cases were publicized, few, even among the legal elite, probably realized that a challenge to the Declaration of 1738 was possible. We have seen that although the Declaration of 1738 was not registered by the Parlement of Paris and was thus withheld from the lower Admiralty courts (including the Admiralty of France and its *sièges particuliers* such as La Rochelle), the king's administration was able to enforce the provisions of the declaration by individual fiat. It probably never occurred to any but a handful of lawyers that the law was challengeable on the grounds of nonregistration.

Given these obstacles, the more meaningful question is: Why did slaves begin to use the Admiralty Court of France to win their freedom in the 1750s? In the first of these cases, Jean Baptiste, a black born in

Cap Français, Saint Domingue, on the plantation of his master, Sir
Stableton, an Irishman, challenged his master sometime after arriving in
Paris. The date of his arrival in France is unknown; his master, Sir
Stableton, never registered him in Paris as required by the Declaration of
1738. He petitioned the Court of the Admiralty for his freedom with the
assistance of his lawyer, Dubourneuf, on November 8, 1752. After an
audience with Sir Stableton, the court awarded Jean Baptiste his freedom on November 13, 1752.[34]

Though the documentation regarding this case is limited, it highlights
the ambiguous status of the Declaration of 1738 within the Admiralty
Court of France in 1752. First, Jean Baptiste's petition, drawn up by his
lawyer, emphasized that his master, Stableton, had neglected to comply
with the terms of either the Edict of 1716 or the Declaration of 1738. The
petition and the Admiralty Clerk's statement both refer to the registers of
blacks in Paris that were begun in response to article 3 of the Declaration
of 1738. So, in some sense, the king's laws were regarded as authorita-
tive in the matter.

Yet Jean Baptiste's petition also points out that neither the Edict of
1716 nor the Declaration of 1738 were registered, casting some doubt on
their validity. In their decision, the judges of the Admiralty Court of
France did not order Jean Baptiste's confiscation, as provided by article
4 the Declaration of 1738, but instead awarded him his freedom outright, in direct opposition to this provision:

> Article 4: Negro slaves of either sex who are brought to France by their
> masters, or who are sent there by them, may not claim to have aquired their
> liberty under the pretext of their arrival in the kingdom; and are required to
> return to the colonies when their masters judge appropriate; but in the event
> of the masters' failure to observe the formalities proscribed by the preceding
> articles, the said slaves will be confiscated at our profit and employed in the
> work that we ordain.[35]

The court's decision to award Jean Boucaux his freedom outright may be
evidence that the judges determined that the Declaration of 1738 was
invalid because unregistered.

Two years after Jean Baptiste won his freedom, the Admiralty Court
of France in Paris heard its first request by a master that an *acte d'affranchissement,* or act of manumission, be registered by the court's
clerk. The request is notable not only for being the first of its kind, but
also because the freedom that it accorded was conditional upon three
additional years of service by the slave:

S. Louis Robert Girand de Cresal, . . . being content with the services rendered him for several years and notably for the past five years by François Durand, his slave, aged 32 years or thereabouts, and born in Martinique, . . . accords . . . to the said François Durand, mulatto, his freedom, and all the more willingly that he has provided for his sustinence, having him learn pastry making at Filleville, pastrymaker and caterer in this city of Paris . . . in the Marais; freedom which he gives him upon this condition, however, that he will serve with zeal, faithfulness and attachment for three consecutive years . . . the Reverend Father de la Valette, Superior General of the French Isles of the Company of Jesus.[36]

It is notable that the clerk of the Admiralty registered this act of manumission despite the fact that the Declaration of 1738 specifically prohibited manumissions "except by testament."[37]

The following year, in the summer of 1755, a flurry of lawsuits came before the Admiralty Court of France. Four slaves were represented by the same lawyer, Antoine Joseph Collet, in four separate petitions.[38] Collet would go on to represent nine more slaves in lawsuits of this type during the next five years, including an important test case before the Parlement of Paris in 1759.[39] Little else is known about the lawyer, though he may have eventually been executed in Lyon during the Terror.[40]

Collet began to collect evidence for the cases as early as January 1755, but his strategy was to bring approximately one petition per week before the Admiralty Court during the month of July 1755.[41] In the first case, he was assisted by the lawyer Mallet who had represented Jean Boucaux in 1738. The first petition, for the *négresse* Corinne, was the most detailed and spelled out the arguments that would be used in each of the subsequent cases.

Born in Guinea, Corinne was taken a slave at the age of ten and transported to Saint Domingue where she was purchased by Dame Marie Catherine Louis de Silvecanne, wife of Sir Joseph Marchand Dumée, a former captain of the infantry. Dame and Sir Dumée brought Corinne to Nantes in 1749. In the service of Dame Dumée, Corinne accompanied her mistress as a lady's maid to Paris. According to her lawyers, Corinne was aware that she might challenge her status as a slave on the grounds that all slaves are free as soon as they set foot on French soil. "But," her petition continues: "She did not want to reclaim [her freedom] because of the sincere attachment that she felt toward the said Dame Dumée; an attachment that would have endured forever if the said Dame had not abused her power over the petitioner as her servant and not as her slave in mistreating her daily."[42] In response to her mistreatment, Corinne

left her mistress. As she left (so we are told), she asked for the linens and
clothes that she customarily used, but Dame Dumée responded with
threats and "a shower of blows," so that Corinne left without them.

Collet and Mallet argued as the basis of their case that Corinne should
be recognized as free since her arrival in France because of a "privilege
of the nation as old as the monarchy (our kings having always had a
horror of tyranny and of slavery)." They added that the Catholic religion, "which the petitioner has the happiness to profess," is also against
slavery.

In conformity with the Admiralty Court's tradition of ambivalence
regarding the Declaration of 1738, Corinne's petition argued both that
Dame Dumée had not made the required declarations with the clerk of
the Admiralty since her arrival in Paris with Corinne in 1750[43] *and* that
the Declaration had never been registered by the Parlement and therefore
"can not have the force of law, nor destroy the original law established
in the kingdom which gives freedom irrevocably to anyone who lands in
France." In consequence, argued the lawyers, "in conformance with
the laws and ordinances of the kingdom registered in the parlement,"
Corinne should be given a hearing to request her freedom, the restitution
of her linens and clothes, and the payment of 500 *livres* in wages for five
years of service to Dame and Sir Dumée in France.

The lawyer's insistence upon following only those laws registered by
parlement is ironic because, as shown, the maxim granting freedom to
slaves upon arrival in France was a custom, never enacted as a royal
decree, and thus never registered by any parlement. Yet, by stressing
that neither the Edict of 1716 nor especially the Declaration of 1738 was
registered, the lawyers clearly hoped to win Corinne's freedom, not her
mere confiscation by the king. The argument that Dame Dumée had not
fulfilled the requirements of registering Corinne annually with the clerk
of the Admiralty was probably offered as a back-up argument, in case
the Admiralty judges decided that the Declaration of 1738 was valid. It
seems possible, even likely, that Collet's series of cases in July 1755
were designed to test the validity of the law in the Admiralty Court of
France.

Conclusion

Unlike the Admiralty Court at Nantes, which ordered Catherine to be
confiscated and returned to the colonies to perform labor in the public

works, the Admiralty Court of France in Paris awarded Corinne, the slave whose test case was introduced in the summer of 1755, her unconditional freedom and 500 *livres* in wages and expenses.[44] Five other slaves won their freedom in the same court that year.[45] In fact, as we shall see, every slave who sued for freedom within the Admiralty Court of France over the next forty-five years won the case either in the initial, provisional sentence, in the sentence resulting from an audience, or upon appeal. As a result of their petitions to this court, 154 slaves won their freedom this way (see Table 3.1).

It appears that their success was due to two factors. First, the Admiralty Court of France never recognized the validity of either the Edict of October 1716 or the Declaration of December 15, 1738, because they had not been registered by the Parlement of Paris. Consequently they relied on the maxim that any slave who entered the French kingdom was free. Second, certain lawyers actively sought out these cases and promoted them in the court. All but one of the slaves who petitioned for their freedom in 1755 were represented by the same lawyer: Joseph Antoine Collet.[46] Little is known about Collet himself, but as we shall see, he was not the only lawyer to champion the right to freedom in France.

Table 3.1. Petitions for Freedom before the Admiralty Court of France, 1730–1790

	Suits for Freedom	Acts of Liberty	Total Slaves Freed
1730s	2	0	2
1740s	0	0	0
1750s	11	2	13
1760s	71	12	83
1770s[a]	23	19	42
1780s	43	58	101
1790s[b]	4	2	6
TOTAL:	154	93	247

Source: "Minutes de Jugement" of the Admiralty of France (Paris: Archives Nationales, Z^1D 126–37).
[a]From June 1771 to July 1775 the Admiralty Court was disbanded and consequently heard no cases.
[b]The Admiralty Court was abolished on November 11, 1790.

Unfortunately for Corinne and several other slaves who won their cases in 1755, however, their freedom was short-lived. As in the case of Jean Boucaux in 1738, the royal administration intervened by fiat.[47] This time the king ordered that four of them (all women) should be arrested, conducted to the port of Le Havre, and returned to Saint Domingue at the expense of their mistresses.[48] The fate of the two male slaves is unknown.

According to Machault, the Keeper of the Seals,

> These orders have been executed, with the exception of the embarkment for Saint Domingue, which has not yet taken place, due to a lack of ships headed for this colony. But the suit which has been brought in the name of these negresses at the admiralty continues to be pursued. Some have even affected to place a very improper passion in this inquiry [*On a même affecté de mettre une chaleur très déplacée dans cette instruction*]. In order to avoid the effects, and to conserve [the slave owners'] propriety in their goods, or to assure them of the King's confiscation if this must take place, I took it upon myself to propose to the King the removal of this case; and I am pleased to inform you that the order has been expedited.[49]

I have found no further indication of the continuation of Corinne's case. It appears, then, that the Admiralty Court of France was initially only marginally successful in obtaining slaves' freedom.

To increase the court's effectiveness, it was necessary to get a definitive ruling on the subject by the highest court, the Parlement of Paris. We turn now to the high court's test case that brought to the jurists' attention for the first time the slippery problem of race.

4

Notions of Race
in the Eighteenth Century

In 1759 the Parlement of Paris rendered a landmark decision that established once and for all the status of slaves who sued for their freedom within the jurisdiction of this court and, consequently, the Admiralty Courts within its domain. This was the case of Francisque.[1]

Francisque's case is significant for several reasons. First, it set an important precedent not only for the suits that would follow it in the same jurisdiction, but also across the channel in England's celebrated Somerset case.[2] Second, it provides a unique window into French thinking on racial difference in the middle of the eighteenth century. For in their attempts to argue that Francisque was not a *nègre*, and thus not subject to the laws of 1716 and 1738, the lawyers revealed some tacit assumptions about the meaning of the term *nègre* and the foundations of racism in eighteenth-century France.

Francisque of Pondicherry

Francisque was in some ways typical of the slaves who traveled to France from its colonies during this period. Purchased as a young boy, he was brought to Paris as a domestic servant for his master. As shown in the following chapter, young males were predominant among Parisian blacks.[3] Francisque was atypical, however, in one important regard: he was a native of Pondicherry, India. The best figures we have for this period indicate that only about 8 percent of the blacks in Paris at this time were born in India.[4] The majority of blacks in Paris (55 percent) originated in the Caribbean colonies of Guadeloupe, Martinique, and especially Saint Domingue. The remainder came directly from West Africa (10 percent); East Africa, including Mozambique, Madagascar, Ile de Bourbon, and Ile de France (17 percent); and French settlements in Canada and Louisiana (6 percent). Thus the majority of blacks in France were—not surprisingly—of African descent. The distinction between black Africans and South Indians became a pivotal point in Francisque's case.

Francisque's master, Sieur Allain François Ignace Brignon, was a native of Saint Malo in Brittany. He came from a modest background, and as a young man he went to sea to seek his fortune. In 1747 he was trading in Pondicherry, a French port on the southeast coast of India, about one hundred miles south of Madras. According to the legal brief filed later on Francisque's behalf, it was there that Brignon, "drunk with the pleasure of astonishing his compatriots with the riches he had acquired," decided to buy two young boys as slaves.[5] He purchased Francisque, age 8, and his brother André, for the sum of eight rupees each.[6] During his return voyage he stopped in Lisbon. Because of the boys' youth, they were not especially useful to him, so he sent them to his mother in Saint Malo, who instructed them in the Catholic faith and arranged for their baptism. Their arrival in France was duly recorded in the registers of the *greffe* of the Admiralty of Saint Malo.[7]

In 1750 Brignon returned to France and built a large mansion in Paris, near the Porte Montmartre. He had prospered during his voyages. His new home included a garden full of flowerbeds and arbors. He brought the two Indian boys to Paris where their exotic backgrounds no doubt added to the sense of luxury and opulence sought in the new quarters.[8] In 1757, Francisque and his brother André, feeling that they were being mistreated, decided to seek work as valets for another employer. According to their lawyer, "As everybody knows, Indian blacks, completely unlike the negroes of Africa, are ordinarily good domestics; consequently they had no difficulty finding a new position."[9]

Their former master, Brignon, obtained an order to have them imprisoned at Bicêtre. On February 4, 1758, the *procureur en la cour* brought suit against Brignon in the Admiralty Court of France on the grounds that the young men were free since their arrival in France. The court found in favor of Francisque and André, but Brignon brought a countersuit, charging that because he had put up 300 *livres* in surety, he should be allowed to seize the brothers. Francisque was transferred to the Conciergerie, but André somehow managed to escape and was never heard from again.[10]

The suits and countersuits between Francisque and Brignon continued through the spring and summer of 1758, culminating in the Admiralty's decision that Francisque should be set free. But Brignon decided to appeal the decision to the Parlement of Paris where it was heard in 1759.[11]

Francisque was represented in the Parlement of Paris by Antoine Joseph Collet, the *procureur* who had already represented five slaves before the Admiralty Court of France,[12] Jean Omer Joly de Fleury, *avocat général* of the Parlement of Paris and brother of the *procureur général,* and De la Roue, an *avocat.* The lawyers based their case on two premises: first, that as an Indian, Francisque was not covered by the laws of 1716 and 1738 that applied only to "negro slaves" (*esclaves nègres*); second, that even if the judges ruled that Francisque should be considered a negro slave under these laws, his master, Brignon, had failed to meet the requirements of those laws and thus had no right to keep Francisque as his slave.

In 1738, the lawyer arguing for the slave owner Verdelin had introduced the question of race to argue that negro slaves were not automatically entitled to enjoy the Freedom Principle due to slave legislation such as the Code Noir and the Edict of 1716. The argument seems to have had little effect, however, because the judges ruled in favor of Boucaux granting him his freedom and back wages.

Since then, the Declaration of 1738 had changed the penalty for slave owners' noncompliance from granting the slave's freedom (1716) to confiscation and return to the colonies (1738). Francisque's lawyers may have reintroduced the racial argument because, if successful, it would have restored Francisque's freedom to him entirely, whereas winning through the second line of reasoning—that Brignon had failed to comply with the Declaration of 1738—would have meant that the justices acknowledged the validity of the law requiring that Francisque be confiscated by the king and resold into slavery in the colonies, perhaps even in the West Indies, rather than in his homeland. Because Francisque's lawyers were so intent on distinguishing their Indian client from the "negro" slaves specified in the Declaration of 1738, they went into detail regarding the characteristics that were supposed to mark the differences between Indians and Africans. But before we look at the spe-

cific usage of the term *nègre* in Francisque's case it is worthwhile to
examine how the word was used more generally for, as with any term
used in casual conversation, its meaning varied with context, usage, and
both the speaker's and listener's intent.

Nègre: An Ambiguous Term

What did the French mean by *nègre* during the eighteenth century? A
logical place to begin is a survey of contemporary dictionaries. Simone
Delesalle and Lucette Valensi have conducted such a study showing that
the word *nègre* carried two entirely separate meanings in eighteenth-
century dictionaries; *nègres* were defined in some instances as a distinct
people, and in others as slaves. For example, Pomey's *Dictionnaire
royal augmenté* (1671) contained this entry:

> *Nègres,* people of Africa, Hi Nigritae, arum. Hi Nigrites, um. Hi Aethyopes,
> um.[13]

Many other entries equated *nègres* with slaves:

> *Nègre.* Black slaves which are taken from the coast of Africa for the farming
> of the land and on the mainland to work in the mines and sugar factories.[14]

The slippage between these two meanings is most evident in the lengthy
entry by Savary des Bruslons in his *Dictionnaire universel de commerce,* which enjoyed several French and foreign editions during the
eighteenth century and was later excerpted verbatim into the *Encyclopédie*:

> *Nègres.* Peoples of Africa whose country extends along the two sides of the
> Niger River. . . . The Europeans have, for several centuries, conducted
> trade in these unfortunate slaves.[15]

As Delesalle and Valensi show, Savary's definition set up a linguistic
equivalence between "*nègres,*" certain "peoples of Africa," and
"these unfortunate slaves," implying that all three terms were identical
in meaning. The linguists further argue that only one eighteenth-century
dictionary accurately distiguished between the various meanings of the
term *nègre*: Abbé Prévost's *Manuel Lexique.* Prevost's dictionary, unlike that of Savary, clearly distinguished between general and specific
uses of the term:

Nègre. Word taken from the Latin, *Niger,* which signifies black. Usage has given this name in general to all human creatures who have black skin; but it is given in particular to those unhappy inhabitants of various parts of Africa that the Europeans buy for the service of their colonies. Physicians have made great studies of the origin of blackness in a great number of nations.[16]

It may be relevant that such a precise definition was first published during the mid-eighteenth century when the circumstances of black slaves in France began to undergo more public scrutiny. It was during this period that the vague term, *nègre,* began to be separated into its constituent parts denoting color *(noir)* and status *(esclave).*

In their valuable analysis of these two different meanings of *nègre,* Delesalle and Valensi overlook a further slippage in meaning of the term. The "people" denoted by *nègre* could be defined geographically ("peoples of Africa") or by appearance ("people with black skin").[17] The case of Francisque, a dark-skinned slave from India, points up the further ambiguity of the term. Was he a *nègre* by virtue of the fact that he was a slave and had dark skin? Or was it also necessary that he be descended from Africans? Let us turn now to the ways in which Francisque's lawyers tackled the ambiguity in the term *nègre.*

Francisque's Lawyers' Racial Argument

The overarching strategy in the lawyers' attempts to define Francisque as "not a *nègre*" was to contrast the civility of Francisque's natal India with African barbarity. The lawyers aimed to show that India was a well-populated, civilized nation, not unlike France, and that despite Francisque's physical similarities to Africans, people of his nation were not meant to be held as slaves. They played on the increasingly popular notion promoted by Buffon that the appearance of Africans made them especially suited to slavery. In so doing, they ignored the writings of Montesquieu that ridiculed the notion that Africans' appearance justified their enslavement.

Following the form established by Boucaux's lawyers' arguments in 1738, Francisque's lawyers began with a brief historical overview of slavery in the Americas. Here they contrasted the supposed underpopulation of the American colonies with conditions in Francisque's natal India. The underpopulation of the Americas was caused in some cases, they claimed, by the fact that no native people lived there and in other cases by the Spanish, who "cruelly exterminated the natives."[18]

This led to colonization and the use of indentured servants, and finally to slavery. Thus the familiar trope of America as an empty wasteland was used to justify its repopulation with African slaves. India, by contrast, apparently needed no slaves because its native population sufficed for labor. The lawyers portrayed India as a densely populated region, whose people practiced customs similar to those of the French: "The city of Pondicherry, Francisque's homeland, has more than 120,000 citizens, of which more than 100,000 are are natives of the country. The Indians of these countries know how to value [*faire valoir*] the land, conduct commerce, begin and maintain manufactures."[19] The East Indies, the lawyer argued, "must be distinguished from these newly populated countries [i.e., America]."[20]

The lawyers went on to accentuate the commonalities between Europe and India. "Indians are a free people," the lawyers asserted, and though the Hindus practice an idolatrous religion they are "ruled by laws, subject to monarchs, rich by the fertility of their lands, [and] perpetuated through an ancient filiation."[21]

In their brief the lawyers do not describe African society at all, so one can only speculate as to the images of Africa that they intended to invoke as a contrast to India. Some historians of European racism have argued that the popular image of sub-Saharan Africans, even in the early modern period, was overwhelmingly negative. They point, for example, to cultural associations between blackness and evil.[22] A review of contemporary travel literature shows that even though Africans were sometimes characterized as lazy, dishonest, and accustomed to slavery, relatively positive images of African kingship, commerce, beauty, and valor were also present.[23] For example, the first volume of Abbé Prévost's extremely popular compendium of travel literature, *Histoire générale des voyages,* contains passages on "the good character of a part of this nation," "the indolence of negroes for work," "the perfidity of negroes," "the civility of a young negro lord," and volume 2 discusses "their ignorance," "their natural goodness," "the avarice of negro kings," and so on.[24]

Yet it should be noted that, although travel literature provided no uniform portrait of African culture or accomplishments, even the most positive portraits of African status and majesty could not compete with French images of India that had been circulating since the end of the seventeenth century at the height of the Mogul Empire. Take, for example, the following passage describing the pageantry of the king of Congo when he received an audience of Dutch emissaries in 1642:

> When the Dutch ambassadors of Loanda were received in an audience of the king of Congo, immediately after having taken this place from the Portuguese, they were introduced to the palace during the night. They were first made to pass through a gallery two hundred paces in length, between two rows of negroes, who carried in their hands torches of wax. The king was seated in a little chapel, held by mats, in the middle of which hung a chandelier full of candles. He was wearing a jerkin of gold cloth, with high breeches of the same material. Around his neck he had for a tie three very massive chains of gold.[25]

The accompanying illustration emphasizes the lowliness of the Dutch in comparison with the power, ceremony, and wealth of the African king (see Figure 4.1). The Dutch grovel as supplicants in shadow at the king's feet, whereas the king and his attendants are elevated above the Europeans and illuminated in torchlight. No doubt the fact that the African king was a Roman Catholic, whereas the Dutch, enemies of the French, formally repudiated Catholicism, had some bearing on the way in which the scene was rendered in Abbé Prévost's compendium.

Contrast this very powerful and positive image of Africans, however, with an image of India presented elsewhere in Prévost's *Histoire générale*: the "Court of the Grand Mogul" (see Figure 4.2). A veritable circus of activity and grand spectacle, this plate suggests that the wealth and power of the Mogul might rival the court of Versailles.[26] Whereas the king of Congo was represented in a rather intimate setting, the Grand Mogul sits remotely on a raised dais surrounded by legions of subjects and soldiers. Elephants, horses, and camels parade through the foreground, and fountains and fighting pachyderms are triumphantly displayed near the horizon. A strange but elegant combination of baroque and Asian, possibly Chinese, architecture adds to the grandeur of the scene.

In both illustrations, the verisimilitude of the images is irrelevant; what matters is the symbolic import that they bring to their French viewers. There can be no doubt that in relative terms the royalty, at least, of India was portrayed as significantly more awe-inspiring than its counterpart in sub-Saharan Africa.

From their social observations, Francisque's lawyers turned to a discussion of the physical differences between Indians and Africans:

Figure 4.1. Don Alvare, king of the Congo, giving an audience to the Dutch, from Prévost, *Histoire générale des voyages,* vol. 5, facing p. 2. (*Courtesy of the Harvard College Library*)

Figure 4.2. Court of the Great Mogul, from Prévost, *Histoire générale des voyages,* vol. 10, facing p. 245. (*Courtesy of the Harvard College Library*)

If, by the color of their skin, the individuals who are born on the banks of the Indus & the rivers which feed it, bear some resemblance to the negroes of Africa, they at least differ from the latter in that they don't have such a flat nose, such thick, protruding lips, and, instead of the woolly, frizzy down which covers the heads of Africans, they have long and beautiful heads of hair, similar to those which decorate European heads.[27]

It should be noted that "the Indus and the rivers that feed it" in north-western India (today Pakistan) are over a thousand miles from Francisque's natal Pondicherry and that the people living there in the eighteenth century were culturally, politically, and socially quite distinct. It is hard to know whether such geographic blurring was deliberate or arose from the lawyers' own ignorance. In any event, the lawyers' strategy was to emphasize the similarities between Indians and Europeans and to draw a strong distinction between Indians and Africans. The legal brief continues: "Such is Francisque: It suffices to see him to know that he has never spent a day on the burning sands of Guinea or Senegal. It is true that his nose is a bit large, his lips a little fat. But, disregarding his color, he looks more European than many Europeans who need only black skin to appear African."[28] The passing references to the "banks of the Indus" and the "burning sands of Guinea and Senegal" recall the climatological theory of racial difference popularized by Buffon in the middle of the eighteenth century. Buffon held that variations in both the customs and appearances of humanity are caused by the physical environment.[29] Yet for Buffon, color differentiation was not value free. He equated lighter skin with industriousness and highly developed culture due to the difficulty in eking food from more barren soil. Dark skin, for Buffon, came about in climates where the land is "rich, fertile in pasture, and produces millet, and trees which are always green"; consequently black Africans tended, in his view, to be "large, plump, and well made but . . . simple and stupid."[30] Buffon's writings were extremely influential during the second half of the eighteenth century, embraced by such figures as Rousseau, Raynal, and Diderot.[31]

If we examine the notions put forward by Francisque's lawyers concerning physical appearance more closely, it is clear that the chain of associations that they wanted to establish between Indians and Europeans is shaky at best. The lawyers acknowledge that Africans and Indians share a common trait: dark skin. But if we subtract from Francisque's lawyers' general list of traits that characterize Africans—a flat nose, thick lips, and wooly hair—those characteristics shared by Francisque—a flat nose and thick lips—the only remaining salient physical difference is woolly hair. Meanwhile, the lawyers' assertion that except for his skin color Francisque looks more like a European than would many Europeans if they were dark, implies that skin color is the only important difference between Indians and Europeans. The lawyers' claim that Francisque looks more like a European than an African is thus, on closer investigation, unsubstantiated.

Immediately after attempting to portray Francisque as physically similar to Europeans, the lawyers linked African features to their servitude: "by their ignoble appearance [*figure ignoble*], the negroes of Africa seem to be more especially destined to slavery."[32] The notion that the lawyers apparently wish to invoke here is the very one ridiculed by Montesquieu in his most ironic passages. In Book 15 of *L'Esprit des lois,* "How the Laws of Civil Slavery Are Related with the Nature of the Climate," Montesquieu mocks the notion that there is a natural relationship between blacks' physiognomy and their enslavement.[33] For example, in his hypothetical "defense" of the French right to own black slaves, Montesquieu includes propositions that are intended to be self-evidently narrow-minded or proposterous:

> Those concerned are black from head to toe, and have such flat noses that it is almost impossible to feel sorry for them.
>
> One cannot get into one's mind that God, who is a very wise being, should have put a soul, above all a good soul, in a body that was entirely black.
>
> It is so natural to think that color constitutes the essence of humanity that the peoples of Asia who make eunuchs continue to deprive blacks of their likeness to us in a more distinctive way.
>
> One can judge the color of the skin by the color of the hair, which, among the Egyptians, who are the best philosophers of the world, was of such great consequence that they had all the red-haired men who fell into their hands put to death.[34]

Most important, Montesquieu associated civil slavery with political despotism. Although conceding that slavery might be "less counter to reason" in tropical climates where "the heat enervates the body and weakens the courage so much that men come to perform an arduous duty only from fear of chastisement," he also makes it clear that slavery weakens masters' ability to participate in the body politic.[35] In short, although Montesquieu granted a natural relationship between tropical climates and enforced labor, he opposed the notion that Africans or other non-Europeans were especially suited to slavery.

In a study of the books owned by eighteenth-century French barristers, legal treatises made up the largest portion of the collections (33 percent), followed by historical works (28 percent), literature ("Belles Lettres," 20 percent), and theology (14 percent). Natural sciences comprised only 5 percent of the collections.[36] Thus it is surprising that Francisque's lawyers chose to evoke the notions of racial hierarchy most forcefully put forward by the naturalist Buffon rather than the certainly more familiar work of comparative law, Montesquieu's celebrated *Esprit des lois*.

The most obvious answer to this anomaly is that Buffon's climatological racial hierarchy most naturally suited the argument that Francisque's lawyers wanted to make: namely, that Francisque was not a *nègre* and was consequently unsuited to slavery because he came from India, rather than from black Africa. But this resolution only begs the question of why such an argument could have been offered as persuasive to judges and the greater French legal community during the mid-eighteenth century. In other words, if not offered within a climate of racist ideology, the lawyers' rather haphazard allusions to the *figure ignoble* of blacks would have fallen apart at the slightest challenge. That Francisque's lawyers merely alluded to these general images of Africans and Indians without offering an explicit rationale for their acceptance suggests that prevailing notions of the differences between Africans and Indians anticipated the images that the lawyers wanted to evoke.

Two recent historians of the French case have argued that a rigidification of French racial ideology occurred at approximately the time that Francisque's case appeared before the Parlement of Paris. Yvan Debbasch, after closely examining the legal system in France's slave colonies in the Antilles, sees 1760 as the point by which a segregational system was fully embraced in the colonies.[37] Pierre Boulle, ranging over a wider variety of sources for metropolitan France has argued that French racism emerges in the second half of the century.[38] My own analysis of French legal and administrative discourse supports this time frame.[39]

It remains to be explained why racial stereotypes became entrenched in public discourse in France during the second half of the eighteenth century. Debbasch argues that the steady increase in the proportion of free blacks (*affranchis* or *gens de couleur libres*) in the colonies caused white colonists to erect the color bar to preserve their status as an elite. Others have argued that the proliferation of racist ideology in France, as opposed to its colonies, is rather a measure of colonial influence on French officials.[40]

There can be no doubt that France's increasing dependence on colonial revenues and a tendency to recruit administrators with colonial connections assisted in a spread of values associated with slave society. However, I would like to suggest another contributing factor: French championship of the abstract notion of freedom coupled with the persistent, indeed expanding, reality of slavery in the colonies necessitated a justification whereby the enslavement of some peoples and not others could be explained.

The historian David Eltis has offered ample evidence that during the early modern period Europeans could not tolerate the notion of enslaving other Europeans. This was based, he argues, on the emergent culture of merchant capitalism that emphasized the value of the individual and the growth of market behavior.[41] Whatever the origins of this cult of liberty, it is clear that it demanded some kind of rationale for the practice of European slavery on others. The combination of historical accidents that led to the transatlantic slave system (indigenous African slavery, the European discovery of the New World, expansion of sugar cultivation) necessitated an ideological counterweight that could justify why, if freedom was an absolute good and slavery an absolute evil, Africans and their children could legitimately be held in perpetual bondage. One answer in the eighteenth century was that Africans were an inferior people, peculiarly suited to slavery.[42] The physiological accidents that made Africans distinctive in appearance from Europeans (hair, skin, facial features) provided the sign by which their destiny as slaves could be known.

Francisque's case posed an anomaly for eighteenth-century racial thought in France in the same way that mulatto children of planters and their slaves posed an anomaly for the slave system in the colonies. In a bipartite system where black equals slave and white equals free, Francisque the Indian and the mulatto child were terms that belonged to neither category, necessitating some kind of justification for their inclusion in either world. That rationale proved, in the short run, to be racism. It was precisely this dilemma, however, that would also fuel the antislavery movements at the end of the eighteenth and into the nineteenth centuries. Proponents of antislavery chose to advocate the extension of freedom, rather than the justification of inequality, as a way out of the contradiction inherent in slaves in a culture valuing liberty.

Having concluded with the racial argument, the lawyers turned to their second line of defense, arguing that Francisque's master, Brignon, had failed to obtain the governor's permission in Pondicherry and neglected to register Francisque with the Admiralty on arrival in Paris.[43] Furthermore, Brignon's actions made it clear that he had no intention of returning Francisque to the colonies once his religious education was complete. In sum, the master, Brignon, was guilty of violating both the spirit and the letter of the laws of 1716 and 1738.[44] Though Francisque's *mémoire* pointed out that none of the relevant edicts or declarations had been registered by the parlement, and thus might not be used as the basis for a decision, this fact was mentioned only briefly in passing.[45] The bulk of the lawyers' arguments dealt with the questions of whether Francisque was a *nègre,* and whether Brignon had complied with the formalities of the law.[46] Their aim was to win their client's freedom from his former master by any workable strategy.

On August 22, 1759, the Grand Chambre of the Parlement of Paris

ruled that Francisque was free.[47] As with other French judicial decisions, the basis of the ruling is unclear. The fact that Francisque was
freed, rather than confiscated and returned to the colonies, suggests that
the laws of 1716 and 1738 were deemed irrelevant, either because
Francisque was deemed not to be a *nègre esclave*, or because the unregistered laws were seen to have no bearing in the Paris court. In a later
case that cited Francisque's win as a precedent, however, the laws' lack
of registration was the focus rather than the debate over Francisque's
questionable status as a *nègre*:

> First of all, the king's declaration of 1738 was never registered by the
> Parlement of Paris. . . . In effect, the Parlement of Paris does not admit the
> provisions of this declaration. This august court has, on all occasions, pro-
> tected the liberty of men. . . . We could recount several examples which
> attest to this jurisprudence. It will suffice [for] us to cite a recent deci-
> sion. . . . Francisque, *nègre*, was purchased at the age of eight by Sir
> Brignon [case then recited].[48]

Although the laws' lack of registration was a relatively minor argument
in the brief by Francisque's lawyers, the impact of the parlement's
decision was to reinforce the notion that unregistered laws were unin-
forceable within the high court's jurisdiction.

Conclusion

By introducing the question of whether or not Francisque was a *nègre*
into their case, Francisque's lawyers exploited an anomaly inherent in
the codification of slavery in the French colonies. The word *nègre* itself
was an ambiguous signifier, designating blackness, but also, in various
texts, specific facial features, geographical origin, and, in some cases,
the condition of being a slave. The enormous corpus of travel writing
generated during the fifteenth through seventeenth centuries offered a
myriad of images of the peoples of Africa, Asia, and the Americas.
Some of these images were positive, some negative, and many exotic,
emphasizing the physical or cultural differences between Europeans and
non-Europeans. The relationship between appearance and behavior, between physiognomy and mores, and, most important, between color and
slave status had not always been assumed.

Francisque's lawyers exploited this ambiguity to argue that their client, a native of India, though dark-skinned, was not a *nègre* and did not

bear the "ignoble appearance" that was the mark of servitude. In the following decades of the eighteenth century the subjects of race and slavery would be explored by such renowned writers as Rousseau, Voltaire, Raynal, and Diderot.[49] Opposition to the institution of slavery would coalesce, but a stronger connection between physiognomy and baseness also would be established.[50] As I have suggested, these two forces, racism and antislavery, were derived from the same ideological origin: the tension between colonial slavery and the cult of liberty in France.

Meanwhile, there is a coda to the story of Francisque. Eighteen years later, a young man from Pondicherry named François Chavry, otherwise known as "Francisque," registered himself with the clerk of the Admiralty in Paris.[51] He gave his age as thirty-two, which makes him about five years younger than the Francisque who served Sr. Brignon (though at this time people were often imprecise about ages). When asked whether he was slave or free, this second Francisque responded that he was born free [*né libre*]. Whether this was the same Francisque or the similarities are merely coincidental we are never likely to know.[52]

5

Crisis: Blacks in the Capital, 1762

Although the Declaration of 1738 had remained unregistered by the
Parlement of Paris and the Admiralty Court of France, the Admiralty
clerk complied with one of the law's provisions: he duly recorded the
declarations of slave owners who brought their slaves to Paris.[1] These
declarations perhaps reflect only a small portion of blacks living in Paris,
but they nevertheless offer a wealth of information about these individuals.[2] The purpose of this chapter is to assess the size and the socio-
logical makeup of Paris' black population, as well as the administration's efforts to control the growth of this group.

Between 1738 and 1776, the number of blacks registered in Paris
increased gradually, with no more than thirty registered in any given
year, except 1762. One factor in the increasing presence of blacks in
France was the Seven Year's War (1756–1763), which interfered with
ocean passage and prevented many colonists from returning to the colonies with their slaves. Many of the declarations of this period state that
the masters intend to return their blacks to the colonies "as soon as
navigation is free." This long interlude—almost a decade—may have
accustomed slave owners to keeping blacks in France as servants.

In the year 1762 alone, however, 159 blacks were registered in Paris.
The reason for this sudden increase lies, in part, with another court case.
The case of *Louis v. Jean Jacques Le Fevre* (or "Febre") spurred the
officers of the Admiralty of France to draft an ordinance that required all
blacks in Paris, free and enslaved, to be registered by the Admiralty's

clerk. The registration drive was a one-time occurrence, designed to give the Admiralty an account of how many blacks were then resident in Paris, perhaps in preparation for a forced return to the colonies. The singular aim of the ordinance accounts for the immediate drop in declarations to pre-1762 levels once the ordinance expired.

The Admiralty Ordinance of April 5, 1762

On March 30, 1762, the Admiralty Court of France rendered a judgment in favor of a mulatto, Louis, against his master, Sir Jean Jacques Le Fevre.[3] Louis was declared free since his arrival in France seven and a half years earlier and Le Fevre was ordered to pay him 750 *livres* for back wages, plus interest.[4]

The case appears to have been decided on the basis of the Freedom Principle, yet the fact that laws of 1716 and 1738 were not registered also loomed large.[5] The *procureur du roi* (king's representative to the Admiralty Court), Guillaume Poncet de la Grave, in a report on the case, charged that the Edict of 1716 was based on the false claim that the colonists needed to bring their slaves to France for training in religion and trades.[6] He called the Edict: "surreptitious and obreptitious, rendered upon false pretexts, without any necessary motive. Under the shelter of this unregistered law, a deluge of negroes appeared in France."[7] The Edict of 1716 was so ineffective, according to Poncet de la Grave, that it had to be renewed in 1738. Even so, more blacks continued to arrive in France: "France, above all the capital, has become a public market where men are sold to the highest bidder. There is not a *bourgeois* or a worker who doesn't have his negro slave."[8] Poncet de la Grave lamented that the influx of black slaves created numerous complications for the police and prisons: "We are continually occupied with opening our prisons to negroes who are being held there without any other formality than the wish of their masters who dare to exercise under our eyes a power contrary to the public order and to our laws."[9] Though Poncet de la Grave seemed to be concerned with the violation of due process and the overburdening of the judicial system, his unflattering portrait of the blacks themselves reveals deeper concerns regarding a multiracial society. And despite the fact that his report was primarily concerned with the history of *slavery* in France, his language—particularly regarding the present state of things—tended to frame the problem in terms of *race*:

The introduction of too great a quantity of negroes in France—whether in the quality of slaves, or in any other respect—is a dangerous consequence. We will soon see the French nation disfigured if a similar abuse is tolerated. Moreover, the negroes are, in general, dangerous men. Almost none of those to whom you have rendered freedom have refrained from abusing it, . . . [they] have been carried to excesses dangerous for society.[10]

The problem the king needed to address, according to Poncet de la Grave, was not the abstract introduction of the institution of slavery into France, but the concrete presence of blacks in the kingdom's capital. This image of blacks as dangerous men who brought disruption to the public order contrasts sharply with the depiction of slaves as victims who could be saved by the French champions of liberty. Poncet de la Grave's reference to the "disfigurement" of the French nation is the first public utterance of a subject that would preoccupy him until his death: the proliferation of interracial, and thus in his eyes illegitimate, sex.[11]

To address the crisis, the lieutenant general of the Admiralty, De la Haye, recommended an expansion of an old tactic—registration—but with a new twist. The Declaration of 1738 had only required "those who have negro slaves" to register them within three months of the law's publication, but Poncet de la Grave recommended that all "negroes and mulattoes"—slave or free—register with the nearest clerk of the Admiralty. If blacks were in the service of someone else, their master should make the declaration. Blacks "of any profession" who were not working for anyone else were required to register themselves in person. The registrations were to include, for each black living in one's residence: "the purpose for which they resided there, for how long, by which vessel these negroes or mulattoes came to France, their age and surname, whether the said negroes are baptized, from which colony or place they were exported."[12] Residents of Paris were required to make these declarations within one month of the publication and posting of the order. The sale and trade of "negroes and mulattoes" was prohibited in France. Thus, in the language of the Ordinance of 1762, the population to be registered shifted from "slaves," to "negroes and mulattoes"—a move from slave status to race.

Poncet de la Grave submitted this proposal to the Chamber of the Admiralty on April 5, 1762. The ordinance was registered by the court, published, and posted throughout the city, suburbs, and neighboring towns of Paris.[13] The ordinance was sent to the provincial Admiralty offices of France.[14]

The appearance of this ordinance explains the sudden surge in the registration of blacks in 1762. The ordinance, in turn, was spurred by the court case of *Louis v. Le Fevre*. The Ordinance of 1762 required blacks to be declared only once; it was not necessary to renew the declarations annually.[15] This helps to explain why the number of blacks registered in Paris dropped off so suddenly after 1762.

The extraordinary gap between the figures preceding 1762 and the year itself strongly suggests that in the preceding decades nonregistration of slaves was the norm in Paris rather than the exception, despite the provisions of the Declaration of 1738 requiring slaves to be declared in Paris.[16] No penalties were established by the Ordinance of 1762, so compliance with the new law must have been essentially voluntary.[17] As we shall see, free blacks and colonial masters each had their own reasons for compliance. Still, it appears that even the registers of 1762 were far from complete because blacks known to be within the Paris Admiralty's jurisdiction do not appear in the registers.[18]

The Registers of 1762

The Ordinance of 1762 generated a tremendous amount of information about blacks who lived in Paris in the middle of the century.[19] The resultant declarations allow us to test some of Poncet de la Grave's assertions: that the presence of blacks in Paris was rapidly increasing, that blacks posed a threat to the social order, and that "every bourgeois and worker has his slave." The sample provided by the registers is small, to be sure, and underregistration appears to have been a persistent problem. Nevertheless, because of the different kinds of information that the ordinance required to be declared with the Paris Admiralty, we can glean a clearer picture of the population that Poncet de la Grave and De la Haye found so threatening.[20]

A total of 159 blacks and other people of color were registered in Paris in 1762. Though this was a dramatic increase in registration over previous years, it nevertheless represents a very small portion of the population of Paris, which, in this period is estimated to have been between 500,000 and 600,000.[21] It is possible—even likely—that some blacks were overlooked in the registration drive, but these figures suggest that Poncet de la Grave's "deluge" was an exaggeration.

Race and Sex

Of the 159 black registrants of the capital, 110, or just over two-thirds, were male and 49 were female.[22] This ratio is consistent with the proportion of male and female slaves transported to the French Caribbean during the eighteenth century.[23]

The registers list the race of each black brought to Paris. More than three-quarters of the registrants were listed as *nègre,* or "negro." An additional 21 people (13.3 percent) were registered as mulattoes. Significantly, whereas the overall ratio of men to women was 2:1, among mulattoes the ratio is reversed. This probably reflects either the preference among white colonial women for light-skinned domestic servants or the arrival of male colonists' mulatto mistresses and children in France, or both. Eleven of the remaining fifteen people of color were variously described as *quarterons, sauvages, indiens,* and *mestiz,* and four of them were described as *créole,* but their race was not specified.

It is important to know what these terms meant to the French in the eighteenth century.[24] The terms *nègre, mulâtre,* and *quarteron* are part of a familiar system for designating race in the French colonial world. They refer to the proportion of black and white ancestors in a person's lineage. If all four of a person's grandparents were black, the person was considered negro. If one parent was white and the other black, then the person was a mulatto. If the person was the child of a white and a mulatto, he or she was considered a quadroon.

In the colonies the racial terminology could be even more complex, tracing blood back for seven generations.[25] In daily life, however, such precise labels were rarely used.[26] They arose primarily within the colonial legal system, such as when an heir made claim to an estate. In Paris, such distinctions were largely irrelevant. The phrase *gens de couleur* (literally "people of color") was used in French metropolitan legislation of the second half of the eighteenth century to cover all possible combinations of European and African ancestry.

The remaining terms, *sauvage, indien,* and *mestiz,* referred to people whose ancestry included non-Europeans and non-Africans. *Sauvage* was the name given to American Indians of Canada, Louisiana, or the Caribbean islands. People from South Asia were sometimes distinguished by the term *indien,* although they were also often designated by the term *nègre* as well. *Mestiz* is a more ambiguous term used in the colonies to describe a mixture that was part American Indian.[27] The

French also used a similar term, *métif,* to describe someone 101 to 112 parts white (out of a possible 128 parts).[28] One woman in the registers was described as a *"négresse,"* but her national origin was given as *"mestiche créole"* of Ile de France (now Mauritius).[29] I have counted her among the negresses because the meaning of the term *"mestiche"* is ambiguous.

The Paris registers for 1762 omitted the race for three men whose nationality was given as *créole.* All of them came from the Caribbean, so it is possible that their racial heritage included both blacks and whites. In all three cases, the men registered themselves with the Admiralty of Paris and the clerk apparently did not ask them to specify their race.

Geographic Origin

When blacks or their masters appeared before the Admiralty clerk in Paris, they were asked for the black's place of birth and the colony from which the black was transported to France. This information helps to paint a picture of the importance of domestic slavery in each of the French colonies as well as their interaction with the metropolis. Admiralty officials recorded both the place of birth and the point of colonial departure, allowing us to determine the relative proportion of creoles and blacks of African or other origin.

The sugar colonies of the Caribbean, particularly Saint Domingue, were an important source of blacks in Paris. Whether measured by place of birth (45.9 percent), or most recent colonial origin (54.7 percent), it is important to note that blacks from the Caribbean colonies were the dominant presence among Parisian blacks. What is perhaps more surprising is the relative importance of blacks from the Indian Ocean region, namely, Mozambique, Madagascar, Ile de Bourbon (today called Réunion), Ile de France (Mauritius), and India.[30] Nearly a quarter (24.6 percent) of Parisian blacks were born in this Indian Ocean region. The plantations off the coast of East Africa provided sugar, coffee, and indigo during the eighteenth century, and the French slave trade, though minor when compared in volume with Atlantic trade, was nevertheless an important aspect of the region's economy.[31] Although the French presence in India was primarily mercantile rather than agricultural, the enslavement of Indians seems to have been not unusual.

A relatively large proportion of blacks (sixteen, or 10.1 percent) came to France directly from West Africa, but this figure may be misleading because it includes ten who gave their birthplaces in West Africa without stating their most recent colonial origin (that is, they may have spent time in other colonies, such as those of the Caribbean, before traveling to France).[32] Ten of the remaining blacks had recently come from North America (6.3 percent); one fourteen-month-old infant was born in France; and the registers list no place of origin for the remaining three blacks.

It is perhaps not surprising that the vast majority of French blacks (78.6 percent) were creoles or probable creoles of their respective colonies because these would have been most likely to learn the French language and manners useful to their masters. The remaining 20.7 percent of Parisian blacks whose origin is known spent some time in a colony other than their place of birth before traveling to France. Of these, only fourteen, or 8.8 percent, of the total 159 blacks in Paris, were taken as slaves in West Africa and sold to Caribbean owners who then brought them to France. Studies of the Caribbean colonies have shown that creoles were more likely to be employed as domestic servants because of their familiarity with the French language and customs and because they were seen as more docile.[33]

Age

The Edict of 1716, the Declaration of 1738, and the Ordinance of 1762 all required that blacks give their ages upon registration. For the purposes of this study, a person's age was subtracted from the year of registration, yielding a year of birth. By comparing the declarations of blacks who were registered more than once over a period of years, we can see that age estimation was inexact. A slave's projected year of birth could vary by three or four years over several declarations.

The median age of the 135 Parisian blacks whose age is known was twenty years in 1762.[34] Ninety-two, or 57.9 percent, were between the ages of eleven and thirty. Within this age group, males outnumbered females by a factor of nearly 3 to 1. Perhaps the dominance of young males helps to explain the Admiralty officials' preoccupation with public order.[35]

By contrast, "women of color" in their thirties and fifties nearly equaled or outnumbered men. There is some suggestion that these women were the partners of the white male colonists who registered them. For example, Jean DuBuq, a colonist of Martinique registered

Amaranthe, a fifty-five-year-old negress of Guadeloupe, along with Barbe, a mulatto woman, thirty-four, and Louis Verdier, thirty-nine, a mulatto man. According to Dubuq, Amaranthe and Louis were free, and Barbe came to France "to accompany and serve" the daughters of Jean Dubuq. It is plausible that Dubuq was married to a white woman, but the age and racial information in the registers is consistent with a portrait of Jean Dubuq and Amaranthe as parents of the mulattoes Barbe and Louis.[36]

On the other hand, contrary to the assertions by Poncet de la Grave, there is little evidence that widespread interracial unions were established in France as a result of black immigration. According to the registers, only one nonwhite was born in France, and she was registered as a negro, rather than of mixed parentage. It seems likely that liaisons between blacks and whites probably did occur without being registered by the Admiralty clerk, but Poncet de la Grave's worries over the "disfigurement of the French nation" appear to reflect his own preoccupations more than the reality of Parisian social life.

Status: Slave or Free

Under the legislation of 1762, blacks in Paris were required to be registered by their master, their master's agent, or, if they were independent, by themselves with the Admiralty's clerk. Although the ordinance did not insist that blacks be identified as slave or free, many declarants (sixty-four, or about 40 percent) volunteered this information on registration. Of the blacks whose status was indicated, most were identified as free (forty-three, or 27 percent). This is not surprising, because free blacks had a stake in registering their status officially.

Neither a free person's sex nor race correlated strongly with their free status in the Paris registers of 1762. This factor contrasts with studies of manumission in the American colonies that have found that female slaves and their children were more likely to be manumitted than adult males.[37] In fact, for France the most significant factor in determining a black's status was his or her age. The mean age of those declared as slaves in 1762 is 22.3 years, and the mean age of free blacks is 30.7 years. Four-fifths of those for whom no status was declared were under the age of thirty (the age of majority for French males).[38] This suggests that blacks were more likely to be manumitted or achieve their freedom in other ways in accordance with age, whereas those under the age of majority may not have been seen in terms of "free" or "slave" at all.[39]

Black slaves might achieve their freedom in France in a number of ways. Only one claimed to be born free (*né libre*) in the Paris registers of 1762.[40] Others were given their freedom by their masters.[41] To prove their freedom, some carried letters, or *actes de liberté,* that legally certified their freedom.[42] On occasion, the registers' declarations reveal affection between a master and his former slave. Jean Jacques le Febvre freed the thirty-year-old negress, Thérèze, as she was the "*sœur de lait*" of one of his own children and "having well merited by her good and faithful services to him."[43]

One of the oldest colonial traditions of manumission was through baptism.[44] However, article 2 of the Code Noir (1685) ruled that "all the slaves who are in our isles will be baptized in the Catholic religion," negating the tendancy to equate baptism with manumission. A letter from the governor general and intendant of Saint Domingue assured a French minister in 1734 that baptismal manumission had no legal standing whatsoever.[45] Nevertheless, as in England, some French masters continued to recognize baptism as a formal act of manumission.[46] For example, Neue Magon brought "a negro, his slave," named Narcisse from Ile de France and Ile de Bourbon. Narcisse was baptized at Montmartre as Dominique Julien, after which M. Neue Magon declared that he kept him in his service, "as a free man."[47]

Some slaves did not wait for their masters to free them and simply ran away to seek employment elsewhere. This was the case with "Joseph, *dit* Paul," who came from Martinique and was sold at Le Havre to a merchant ship captain "whom he left because of his bad treatment."[48] Others received their freedom via tribunals, as we have seen.[49] One Augustin received his freedom "from his majesty, in consideration of the services rendered by him."[50]

Literacy

Among the twenty-one blacks who registered themselves in Paris, seven signed their names, implying at least a minor degree of literacy. All of those who signed were free negro men.[51] Four of them did not give their ages, but the remaining three were twenty-seven, thirty, and thirty-six, which are within the upper third of the range of ages. Three were creoles of Saint Domingue, three were born in West Africa (Guinea, Arada, and

Senegal), and Pierre Fidel's place of birth is unknown. One was a tailor, two were fencing masters, and one appears to have been a servant.[52]

An analysis of literacy rates among blacks in Bordeaux from 1740 to 1787 shows that literacy was more prevalent among males than females and that the highest rate was among teenagers and men in their twenties.[53] All but one of the eighty-five individuals in this sample were creoles and all but five were mulattoes. The sample for Paris is admittedly small, but a comparison of data for Paris and Bordeaux suggests that a far greater proportion of literate blacks in Bordeaux were in fact planters' and black women's sons who were in Bordeaux to receive an education. By contrast, independent negro tradesmen constituted the greater portion of literate blacks in Paris.[54]

Purpose and Trade

Both the Edict of 1716 and the Declaration of 1738 specified that the only legitimate purposes for bringing black slaves to France was for them to receive religious instruction or to learn a trade. As we have seen from the cases of Jean Boucaux and Francisque, employing blacks as servants in France (rather than tending to their souls or providing them with skills that were beneficial to the colonies) could be construed as merely pampering the vanity of colonial masters. Yet, unless a slaveowner also declared that the slave was brought to France for one of the authorized purposes, he or she ran the risk of having the slave freed or confiscated *au profit du roi*.

The legislation of 1762 changed several factors. First, the new ordinance did not reiterate the formulation that religious and technical instruction were the only legitimate reasons for bringing blacks to France. Second, the legislation of 1762 applied to all blacks in France, not just slaves. Consequently, for the first time free blacks who were unattached to any master declared themselves in the registers. As we have seen, a large number of the registrants made use of the Admiralty's registrations to formally declare themselves free.

Most free blacks (62.8 percent) did not specify a purpose for their travel to France. (This was especially true of those who registered themselves, as opposed to those who were registered by someone else.) Otherwise, the percentage of blacks for whom a purpose was declared remained over 90 percent. In most cases the registers indicated more than one purpose, the most common being instruction in the Catholic faith and training in a trade. In fact, the phrasing *"pour le faire instruire dans la religion catholique, apostolique et romaine et apprendre un métier"* became virtually standardized in the declarations. Prior to 1762, either one or both of these purposes was given for 93.3 percent of registered blacks. Although this proportion dropped to 80 percent in 1762 (excluding those registered as free), this figure still represents a significant majority of declarations. No doubt these purposes were so popular because they were the only legitimate purposes stipulated by the Edict of 1716 and the Declaration of 1738.

These patterns suggest that many Parisians—both black and white— were using the act of registration for their own purposes. Masters complied with the laws of 1716, 1738, and 1762 in order to ensure the retention of their slaves who might seek their freedom either through escape or lawsuits.[55] Similarly, it appears that many free blacks complied with the law of 1762 to register their freedom with the Admiralty, thus ensuring that status officially.

Education apparently played a relatively minor role in the purposes for which blacks were brought to Paris. None of the registers prior to 1762 records this purpose, and only three declarations mention this purpose in 1762. These include Peter, a seven-year-old quadroon, the son of Sr. Granville, who was charged to M. Rouvray to give him *"toute l'éducation possible"*; Charles Jean Baptiste Joseph, called "Aza," a ten-year-old negro of Madagascar, who was in pension at Versailles for his education; and Joseph Ritodame, a fifteen-year-old mulatto from Guadeloupe, who was brought to France "to give him all the education suitable to a young man."[56]

Only forty-five (28.3 percent) of the blacks registered in Paris in 1762 were registered as baptized. Of these, only eleven were baptized in France, and twenty-one were baptized in the colonies, including Saint Domingue, Ile de France, Louisiana, and Martinique.[57] The fact that basic religious instruction was available in the colonies suggests that, despite claims to the contrary (and as Poncet de la Grave suspected), the claim to provide religious instruction was used as a smokescreen for retaining enslaved domestic help in France.[58]

According to the law of 1738, those who were brought to Paris to learn a trade were supposed to specify the proposed trade and the master to whom they would be apprenticed.[59] This requirement was frequently ignored in declarations up to and including those of 1762. Of the 147 blacks who came to Paris prior to 1762 with the declared purpose of

learning a trade, only eighty-one, or 55 percent, specified the trade that
he or she was to learn. Moreover, of the fifty-nine blacks who were
supposed to learn a trade in Paris in 1762, only twenty, or 33.9 percent,
specified the trade. Only four declarations named the master to whom
the black would apprentice.[60] These figures confirm the administration's
perception that colonial masters were abusing their privileges by bringing their slaves to France for reasons other than learning a trade that
would be useful to the colonies.

The 1762 registers for Paris do not indicate a trade for the majority of
blacks (see Table 5.1). This may result, in part, from the disproportionate number of blacks under the age of twenty. For the remaining registrants, the most important occupation for both men and women is that of
domestic servant (20.1 percent of the total 159 blacks). The average age
of the chambermaid is fairly high (twenty-nine years), but butlers and

Table 5.1. Trade by Age and Sex for Blacks in Paris, 1762

	Male	Female	Total	Percent	Age Range	Mean Age
No trade registered	67	30	96	60.4	1–55a	20.9
Servant (total)	19	13	32	20.1	11–46	26
Butler	1	0	1	0.6	22	22
Chambermaid	0	7	7	4.4	18–46	29.3
Valet	2	0	2	1.3	20–30	25
Wigmaker	13	0	13	8.2	8–31	17.3
Cook	7	1	8	5.0	14–42	25.4
Hairdresser	0	4	4	2.5	18–46	28
Nurse	1	2	3	1.9	12–14	13
Seamstress	0	3	3	1.9	14–21	18
Fencing master	2	0	2	1.3	?	?
Arquebusier	1	0	1	0.6	40	40
Cooper	1	0	1	0.6	20	20
Hatmaker	1	0	1	0.6	15	15
Musician	1	0	1	0.6	19	19
Tailor	1	0	1	0.6	27	27

Source: Archives Nationales, Paris, Z¹D 139. The registers list more than one trade for
some individuals.
aThe distribution for those blacks with no registered trade is: ages 1–10, 15; 11–20, 29;
21–30, 20; 31–40, 9; 41–50, 3; and 51–60, 2.

valets tend to be younger (average, twenty-two to twenty-five). Women dominated the trade of hairdresser, and teenaged boys were frequently employed in wigmaking.

It appears that relatively few of the trades practiced by blacks were strictly useful to the colonies, as required by law. Most blacks, as has been suggested, were employed in servicing the domestic comforts of their masters. Only four Parisian blacks were registered in skilled trades that could unequivocally be seen as useful to colonial commerce and defense. The cooper, L'Eucille, aged twenty, would certainly have been useful to the colony of Saint Domingue, whence he came.[61] The arquebusier and the two fencing masters, however, were all registered as free and presumably had no intention of returning to the colonies.[62]

Residences

When a black, a master, or the master's agent registered a black with the Admiralty clerk, it was the registrant's address (though not necessarily the black's) that was most often recorded. On one hand, this makes it difficult to say with certainty where most Parisian blacks resided. On the other hand, if we assume that the majority of Parisian blacks for whom no trade was specified were probably employed as servants, it seems likely that they lived in Paris with their masters.[63] Consequently, when it appears, the master's residence most likely indicates the black's residence as well.

Addresses for blacks, their masters, and their masters' agents were scattered throughout Paris, but two of the largest parishes, St. Eustache and St. Roch, held the greatest concentration (thirty-three and twenty-one blacks, respectively).[64] St. Eustache, adjoining the markets, Les Halles, was one of the wealthiest parishes in Paris. St. Roch, located in the Palais Royal *quartier,* served some of Paris's wealthiest noble families.[65] When we look at the residences of those blacks who were known to be employed as domestics (including cooks), a significant majority resided in St. Roch, and the remainder were scattered around other parishes.[66] Poncet de la Grave, the author of the report lamenting the presence of blacks in Paris, lived in the Marais district, at the corner of the rue Ste. Croix de la Bretonnerie and the rue du Bourg Tibourg.[67] Even though this area was not especially densely populated with blacks, he may have had the experience of passing the blacks Marie and Augustin (both of the Ile de France) who actually lived and worked in his neighborhood.[68]

It is impossible to give precise statistical information regarding the status of the owners. However, the registers for 1762 do name eight counts and countesses, and three marquis and marquises who each employed one or two blacks in their service. Others bear the title of Sieur, Dame, Monsieur, or Madame; some were also military officers (chevalier, captaine). One former attorney was listed amongst those who declared blacks in their service. Many masters lived in hotels, suggesting that they were in Paris temporarily to do business.[69]

Among the blacks who registered themselves, a significant proportion lived on the left bank, in the parishes or the *faubourg* of St. Germain.[70] Those blacks who performed a skilled trade (wigmaker, seamstress, fencing master, arquebusier, cooper, hatmaker, musician, and tailor), were fairly evenly distributed between the parish of St. Eustache, on the right bank, and several parishes of the left bank.[71]

These findings indicate that Poncet de la Grave's overstated assertion that "every bourgeois and worker has his slave" does not reflect the reality of employment for blacks in Paris. On the contrary, people with blacks in their service appear to have come primarily from the higher echelons of society. Yet, since Poncet de la Grave was, himself, of the Paris elite, he may have encountered blacks more frequently than did the average "bourgeois or worker," causing him to overestimate the presence of blacks in the capital city.

Follow-up to the Ordinance of 1762

With the conclusion of the Seven Years' War in February 1763, the Duc de Choiseul, Louis XV's minister of the marine, was free to turn his mind to other matters. On June 30, he issued a circular letter to all administrators in France and in the colonies, outlining his plans to return all slaves to the colonies and to prohibit all blacks, free and unfree, from traveling to France. The reason for the new crackdown was stated in the letter: instead of receiving instruction in religion or a trade, "The number of slaves has increased so much in France . . . that it has resulted in a [population of] mixed blood [*un sang mêlé*] which multiplies every day, by the [sexual] communication that they have with the whites."[72] In compliance with this directive, the intendant of Metz (and presumably many other intendants) ordered a poster to be displayed around the city requiring those with black slaves to send them back to the colonies by October 15, 1763, under penalty of confiscation by the king. The poster further enjoined slaveholders to declare their slaves by August 15 with the district Marine officer.[73] The minister's letter of June 30, 1763, indicated that measures would be taken "for the expulsion of free negroes who are in France."

Despite these grand plans, there is no evidence that such an expulsion—whether of slaves or free blacks—was ever undertaken. Presumably, some slave owners voluntarily complied with the June 30 directive, but by April 1764, it appears that the government had not yet followed through with confiscation. We know that at least one colonial administrator objected strongly to the measure. In April of 1764, Fénelon of Guadeloupe explained the reasons for his objections:

> 1. One should not flatter oneself that, accustomed to the idleness and the ease of being a domestic, [a negro] can be of a great profit to agriculture. . . .
> 2. The return of the negroes from France to the colonies would inundate us with very bad subjects, too instructed by their stay in France which would give knowledge and light [*des connaissances et des lumières*] to negroes of the land, the consequences of which would be very dangerous.[74]

The royal administration might wish once again, as it had following the Declaration of 1738, to make a clear separation between colonial slavery and French freedom—in effect, a kind of quarantine—but, as before, the strong colonists' lobby opposed the return of "contaminated" slaves to the colonies.

The other half of the June 30 directive, prohibiting the transport of blacks to France, was perhaps slightly more effective, at least at first. On March 1, 1764, the intendant of Guadeloupe issued an ordinance prohibiting the transport of all people of color, free or enslaved, to France. A circular letter from Choiseul to the administrators of Martinique in January 1765 reminded them to prevent blacks from traveling to France.[75] Yet their migration persisted, despite the government's efforts.

A look at the Paris Admiralty clerk's registers confirms this. The registers record an uneven drop in the number of blacks registered in Paris for the years 1763–1776.[76] The drop between 1763 and 1764 is likely the consequence of the minister's circular letter of June 30, 1763, and the resurgence in 1765 and 1766 suggests that the effort to keep black slaves out of France was not strictly enforced. A circular letter of

September 30, 1766, then reinstituted the payment of 3,000 *livres* for each black brought to France who was not immediately returned. The intendant of Saint Domingue raised this figure to 4,500 *livres,* payable in advance, with the requirement that the slave be returned within eight months.[77] A new round of ministerial letters in 1769 enjoined colonial administrators not to let any slaves embark for France unless they were to be returned to the colonies within eight months.[78] The continual reiteration of these measures, however, points to the difficulties of policing migration.

Conclusion

Clearly, Poncet de la Grave's 1762 lament regarding the "deluge" of blacks "disfiguring" the city of Paris was an exaggeration. Even if underregistration occured in the extreme, the proportion of blacks in the population of the capital was minor. Yet Poncet de la Grave appears to be correct in his assertion that colonists were taking advantage of the laws of 1716 and 1738. Despite the fact that many masters claimed they brought blacks to France for religious or technical instruction, few were baptized in France and fewer specified the trade they were to learn. The preponderance of blacks who worked as domestic servants suggests that colonists and the Parisian elite were taking advantage of the laws of 1716 and 1738 to supply themselves with servants.

At the same time, the registers of 1762 indicate that a disproportionate number of Parisian blacks were young, possibly unemployed, males. One can imagine that, as the most visible segment of the black population, they attracted the attention of Poncet de la Grave and other officials concerned with maintaining the public order. On the other hand, historians of eighteenth-century Paris, such as Daniel Roche and Arlette Farge, take little notice of blacks in their studies of social order and disorder, which further suggests that a certain amount of official exaggeration took place.[79]

In the legal arena, however, blacks achieved real prominence. During the decade following the Admiralty Ordinance of 1762, in Paris at least, the number of slaves who won their freedom through lawsuits and manumissions in the Admiralty court multiplied eightfold. It is to these efforts that we now turn.

6

Antislavery and Antidespotism: 1760–1771

The years that elapsed between the Admiralty's ordinance of 1762 and the 1777 *Police des Noirs* were an absolutely crucial period for slavery in France. First, as the number of blacks registered in Paris returned to its pre-1762 levels of fewer than thirty per year, the number of those suing for their freedom in the Paris Admiralty Court increased dramatically.[1] Second, outside of the Parisian judicial world, some of the best-known authors of the eighteenth century adopted the metaphor of slavery to challenge the excesses of monarchic government in France. The political context in which the lawsuits and discourse proliferated was sharply radicalized from 1770 to 1774 when Louis XV's chancellor Maupeou instituted a series of dramatic judicial reforms. A judicial *mémoire* by Henrion de Pansey on behalf of the slave Roc circulated widely in Paris, linking the injustice of Roc's slavery to the influence of Maupeou on the king.

Lawsuits before the Admiralty Court of France

The number of lawsuits for freedom brought before the Admiralty Court of France in Paris during the 1760s increased sixfold over those of the previous decades. Gradually, as these petitions became more common, the judicial procedure became standardized and, by the end of the decade, routine.

Each case began with a petition, or *requête*, on the part of the slave.[2]

The petition was prepared by a lawyer and followed a standard formula. Most began with the slave's story, including how he or she came to France, identified the master or sequence of masters, and sometimes specified ill treatment or other extenuating circumstances. The petition also frequently cited the slave's justification for the claim to freedom via the Freedom Principle (e.g., *"nul n'est esclave en France"*). It concluded with specific requests: a *délai de l'ordonnance* (that is, a reprieve from the master's power over the slave), recognition of the petitioner as a free person, prohibition against attempts on the petitioner and his belongings, and the protection of the king or of the court. In addition, some petitioners requested the return of their clothing and linens. Finally, some requested a monetary award, most commonly back wages but also occasionally reimbursement for food purchased while in prison or money left with the master for safekeeping.[3]

The petition was sent before the *procureur du roi* or his substitute, who authorized the petitioner's right to have the case heard by the court. Shortly thereafter, usually on the same day, the court issued a provisional sentence. In all slaves' cases before the Admiralty Court of France during the eighteenth century, this sentence affirmed the petitioner's freedom and offered the court's protection. During the early 1760s, these sentences often explicitly protected the petitioner's freedom even when traveling in jurisdictions that had registered the Declaration of December 15, 1738, such as Britanny or Guyenne, although within a few years this practice all but died out.[4] When monetary awards were sought (such as wages), the provisional sentence awarded the petitioner the right to a hearing before the Admiralty Court's *Chambre*.

Most cases stopped at this stage. If the slave wished to pursue his or her request for back wages or another award involving money or property, a hearing was set before the Admiralty Court during which the slave sought the *fin de sa requête,* or the object of his or her demands. At such a hearing, the master was permitted to contest the slave's plea. Frequently in these cases, however, the owner did not show up and the case was decided by default against the slaveowner. Occasionally, especially when a large sum of money was involved, the slaveowner waged countersuits by initiating independent petitions. In its final sentence, known as a *sentence en l'Amirauté,* the court ruled on all the petitions pertaining to the two parties. Decisions were sometimes appealed, but in no case did a slaveowner win a final decision against a slave in the Admiralty Court of France from 1730 to 1790.[5]

The slaves' petitions permit us to see into the conditions of their lives. Slaves came from all reaches of the French empire and beyond.[6] Some had lived in France for as little as three months, some for as long as eighteen years, with a median term of about five years.[7] Two of the women described marriages that seem suspiciously like the conditions of slavery.[8] In the years following the Treaty of Paris (February 10, 1763) that concluded the Seven Years' War, several petitioners recounted their service in black regiments, their capture by English forces, and their subsequent arrival in France as prisoners of war.[9]

Most petitions cited juridical grounds for the petitioners' claim to freedom. Some petitioners claimed to have been born free.[10] Others pointed out that their masters had not properly registered them with the Admiralty clerk upon arrival in France.[11] In a number of cases, petitioners pointed to their ill treatment at the hands of their masters.[12] The most common justification for the claim to freedom, however, was some formulation of the Freedom Principle that slavery does not exist in France.[13] During the late 1760s some petitions began to treat this principle as a basic tenet of French public law, even (inaccurately) in the sense of its written statutes.[14]

In 1767, the lawyer Pierre Etienne Regnaud, who had by now drafted dozens of such petitions, inexplicably began introducing the following phraseology into the petitions he drafted: "There is no slavery in France by the terms of the edicts, ordinances and declarations of his majesty."[15] It is not clear whether Regnaud introduced the notion of the king's *written* law inadvertently or whether he was trying to make the point that slavery was not acknowledged in any of the statutes registered by the Parlement of Paris and thus recognized by the Admiralty Court of France. In fact, by the king's written law, that is, the Declaration of 1738, which was duly registered by every other parlement in France besides that of Paris, slavery *was* acknowledged in France, and no slave could hope to win his or her freedom on the basis of that statute. Still, for whatever reason, the phrase, "*aux termes des édits et déclarations du roi,*" was picked up by other lawyers as they drafted petitions for the slaves they represented.[16] This inaccuracy probably reflects how routine such petitions had become by the late 1760s.

Owners rarely contested the provisional sentences that awarded slaves their freedom. The petitioner was given a sheet of paper with the court's sentence on it that could be used as protection if he or she was threatened with arrest or abuse.[17] If the petitioner sought and won a monetary

award in an audience before the Admiralty Court, however, it was
not uncommon for a master to file countersuits in an effort to derail
the petitioner's plea. Dame Julie d'Utrousset d'Héricourt, widow of
Sr Butler, for example, offered to have her former slave, Pélagie, conducted to Rochefort "or any other port" when Pélagie won her freedom
and 1,200 *livres* in back wages.[18] The Admiralty judges denied her
petition. In another case, Jacques Medor won his freedom in an original
sentence and an unspecified sum for back wages (to be calculated at a
rate of 120 *livres* per year) but lost the monetary award when challenged
by his former master.[19] Yet Medor successfully achieved his freedom,
as did all slaves who sued through the Paris Admiralty Court.

In the early 1760s before the court's actions on requests for liberty
became a matter of routine, there was some confusion about due process. One case that did not follow the formal channels (i.e., a petition
drafted by a lawyer resulting in a provisional sentence) originated in a
complaint of brutality to the Admiralty clerk. Joseph Louis of Bengal
complained that his master, Sr. Cottel, an officer in the Compagnie des
Indes, beat him and threw him out on the streets without any resources.
Poncet de la Grave, the *procureur de roi,* took Joseph Louis's complaint
and made it the basis of a claim to freedom that was awarded by the
Chamber on July 28, 1762.[20] In response to the court's decision, Cottel
apparently decided to emancipate Joseph Louis, perhaps in exchange for
a promise from Joseph Louis not to seek back wages.[21]

Subsequent manumissions, however, were not acknowledged as such
by the court, at least not at first. When Camille and Marie Anne petitioned for their freedom in December 1762 on the basis of a notarized
acte de liberté, Poncet de la Grave gave his formal approval of their
claim to freedom with a caveat: "I do not prevent for the king the
conclusions of the present petition to be judged for the petitioner,
. . . without regard for the stated act of manumission because of the
constant maxim that every slave entering France is free like all other
subjects of the king."[22] In other words, Poncet de la Grave, as the
representative of the king's power in the court, was willing to extend the
king's permission to the women to seek their freedom irrespective of any
acte de liberté granted by their masters. Poncet de la Grave repeated the
caveat in response to similar requests in 1763.[23] In 1764, however,
when Poncet de la Grave was temporarily replaced by the substitute
procureur du roi, acts of manumission began to be accepted unconditionally.[24] When a similar request next came before Poncet de la Grave

in 1766, he signed it without reservation.[25] In this way manumission came to be established as a second legitimate path to freedom through the Admiralty Court of France.

It is significant, however, that as the court gradually came to accept manumission as a legitimate process in Paris, it was unwilling to accept conditions on the process of manumission. For example, in 1768 René Jacques de Loubes, a lieutenant colonel of the infantry in Martinique, granted Jean Baptiste, *dit* Honoré, his freedom on the condition that he serve his master for the rest of his life. Such conditional manumissions were not uncommon in the colonies, but the Admiralty Court would have no part of them. In its provisional sentence, the court struck down the *acte*'s wording and awarded Jean Baptiste his freedom unconditionally.[26]

By the end of the 1760s, then, two distinct routes to freedom had emerged within the Admiralty Court of France: petitions initiated by the slave (occasionally contested by the master), and manumission by the master, to be registered with the Admiralty Court.

To what can we attribute this increase in court activity promoting freedom? One factor is almost certainly the success of Francisque's case heard before the Parlement of Paris in 1759, as discussed. Interest in that case likely would have been stimulated by the *mémoire* composed on his behalf and circulated in Paris. Catherine's case, also discussed, showed how an informal network among blacks could have helped to inform slaves of Francisque's success, thereby encouraging others to sue. Similarly, the favorable precedent likely would have predisposed lawyers to accept these cases, knowing that their own success was virtually assured.

Second, the actions of the Admiralty Court in 1762 and the marine ministry in 1763 also drew slaves' attention to their unfree status and to the advantages of changing it. The Marine directive of June 30, 1763, publicized the government's intent to expel all slaves from France by October 15 and provided a powerful motive to both slaveholders and slaves to change slaves' status. An annual breakdown of the number of lawsuits for freedom supports this hypothesis. As shown in Table 6.1, both slave-initiated lawsuits and master-initiated acts of liberty (manumissions) increased in 1762. The number of slave lawsuits dropped off after 1767. What is more, statements from slaves' own petitions confirm the fact that after years of service in France, many slaves were now threatened by their masters with return to the colonies.[27]

Table 6.1. Petitions for Freedom before the Admiralty Court of France, 1760–1770

	Suits for Freedom	Acts of Liberty	Total Slaves Freed
1760	5	0	5
1761	1	0	1
1762	5	2	7
1763	13	3	16
1764	11	1	12
1765	9	0	9
1766	10	4	14
1767	7	0	7
1768	4	1	5
1769	6	0	6
1770	6	3	9
1771[a]	1	0	1

Source: "Registres pour servir à l'enregistrement des dèclarations qui se font au sujet des noirs amenés des colonies en France, 1739–1790" (Paris: Archives Nationales, Z¹D 139). When a slave initiated more than one petition against the same master, I have counted only the first.

[a]The Admiralty Court was disbanded by Maupeou's reforms in June 1771.

A third reason for the increase in lawsuits for freedom may have been the predispositions of lawyers themselves. Two kinds of lawyers represented slaves: *procureurs* and *avocats*. The *procureurs* were the workhorses of the French judicial system, responsible for collecting evidence, filing motions, and generally managing procedural matters. *Avocats,* on the other hand, were responsible for the oral and written arguments that touched only on questions of law.[28] It seems likely that during the 1760s, when lawsuits for freedom became virtually commonplace, *procureurs* did the greatest part of the work, drafting slaves' petitions and so on. Only when a petition was contested by a master was an *avocat* likely to be called in.

There are many possible motives that may have induced *procureurs* or *avocats* to take on a slave's case. The three most important of these are remuneration, experience, and sympathy for their clients' cause.

At first glance, remuneration stands out as the most obvious motive. Catherine's lawyer, for example, charged 146 *livres* (or the approximate equivalent of fourteen months of a servant's wages) for his services in Nantes in 1747. *Avocats'* principal source of revenue were the honoraria received from their clients, although they were not permitted to collect such fees as a percentage of their clients' winnings or to sue for lack of payment.[29] The less prestigious *procureurs* also charged for their services because it was they who did the bulk of the drudge work for their clients. The fact that they had to purchase their offices meant that many lived in a constant state of debt. During the eighteenth century, they developed a reputation for greed that "Shylock might have pitied."[30]

Yet slaves were not likely to own much in the way of property or cash.[31] Many of the Admiralty Court sentences specified that petitioners should be awarded their "linens and clothing," which suggests that all that they owned upon winning their freedom was literally the clothes on their backs. Cases where monetary awards were judged (when, for example, a slave won back wages), were relatively rare. It therefore seems likely that at least some of the lawyers' services were provided, in effect, pro bono.

If we grant that cash rewards were not likely to be a strong or frequent incentive, we must nevertheless acknowledge that, as the pattern of winning developed, lawyers may have been drawn to representing slaves simply for the experience and the likelihood of winning. Contemporary observers felt that the number of *procureurs* practicing during the 1760s had grown out of proportion, whereas their offices objectively declined in value.[32] Perhaps attorneys were desperate to take on any work, simply for the experience.

Many *avocats* gravitated toward clients whom they found sympathetic for one reason or another.[33] This would certainly seem to be the case in one of the most important lawsuits for freedom of the eighteenth century, that of *Roc v. Poupet*. Before we can explore the reasons why Henrion de Pansey took on the case of Roc in 1770, however, we must review the political and ideological context of the case.

Secular Critiques of Despotic Monarchy

Beginning in 1749 and continuing intermittently until his death in 1774, Louis XV experienced a series of crises involving the parlements of France. First, the king met with stubborn resistance in the Parlement of

Paris over the refusal of sacraments controversy, culminating in two
judicial strikes, exile for the magistrates of two chambers of the court,
and the ultimate adoption of a compromise measure known as the "Declaration of Silence."[34] No sooner had this conflict been resolved, however, than an explosive rivalry broke out between the *Grand Conseil* and
the Parlement of Paris that grew to encompass many important provincial parlements.[35]

During the 1760s the king's administration met with additional judicial resistance in Paris and the provinces concerning the government's
taxation policies. The Parlement of Rennes in Brittany chafed under the
rule of the crown's provincial governor, the Duc d'Aiguillon, and re-
signed as a group in 1765. Louis XV replaced the Breton court with his
own men, but the Parlement of Paris protested the king's action, accus-
ing him of despotic rule. Louis XV convened a *lit de justice* on March 3,
1766, reprimanding the parlement's resistance, but this ceremonial
show of power did not have a lasting effect.[36]

Polarization between the Parlement of Paris and the crown erupted in
its most virulent form in the fall of 1770, when, in the course of trying
the Duc d'Aiguillon, the magistrates began to question aspects of the
king's governance in Brittany. The king responded with an edict, drawn
up by his new Chancellor Maupeou, severely castigating the Parlement's actions, which was registered by the Parlement in a *lit de justice*.
However, the court retaliated with another judicial strike. Maupeou
persuaded the king that drastic action was necessary. On the night of
January 20–21, 1771, the king sent armed guards to each of the magis-
trate's homes along with a *lettre de cachet*. Those who refused to return
to the bench—nearly the entire court—were sent into exile.[37] Maupeou
divided the Parlement of Paris's former jurisdiction into six new districts, each headed by its own *conseil supérieur*. Some contemporaries,
such as Malesherbes, protested the abolition of the Parlement of Paris on
the grounds that the parlement protected France from despotism.[38] But
others lauded the accompanying judicial reforms, such as the abolition
of the venality of offices and of the *épices,* or legal fees, which, they
felt, had become exorbitant.[39]

For the following four years, Maupeou's courts slowly ground the
wheels of justice, challenged on all sides by a political campaign aimed
at swaying public opinion against the administration's reforms.[40] By
threatening those lawyers who refused to cooperate with the new *conseils* and offering enticements to those who complied, Maupeou was

able to drive a wedge between members of the Parisian legal community. Ultimately Maupeou lured 130 striking *procureurs* back into practice with the offer of 100 new venal offices.[41] As for the more prestigious *avocats,* half of the 532 members of the Parisian Order of Barristers returned to serve under Maupeou, but the other half continued to strike until the parlement was ultimately restored in 1774.[42] Those most likely to return to work were the younger lawyers who lacked the financial resources to support the strike and those who were ideologically predisposed to resist the old guard Jansenist party line, including royalists and those under the influence of Enlightenment skepticism.[43]

In the midst of these decades of political tumult some of the most important eighteenth-century tracts on freedom were penned. In the early 1750s Jean Jacques Rousseau composed two essays, known now as the First and Second Discourses, which set forth his notion that man in a state of "nature" was the most free and that civilization, especially the state, had severely restricted his freedoms.[44] More important, in 1762 Rousseau published *On the Social Contract,* whose opening words invoke slavery as a metaphor for political domination: "Man is born free and everywhere he is in chains."[45] Book 1, Chapter 4, of *The Social Contract* is ostensibly about personal slavery, yet Rousseau glides immediately from the particular instance of the civil slave who alienates himself and enslaves himself to his master to the general question of whether an entire people can alienate its freedom and subject itself to a king.[46] In other words, Rousseau is interested in the slave, white or black, only as a *symbol* of political domination, rather than in the actual condition of slaves in the French colonies of the time. Although *The Social Contract* would not become widely read until the Revolution, it shows how a critique of monarchy via the metaphor of slavery was already being formulated by mid-century.

Voltaire, whose antitheological stance led him to support the notion of separately created, and thus fundamentally distinct, human races, nevertheless opposed slavery as an institution on political grounds. His correspondance reveals how his antislavery position influenced other artists of his time. In July 1763, Voltaire received a letter from the sculptor Pigalle, who had read *Le Siècle de Louis XIV,* wherein Voltaire had criticized the tradition of portraying enchained slaves at the base of statues of kings, "as though one could not extol the great except through the evils by which they had crushed humanity."[47] Pigalle proposed to create, instead, a statue of Louis XV standing on a pedestal:

On the two sides of the pedestal are two emblematical figures, the first of which expresses the Gentleness [*Douceur*] of the government and the other the Felicity of the peoples. The gentleness of the government is represented by a woman, holding in one hand a rudder [*gouvernail*], and driving with the other, by the mane, a lion in liberty to express that the Frenchman, despite his strength submits himself voluntarily to a gentle government. The felicity of the peoples is rendered by a happy citizen, enjoying a perfect repose in the middle of abundance, designated by the cornucopia which pours out fruits, flowers, pearls, and other riches.[48]

In other words, Pigalle was inspired by Voltaire to replace the slaves at the base of the king's statue with symbols of a voluntary, contractual relationship between the crown and its subjects.

One final pair of authors injected an important strain into the discourse on slavery during this turbulent period. In 1770, Guillaume Thomas Raynal published his *Histoire des Deux Indes,* the first major French-language attempt to narrate the European conquests of and commerce with Asia and the Americas.[49] Michèle Duchet has shown how portions of the *Histoire des Deux Indes* were written by Diderot and incorporated by Raynal into the text.[50] Several themes are significant in this work. First, the Spanish are portrayed as monsters for their devastation of American Indians in Central and South America (a view already cited by Francisque's lawyers in 1759). By the same token, native Americans are portrayed as innocent victims of the Spaniards' brutality.[51] Second, the book is uncompromising in its stance against slavery.[52] Developing a theme originating in Montesquieu's *Esprit des lois, Histoire des Deux Indes* argues that black slaves are dull because of their experience as slaves rather than because of inherent character faults.[53] Finally, like the writings of Rousseau and Voltaire, *Histoire des Deux Indes* links colonial slavery to all kinds of oppression: "Who, barbarians, will you make believe that a man can be the property of a sovereign; a son, the property of a father; a woman, the property of a husband; a servant, the property of a master; a negro, the property of a colonist?"[54] Thus *Histoire des Deux Indes* advocated a radical equality whereby all social hierarchies would be leveled. In this way, the condition of the Frenchman under a despotic ruler was linked metaphorically to that of a slave.

Roc v. Poupet, 1770

Given such a turbulent and ideologically charged atmosphere, it is perhaps not surprising that arguments for the freedom of slaves in Paris took on a new, highly politicized tone. One year prior to Maupeou's dismissal of the Paris courts, one case attracted a tremendous amount of attention in Paris (and may have spurred several other slaves to initiate similar suits) when the slave's lawyer, Henrion de Pansey, published an eloquent *mémoire* pleading for his freedom. Henrion's representation of lawyers as the great protectors of the nation from the evils of despotic tyranny resonated strongly with growing critiques of despotic power.

The original petition for Roc (also spelled "Roch") was filed by his *procureur,* Nicolas De Foissey, on January 5, 1770. It stated that Roc was born free and appealed the declaration made by his master Michel Poupet, a merchant from Louisiana, to the clerk of the Admiralty of La Rochelle on June 16, 1769. The declaration made in La Rochelle (in conformity with the Declaration of 1738) stated that Roc was a slave. Roc's petition requested that his status as a free man be recognized, that he be permitted to return to La Rochelle, "and to dispose of himself as he wishes." In a provisional sentence, the court awarded Roc his freedom and the protection of the king.[55]

Poupet retaliated by filing petitions of January 18 and January 20 requesting that the court's provisional sentence be overturned and that Roc be required to "follow the said Poupet, his master, to Louisiana, or to any other part of America where it pleases the said Poupet to go; and to this effect to board the ship *The Two Brothers* which is equipping itself in La Rochelle, and on which Poupet has booked his passage. . . . In default of which the said Poupet be authorized to make him board by force by chaining hands and feet."[56] In response, Roc and his *procureur* filed petitions on February 13 and 16 requesting that Poupet's petitions be dismissed, that Roc be declared a free man, and that Poupet be condemned to pay 3,000 *livres* for Roc's food "since it is impossible for him to earn it" (presumably Roc was imprisoned until the court made a ruling on Poupet's petitions), and the same amount for damages, interest, and the costs of the appeal.[57]

The court heard the arguments by Roc's *avocat,* Henrion de Pansey, Poupet's *avocat,* Guillon, and the *procureur du roi,* Poncet de la Grave in four separate hearings of January 30, February 7, February 12, and March 2, 1770.[58] Roc's lawyer Henrion de Pansey, is an interesting figure.[59] According to his biographer, Roc's case was the first and only one that Henrion pleaded before a French court. His biographer implies that this was because Henrion found the "tumult" of the courtroom distasteful, opting instead for the career of an *avocat consultant.* But the

fact that Henrion never pleaded a case after Roc's coincides perfectly
with an abandonment of his fledgling practice during the Parisian judicial strike of 1771. Furthermore, the writings of his early career suggest
that Henrion's political sentiments, rather than his personal demeanor,
may have kept him from the courtroom.

During the reign of Maupeou's court, Henrion "kept his practice
closed" but was hard at work on a number of other projects. One of
these was his *Traité des fiefs de Dumoulin,* published in 1773. Henrion
dedicated the work to Matthieu Molé, son of the first president of the
parlement who would have inherited his father's office were it not for
Maupeou's reforms. Maupeou considered this dedication a protest
against his reforms and ordered the censure of the dedication. It was
published separately, however, as *L'Eloge de Mathieu Molé* in Geneva
in 1774.[60] Finally, when Maupeou lost favor with the new king in 1774
and his reforms were overturned, Henrion was selected by the Paris bar
to compose the speech delivered on the occasion of the parlement's
return.[61] These facts suggest that Henrion de Pansey was very likely
involved in the opposition to the Maupeou court.

According to Henrion's biographer, the *Mémoire pour un Nègre qui
réclame sa liberté,* "was read with much eagerness" in Paris.[62] Legal
mémoires were virtually the only form of publication that escaped censorship during this period and contributed significantly to the circulation
of anti-Maupeou opinion.[63] Close examination of the *mémoire* reveals
that the text can be read on two levels: on one level it is ostensibly about
Roc and his claim to freedom; on another level it gives voice to anti-
Roman and antidespotic sentiments.

Henrion's *mémoire* describes the misfortune of Roc, a freeborn negro
of Cayenne, who supported himself by fishing. One day a Spanish ship
drew near, and Roc, thinking to sell the sailors some of his catch,
boarded the vessel. The Spanish kidnapped Roc and sold him to French
colonists in Louisiana, where he was held as a slave for eight years.
After being sold from one master to another, Roc was selected to accompany Sr. Poupet on a voyage to France, because of his "faithfulness,
his intelligence, and his cleverness." Poupet and Roc arrived in La
Rochelle in June 1769, where Roc was duly registered with the Admiralty of that port.[64]

Henrion's *mémoire* argues for Roc's freedom on the grounds that Roc
was born a free man and though enslaved, his freedom should be restored on his arrival in France.[65] Henrion reiterated that the laws regulat-

ing slavery in France (1716 and 1738) were unregistered, making them
inapplicable for the case. Nevertheless, if the court found these arguments unpersuasive, Henrion charged in addition that Roc's master,
Poupet, failed to fulfill the formalities of these laws.[66] In many ways,
the technical grounds of Roc's claim to freedom are similar to the
arguments presented in the cases of Boucaux (1738) and Francisque
(1759).

In some important ways, however, Henrion's arguments in this case
differ from those in earlier *mémoires*. First, Henrion's history of the
abolition of slavery in France during the Middle Ages reflects a more
secular notion of historical change. As shown, lawyers on both sides of
the 1738 case, *Jean Boucaux v. Verdelin,* credited Christianity with
abolition of French slavery, itself a holdover from Roman times. The
mémoire for Francisque (1759) represented Christianity and a national
spirit as the forces that hand in hand dismantled slavery in France centuries after the fall of Rome.[67] Poncet de la Grave, in his 1762 report on
the case *Louis v. Le Febvre,* also credited the "monarchs of the third
race, secured on the throne by the Christian religion, now recognized
universally by all the French" with abolishing "an odious power, contrary to divine and natural law."[68]

In his 1770 *mémoire,* Henrion continues to link Christianity with
liberty, but he does not credit it with the decline of slavery in medieval
France. In fact, unlike earlier writers on the subject, Henrion claims that
"the Franks never had any slaves," though he acknowledges the presence of French serfdom until the fifteenth century.[69] On the contrary,
Henrion subtly hints that Christian missionaries may have been responsible for introducing modern slavery to French territories. He notes that
Louis XIII: "rejected with indignation the idea of introducing slavery
into the places subject to his empire. It was necessary to interest his
piety, it was necessary to bring it into conflict with his justice; it was
necessary to persuade him that it was the unique means to put these men
under the yoke of faith."[70] The phrase "yoke of faith" suggests an
ironic attitude toward the Catholic Church and its influence on the king.
At the end of this passage, Henrion cites Père Labat's *Nouveau voyage
en Amérique* as a source for the idea that slavery could be used to spread
Christianity. Indeed, Labat, a Dominican friar who purchased slaves to
build a mission in Martinique, states that Louis XIII was only persuaded
to permit slavery in the French colonies when it was shown to him that
"it was an infallible means, and the only one he had, to inspire the

worship of the true God to the Africans."[71] In other words, unlike the writers of earlier *mémoires,* Henrion implies that the Catholic church was the cause of slavery in seventeenth-century France, not the reason for its abolition during the Middle Ages.

Henrion's history of the origins of French slavery differs from earlier accounts in another significant way: his is the first *mémoire* to challenge the institution of slavery in toto, rather than excusing it as a necessary evil in the French colonies. Whereas earlier lawyers had claimed that slavery in the French colonies was a necessity,[72] Henrion refuted that claim: "But it is not true that the slavery of Negroes is necessary to the prosperity of our colonies. This is the reasoning of a politic as strict as it is cruel. Servitude, like a destructive volcano, dessicates, burns, engulfs everthing it surrounds: liberty, on the contrary, always brings in its wake happiness, abundance and the arts."[73] The notion that slavery is the only way to enforce labor in the hot climate of the tropics strikes Henrion as hypocritical and absurd: "Does the morality of our actions vary like the climates? Can that which is unjust under one latitude be just under another?"[74] Unique among the lawyers who wrote these *mémoires,* Henrion calls attention to the Quakers in Pennsylvania who free all slaves.[75] This *mémoire* contains the most straightforward antislavery rhetoric to date: "Everything is disastrous under slavery; it renders the master cruel, vindictive, proud; it renders the slave sluggish, deceitful, hypocritical; sometimes it brings man to atrocities which, without it, he would never have been capable."[76] In sum, Henrion's challenge is one of the first recorded denunciations of the entire institution of slavery to be heard in the French courts.

Henrion's antislavery position is informed by a host of antislavery writings published in the seventeenth and eighteenth centuries.[77] Most important, the idea that the institution of slavery corrupts both master and slave is present in the first paragraph of Book XV in Montesquieu's *Esprit des Lois*:

> [Slavery] is not good by its nature; it is useful neither to the master nor to the slave: not to the slave, because he can do nothing from virtue; not to the master, because he contracts all sorts of bad habits from his slaves, because he imperceptibly grows accustomed to failing in all the moral virtues, because he grows proud, curt, harsh, angry, voluptuous and cruel.[78]

This passage is particularly significant because it is immediately followed by text that links slavery to despotism: "In despotic countries, where one is already in political slavery, civil slavery is more bearable than elsewhere." Montesquieu goes on to state that slavery does not belong in a monarchy, still less in a democracy:

> But in monarchical government, where it is sovereignly important neither to beat down nor to debase human nature, there must be no slaves. In democracy, where everyone is equal, and in aristocracy, where the laws should put their effort into making everyone as equal as the government can permit, slaves are contrary to the spirit of the constitution; they serve only to give citizens a power and a luxury they should not have.[79]

By recalling the familiar arguments of Montesquieu, Henrion de Pansey implicitly warned that slavery in France, if tolerated, would turn a monarchy into a despotic government.[80]

Elsewhere, Henrion was more explicit in his linkage between despotism and slavery: "Everyone is free in a kingdom where liberty is seated at the feet of the throne, where the meanest of the subjects finds in the heart of his king the feelings of a father; where one encounters neither the despotism of monarchies nor the storms of republics. *No one is [a] slave in France.*"[81] Henrion's political vision is far from revolutionary (he clearly favors monarchy over republicanism), but he nevertheless supports limitations on the absolute power of a despot substituting the image of a benevolent, paternal kingship that characterized French monarchy at its best. Citing as precedent the case of 300 Spanish slaves who threw themselves at the king's feet requesting freedom, Henrion notes that Henry II "assembled his council," and "despite the opposition of the Spanish ambassador" freed the slaves.[82]

In another important passage concerning the role of the king, Henrion underscored the importance of Parlement in offsetting the bad influence of the king's courtiers. This passage merits quotation at length:

> The highest wisdom makes itself heard by the mouth of our Kings. They said: "We are the most cherished of the princes, let us be the best; we are the greatest, let us be the most just. But the more we are elevated, the more we will have ambitious flatterers, greedy courtiers, deceitful and mistaken advisors. One mistaken word could make twenty million Frenchmen unhappy; if this word escapes us, will there be a citizen general enough, powerful enough, to send the truth to us? It is you," they said to the Parlement, "whom we charge with this formidable and sacred function. Born in the cradle of the monarchy, always wise, always resolute, always incorruptible: surround the throne, guard the glory of the master and the happiness of the

subject. Be the first depository of our sovereign wishes and [let] the legislative power speak to the people by your voice.'' In this way our kings showed themselves greater than their own dignity; in this way their prudence became a shield against deceit; in this way our public law was formed. To scorn the formality of registration, to cite in the tribunals a law which has not been invested with it; this is to shock the constitution; it is at the same time to break the nation and to disobey the prince.[83]

In this crucial passage of the text, Henrion appealed to the parlements as the guardians of the French legal traditions against corrupt courtiers (such as Maupeou) who might try to mislead the king. He justified their right to refuse registration of laws that they believed might damage the French nation. Using the language of nationalism (*citoyen, nation*), Henrion portrayed the parlements as the true defenders of the interests of the "twenty million Frenchmen" of the realm.

By justifying the Parlement's role in registering new legislation, Henrion dramatized the important victories won by the Parlement over the previous decades. At the same time he linked the injustice of slavery with the injustice of a despotic kingship, in which the king was not accountable to the people for the exercise of his powers. This was heady stuff. Not surprisingly, as in all previous decisions, the Admiralty Court ruled in favor of Roc, granting him the status of a free man, return of his linens and clothing, and wages since his arrival in France. Poupet was sentenced to pay for the expenses of the trial.[84]

Lawyers and Their Motives

Earlier I suggested that three primary motives induced lawyers to take on slaves' cases: remuneration, experience, and sympathy. Roc's case provides an example of two of these in action. On April 2, Roc's *procureur*, Nicolas De Foissey, submitted a list of expenses to the court. Much of the bill is illegible, but it appears that De Foissey had advanced 193 *livres, 9 sous,* and 6 *deniers* to Roc and now requested repayment out of the costs judged against Roc's former master, Poupet.[85] It is not clear whether the orginal sum represented a cash advance paid by De Foissey to Roc or whether the amount represented De Foissey's legal fees. In either event, the fact that the court was willing to support De Foissey in the recovery of his expenses confirms that financial motives contributed to the reasons why lawyers, especially *procureurs,* took on similar cases.[86]

Henrion de Pansey's *mémoire* is eloquent testimony to the idea that higher ideals could propel lawyers into the service of slaves. Clearly Henrion deserves recognition as one of France's first abolitionists. He took a strong public stance against the institution of slavery more than a decade before the celebrated *Amis des Noirs,* and his arguments against slavery circulated in Paris at precisely the same time that Granville Sharp brought Somerset's case to court in London.

A third lawyer, who was not involved in Roc's case, nevertheless demands attention because he represented, by a wide margin, more slaves than any other lawyer in the Admiralty Court of France. Given that nearly all of his work was conducted during the 1760s and 1770s, we might expect to find that Pierre Etienne Regnaud was motivated by the profound sentiments that induced Henrion to represent Roc in 1770. Yet this seems not to be the case.

Born and educated in Paris, Regnaud was the son of a *procureur au parlement.* He practiced as an *avocat* until 1766 when he inherited his father's position as a *procureur.*

His first judicial encounter with the issue of slavery occurred in 1760 when he argued unsuccessfully for a slaveowner.[87] Regnaud seems to have learned his lesson well: he changed allegiance and went on to represent fifty-two slaves in their successful suits for freedom over the following two decades.

Outspoken and prolific, Regnaud was a fierce opponent of Maupeou's reforms in the 1770s. It has been argued that the decision to practice law under Maupeou can be offered as an ideological litmus test for lawyers of this period.[88] Those who refused to return to practice usually shared the strong Jansenist sympathies of the parlementary leadership or were strongly committed to the idea that the legal community represented the voice of the French nation. Regnaud was one of the dedicated who refused to practice law under Maupeou.

Nevertheless, Regnaud seems to have been neither a Jansenist sympathizer nor especially patriotic. During the Revolution, for example, Regnaud was an ardent royalist. His published memoirs proclaim his relentless efforts to protect Louis XVI and Marie Antoinette from the uprising.[89] He was knighted by Louis XVIII in 1814 for his efforts on behalf of the crown.[90] Regnaud's deep royalist sympathies after the Maupeou affair make it difficult to see his efforts on behalf of the slaves as part of an incipient republicanism. Furthermore, there is no evidence linking him with the Jansenists. Rather, it appears that his resistance to

Maupeou was entirely self-interested: he opposed Maupeou's abolition of venal offices in the courts (most especially the one he had inherited from his father).

Regnaud's expertise in the field of slave law appears instead to be more mundane. Apparently, as he took on more slave cases, he became known as a specialist in the field and consequently received referrals from officials in the Paris admiralty court and perhaps his former clients. Despite all his efforts on behalf of slaves, Regnaud, unlike Henrion de Pansey, cannot be called an abolitionist. Instead, Regnaud appears to have taken advantage of France's peculiar legal anomaly to develop a profitable business in freedom.

Conclusion

Henrion de Pansey's *mémoire* on behalf of Roc the slave stands out as unique in several ways. First, it cast Christianity as a force that extended and justified colonial slavery in contrast to earlier accounts that had stressed Christianity's role in leading the French out of Roman slavery. Second, it went beyond the Freedom Principle, which stressed only that slavery could not be permitted in France, to a more extreme position that advocated the abolition of colonial slavery in its entirety. Third, it represents a conjuncture between the Parisian jurists' resistance to Maupeou, a growing secular critique of despotism, and the rhetoric of antislavery.

It has been argued that the Maupeou reforms broke the back of traditional discipline and authority in the Parlement of Paris and that the subsequent generation of Parisian lawyers practiced a new style of argumentation based on sentimental flourish rather than judicial erudition.[91] In the following chapter we will see how this new discourse shaped the pleas of French slaves. In the meantime, however, Maupeou's ascendancy had a more concrete effect: the Admiralty Court of France was disbanded in June 1771 and did not resume business until July 1775.[92] During this four-year hiatus slaves in Paris had no recourse to the French courts.

7

The *Police des Noirs,* 1776–1777

On August 9, 1777, Louis XVI issued the third and final major piece of legislation regulating the entry of black subjects to the kingdom of France. Known as the *Police des Noirs,* this royal declaration differed significantly from its predecessors, the Edict of October 1716, and the Declaration of December 15, 1738, by prescribing actions based on skin color alone, rather than slave status. Another important difference was that, unlike earlier laws, the *Police des Noirs* was registered by the Parlement of Paris. These two facts are not unrelated. In fact, Minister of the Marine Sartine deliberately advocated the use of racial language as a way to circumvent the parlement's opposition to legislation containing the word *slave.* As with previous legislation, the *Police des Noirs* was prompted by specific court cases in which slaves sued for their freedom.

Among the first cases heard by the Admiralty Court of France when it resumed its hearings on August 23, 1775, was a slave's petition for freedom.[1] This was followed by two more in 1775 and seven in 1776.[2] One of these was the case of *Gabriel Pampy and Aminte Julienne v. Isaac Mendès France,* which received widespread publicity the following year through its inclusion in a collection of celebrated cases.[3] The *mémoire* on behalf of Pampy and Julienne demonstrates the new flamboyant rhetorical form that developed out of the Maupeou crisis. At the same time, royal administrative reactions to the *mémoire* show just how powerful an inciter of public opinion the legal brief had become.

106

Pampy and Julienne v. Mendès France

The case of *Pampy and Julienne versus Isaac Mendès France* has been well documented.[4] Pampy, a creole of Saint Domingue, and Julienne, enslaved in the Congo, were both sold to Isaac Mendès France, a Jew of Portuguese descent born and raised in Bordeaux. Mendès France was one of many Frenchmen who moved to Saint Domingue after the Seven Years' War to see seek their fortune. He was successful in the export trade and built on his successes by investing in cotton and coffee plantations.[5]

Mendès France brought Pampy and Julienne to Nantes in June 1775.[6] Also in the group was the sister of Mendès France's daughter-in-law, Mlle. Brunswick. The party stayed in Nantes for a short time before traveling to Paris.[7] In Paris, however, Mendès France and Brunswick were arrested and imprisoned for two months. They took their servants Pampy and Julienne with them to their respective prisons.[8]

Des Essarts's account of the story of Pampy and Julienne is a wonder of rhetorical flourish: Pampy and Julienne are portrayed as the hapless victims of the avaricious and cruel Jew, Mendès. Des Essarts reports that while in prison, Pampy contracted a severe illness because "the sadness and contagious air that he breathed in the prison inflamed his blood."[9] Mendès France refused to pay for Pampy's food, but a prison turnkey nourished Pampy back to health by feeding him bouillon. Des Essarts also claimed that Mendès France refused to give the servants clothes appropriate to the climate and beat them frequently.[10]

There is no reason to doubt that Pampy and Julienne were beaten (treatment sometimes accorded to social subordinates in the eighteenth century), but the obvious bias of Des Essarts's account makes it difficult to get a balanced portrait of the individuals. Pampy and Julienne are portrayed as two-dimensional symbols of injustice. Whereas Henrion de Pansey also used Roc's story to portray political ideas in 1770, his caricatures of the master and slave were not as extreme. For example, Henrion de Pansey wrote of Roc's seizure and sale into slavery: "One day he was throwing his [fishing] lines into a place in the river; a Spanish vessel passed; the captain called him, flattered him with the hope of selling his fish, by these means lured him on board and seized his person. The vessel continued on its route, arrived in Louisiana, where the cruel Spaniard sold this unfortunate to a Frenchman just as cruel as he."[11] Though the Spaniard and the Frenchmen are described as "cruel" by the lawyer, and Roc is clearly represented as an innocent dupe, these portraits are not as extreme as those drawn by Des Essarts in his account of Pampy and Julienne:

> the most hard-hearted of masters wanted to snatch from [Pampy and Julienne] the unintended benefit of having brought them to a land which does not recognize slavery. He pursued them, he threatened them, he struggled for their mastery with the laws that protected them. . . . The idea of death is less horrible for them than that of wearing the chains that they ask the magistrates to shatter. Their position is terrible; it is humanity itself which presents them to justice.[12]

Throughout Des Essarts's text, Isaac Mendès France is portrayed as an evil, greedy, arrogant master, and Pampy and Julienne are nothing but innocent, long-suffering victims. Compared to Henrion's assertive portrait of Roc as a servant chosen for his "fidelity, his intelligence, and his cleverness," or Le Clerc du Brillet's 1738 description of Boucaux as "a man equal to us," Des Essarts's account of Pampy and Julienne shows them to be passive martyrs unable to resist their fate.[13]

   This contrast in rhetorical styles exemplifies what has been called the "new, more literary directions in legal writing" that developed at the time of the Maupeou crisis.[14] During the crisis a new generation of lawyers entered the Parisian bar, and they favored sentimental rhetorical flourishes over the traditional forms of legal oratory that emphasized erudition and understanding of France's complex legal traditions. Pierre Louis Claude Gin, author of *The Eloquence of the Bar* (1767), for example, counseled his readers that "All the rules can be reduced to a simple principle: . . . feel vividly, and you will express yourself vividly as well."[15] It appears that Des Essarts heeded Gin's advice.

In Des Essarts's account Pampy and Julienne discovered that they might claim their freedom by virtue of being in France. The text does not specify how they came to this knowledge, but there seems to have been a veritable explosion of publicity surrounding the freeing of slaves during the 1770s. By January 1776, when Pampy and Julienne submitted their first petition for freedom, two others had obtained their freedom in the same manner.[16] In his 1777 report to the Conseil des Dépêches, Antoine de Sartine wrote: "Some published *mémoires,* full of declamations against slavery and against the tyranny of masters are scattered with profusion in Paris. The judgments rendered public by posters inform the Negroes that they are free, independent, and even equal to those whom they regard as superior beings, and whom they were destined to serve."[17] The phrase "*mémoires imprimées*" almost certainly refers to Des Essarts's own account, which was published for public circulation after the trial, but it also may refer to Henrion de Pansey's *mémoire,* published in 1770.[18] It is difficult to say when the posters began to announce the courts' verdicts publicly. Any of the decisions by the Admiralty court since its resumption in 1775 might have been publicized in this way. Sartine's comments suggest that there may have been an active antislavery movement in France more than a decade prior to the formation of the celebrated *Société des Amis des Noirs* (1788).

However Pampy and Julienne came to know of their rights, they made contact with the lawyer, Dejunquières, a *procureur* at the Admiralty Court of France. Dejunquières sued for their freedom in the Admiralty Court, and a judgment was rendered in their favor on January 19, 1776. The court named Dejunquières their guardian and placed the two former slaves under the safeguard of the king; Mendès France was prohibited from seizing their persons or their goods. Yet Mendès France was not to be undone. He filed a *requête* on January 25 to overturn the court's judgment. However, on February 5, Mendès France did not appear in court, and the magistrates awarded Pampy and Julienne 100 *livres* for back wages and 60 *livres* for food.[19]

Despite the two sentences, Mendès France arranged for Pampy and Julienne to be arrested once again, flaunting the authority of the Admiralty Court. De la Haye, Lieutenant General of the Admiralty, wrote to Antoine de Sartine, minister of the marine, requesting him to intervene with orders from the king.[20] It is not clear whether Sartine complied.

On February 17, Mendès France renewed his earlier *requête* against Pampy and Julienne, and it was this final challenge that prompted Des Essarts to write his *mémoire* on their behalf.[21] The arguments presented in Des Essarts's *mémoire* differ significantly from those of Henrion de Pansey published six years earlier. First, Des Essarts returns to the familiar notion that slavery was "necessary" to ensure cultivators in the American colonies.[22] Thus Des Essarts retreated from Henrion de Pansey's absolute opposition to slavery as an institution, emphasizing instead the cruelty of particular masters.

Unlike any previous legal history of slavery in the *mémoires,* Des Essarts dwells upon Jewish slavery law: "The Jews combined personal and real slavery at the same time. Foreigners, among this fierce people, were condemned to endure the yoke of slavery, and when Moses called to them, *'You will never have harsh dominion over your slaves; you will not oppress them at all,'* they exercised the hardest treatment against their slaves."[23] This addition probably develops out of Des Essarts's rhetorical strategy, which was based on anti-Semitism. Elsewhere in the brief he refers to the Jews of Metz, accused of poisoning wells and sacrificing children.[24]

On the other hand, Des Essarts maintains the secular interpretation of the abolition of slavery in France established by Henrion de Pansey in 1770. Here the kings of France are celebrated for setting their own slaves free and for "abolishing slavery entirely from [their] states."[25] Des Essarts quotes Louis X's edict of 1315 but omits the passages that make the franchise conditional. In this regard, Des Essarts helps to maintain earlier lawyers' mythical origins of the Freedom Principle.

Pampy and Julienne won their freedom like so many French blacks before them. The Admiralty Court of France rendered its decision on February 23, 1776.[26]

Meanwhile, De la Haye's February 7 request for ministerial intervention seems to have spurred the government into action. Soon thereafter, Poncet de la Grave submitted a report to Sartine on the issue of blacks brought to France by their masters.[27] His primary complaints are strikingly similar to those he voiced in 1762, namely, that blacks intermarry with whites or engage in prostitution and that, because the earlier laws of 1716 and 1738 were not registered, the slaves are judged free by the courts. To rectify these problems, Poncet de la Grave proposed an independent commission that would judge the status of blacks and a series of "*hospices*" at port cities to retain black domestic servants once their colonial masters arrived in France. These ideas formed the kernel of what eventually would become the new law known as the *Police des Noirs.*

Miromesnil, the keeper of the Seals, seems to have been designated to interpolate between the Admiralty officials (De la Haye and Poncet de la Grave) and Minister Sartine.[28] Commenting on Poncet de la Grave's suggestions, he counseled Sartine against most of the *procureur*'s innovations—the commission, the hospices—arguing that new legislation, based on the laws of 1716 and 1738, would be sufficient to deal with the problem. The most important thing, according to Miromesnil, was to register the new law "in all the courts of the Kingdom, and in all the tribunals of our colonies."[29]

A month later, Sartine issued a letter designed to quell a rumor that the government intended to free all French slaves. In a letter to the chambers of commerce of Bordeaux, La Rochelle, Nantes, St. Malo, Le Havre, Rouen, Marseille, and Dunkerque, the minister wrote:

> Some evil-minded people have circulated in various ports of the kingdom [the rumor] that the government plans to free the negroes, and I don't doubt that this absurd proposal has made its way to your place. However I am persuaded that a similar piece of news can only excite scorn for those who are its authors. I thought that I should inform you so that if some feeble mind had imagined some uneasiness about it [*en avoit conçû de l'inquiétude*], you could dissuade him. You merchants, who contribute to the prosperity of commerce, can expect nothing but acts of benevolence and new tokens of the king's attention.[30]

The phrase, "new tokens of the king's attention," was the first public hint that Louis XVI intended to address the problem of slavery in France.[31] Even before Pampy and Julienne's case was decided, the king's administration was attempting to create new, more stringent legislation that they hoped would stop the influx of blacks into France once and for all. The new legislation, known as the *Police des Noirs,* would not be formally declared for another year and a half, but, once in effect, its provisions would be more sweeping than either the Edict of 1716 or the Declaration of 1738. What is more, the king's administrators would be successful in registering it in all of the parlements of the kingdom.

The Drafting of the *Police des Noirs*

Although Poncet de la Grave continued to be an important figure in articulating the problems posed by blacks and slaves in the metropolis, he was subordinate to a new administrator in the king's cabinet. Antoine de Sartine became secretary of state and then minister of the marine and colonies within a few months of Louis XVI's accession to the crown.[32] His earlier offices as *lieutenant criminel* of the Châtelet and *lieutenant général de police* of Paris, gave him a wide range of supervisory experience and responsibility, but little in his background prepared him for the management of colonial affairs. To understand both the innovations of the *Police des Noirs* and the tenacity with which it was implemented, it is useful to review the career and character of the man who would oversee its implementation.

Antoine Raimond Jean Gualbert Gabriel de Sartine began his mete-

oric career as a *conseiller,* or judge, in the Parisian Châtelet court in
1752 at the age of 23. Such an appointment was technically illegal
because of his youth, but Sartine received a special dispensation from
Louis XV to hold the office. There he heard and decided cases concerning, among other things, Jews and Protestants, beggars and prostitutes,
publishers and Jansenists. He rose rapidly through the ranks to *lieutenant criminel* (1755) and *maitre des requêtes* (1759), ultimately achiev-
ing the position of *lieutenant général de police* in December 1759.

The office of lieutenant general of the police encompassed far more in
the eighteenth century than the title suggests to us today. The of-
ficeholder was essentially the *intendant* for Paris, carrying out the functions of the prefect of police, some of the duties of the prefect of the
Seine, and those of the mayor of the capital. In 1762 Sartine oversaw the
formation of a centralized system for locating and supervising wet-
nurses. In 1768 he introduced a citywide system of streetlighting in
Paris.[33] Sartine also counted among his duties the supervision of the
markets of Paris, including the trade in grain, wine, and livestock in the
capital.

Sartine became best known in this role for the expansion and profes-
sionalization of the surveillance of Paris. Under Sartine, a complicated
network of undercover informants honeycombed the city and beyond,
reporting on both domestic and foreign intrigues. One story, perhaps
apocryphal, gives an indication of Sartine's reputation as a thorough
spymaster:

> Having received a letter from a minister of the emperor of Germany that
> requested him to order the arrest of a famous thief believed to be hiding in
> Paris, [Sartine] responded, a few days later, that the man in question was in
> Vienna itself, in a house in one of the suburbs of the city, whose number he
> designated, indicating the hours at which this individual habitually came and
> went, and the disguises he used. The information proved to be correct and
> made it possible to seize the guilty party.[34]

Thus Sartine was in a position to monitor much of the Parisian under-
world through his network of spies and moles.

In addition to overseeing the practical matters of the city—legal and
material—Sartine also supervised the *librairie de police,* one of two
censors operating in Paris. In this capacity Sartine monitored theatrical
plays and shorter works, such as lampoons, pamphlets, brochures,
posters. Since 1750, the other branch of the censor, the *librairie gra-*

cieuse, which monitored longer works of literature, philosophy, law, theology, mathematics, and the like, was run by Malesherbes. In October 1763, Maupeou maneuvered Malesherbes out of the post, and the position was transferred to Sartine who then oversaw both censorship bureaus. Sartine, however, followed in the tradition of Malesherbes, indulging a certain amount of freedom of expression. Shortly after Sartine was appointed, the Parlement of Paris virtually prohibited the publication of the *Encyclopédie* in 1759, yet he remained friends with one of its principal authors, Diderot, throughout the 1760s. During the exile of the Parlement of Paris in 1771–1774, Sartine was complicit with the anti-Maupeou propagandists, prosecuting only the minor figures. It is speculated that he warned major anti-Maupeou figures before a police raid.[35]

Prior to his appointment as minister of the marine and colonies in 1774, therefore, Sartine had developed a minute familiarity with the workings of the city of Paris, from both administrative and regulative perspectives. A friend of the Encyclopedists, and an experienced chief of surveillance, Sartine brought a methodical passion for observation and organization to his new post. Finally, his complete lack of experience outside of Paris seems to have led him to exaggerate his capacity to control the entry of blacks into France.

As minister of the marine, Sartine attended the king's high council twice weekly to deal with the government's most pressing problems, especially in foreign affairs. Sartine was at the top of a chain of command that supervised all French activities in Africa, America, and the Indian Ocean as well as the three primary navy bases of Brest, Rochefort, and Toulon.[36] Consequently, Sartine's role in the formation of the *Police des Noirs* was only a minor aspect of his new position, yet it appears to have been a problem that he took very seriously.[37]

During the spring of 1776, an anonymous proposal was drafted for a new edict that would address the problem of blacks in France.[38] The proposal itself has been lost, but something of its nature can be gleaned by the response of De la Rivière, who critiqued the proposal for Sartine.[39] Consisting of more than thirty-two articles, the proposed edict attempted to address numerous issues relevant to the presence of black slaves in France. But, according to De la Rivière, the plan was peppered with "superfluous, incoherent, contradictory, unjust, and poorly designed" provisions. These include plans to baptize all new blacks in the colonies by rounding them up for instruction. De la Rivière objected that this proposal "undoubtedly ignores the danger in regularly amassing a large number of blacks native to different countries and belonging to different plantations. Furthermore it overlooks the hardships to masters that a supposed instruction would cause to the negroes' work."[40] De la Rivière also criticized the proposal to set up an independent tribunal to judge the status of all blacks in France, as well as the proposed additional penalties (including fines and corporal punishment) for manumission, marriage, sale, trading, or giving away of slaves during the Atlantic crossing. De la Rivière argued that the loss of a slaveowner's deposit should be sufficient in most cases and that marriage was already prohibited without the master's consent. De la Rivière was particularly scornful of article 32, which, in effect, prescribed different penalties for white men who impregnated black women depending on whether the man owned the woman. How, De la Rivière wondered, was the paternity to be determined?

In sum, the proposed edict was a resounding failure. Meanwhile, the Admiralty Court of France continued to hear the cases of blacks seeking their freedom until it adjourned for the summer. Shortly after the court reconvened in August 1776, Louis XVI issued *lettres patentes* decrying the proliferation of court cases in which blacks sued for their freedom.[41] Five days later he established a committee to look into the matter and to draft new legislation.[42]

There are several notable things about the *lettres patentes* of September 3. First, in contrast to previous legislation, the administration seems finally to acknowledge that the majority of blacks brought to France come as domestic servants, rather than to gain religious or technical instruction. In fact, Emilien Petit, a lawyer who published his comparative study of international slave law this same year, noted that the requirement of religious instruction was regularly flouted by masters who brought their slaves to France.[43]

Second, the term *noirs* has begun to replace *nègres* in official documents, a linguistic convention that may mark a corresponding conceptual clarification of the difference between free and enslaved blacks. That is, the use of the new term *noir* may arise at this juncture precisely because metropolitan officials wanted to overcome the ambiguity of the term *nègre* and address the status of both free blacks and slaves. Notably absent from the *lettres patentes* is the word *esclave*. It is possible that the terminology of the *lettres patentes* constituted a "trial balloon" by

Sartine to see whether the parlement would accept racial categories in lieu of slave status in new legislation.

Third, and most significant, the *lettres patentes* display a new antiblack, proplanter stance. For example, the letters characterize the blacks' lawsuits as "inconveniences" that delay the colonists' return to the colonies and cost them money. The presence of blacks in France, "especially in Paris" is portrayed as disruptive to public order. One sentence implicitly distinguishes between the blacks of Paris, who apparently do not deserve their freedom, and "those who inhabit [the colonies] with the grace that merits liberty."[44] The author even includes the old chestnut about depleting the colonies of fieldworkers, as though the estimated 4,000 blacks then in France, trained as domestic workers rather than agricultural laborers, might have contributed significantly to the labor pool of over 500,000 in the French American colonies of Louisiana, Saint Domingue, and so on. The authorship of the *lettres patentes* is not clear, but it is evident that the new trend in Louis XVI's administration was to dismiss blacks' claims to liberty and to support colonists' efforts to reclaim their slaves and return them to the colonies.

Perhaps the most damning provision of the *lettres patentes* was its suspension of all lawsuits for freedom—present or future—that might come before the courts. Anyone who had not yet received his or her freedom through the courts was to remain in the same state they held previously, that is, they were to be considered slaves.

The *lettres patentes* recognized that the ineffectiveness of previous legislation concerning black slaves in France was due to the fact that neither the edict of 1716 nor the declaration of 1738 were registered by the Parlement of Paris and several other high courts. To remedy this situation, Sartine sought to have the *lettres patentes* registered immediately. The Parlement of Paris complied right away, registering the letters on September 6, 1776.[45] If I am correct in hypothesizing that the use of racial terminology instead of slave status in the *lettres patentes* constituted a trial balloon, it would seem that it flew. Meanwhile the Admiralty Court of France delayed registration of the letters until October 2, 1776, permitting one last petitioner, Paul de Manouevrer, to register his manumission with the Paris court.[46]

On September 8, the king's council of state issued an *arrêt du conseil* that established a commission to draft new legislation for the policing of blacks [*police des noirs*].[47] Named to that commission were Chardon, d'Aguesseau, Joly de Fleury, de Bernage, Taboureau, and Lenoir.[48] Sartine apppointed Chardon the *rapporteur* of the commission.[49] Poncet de la Grave, though not officially appointed to the commission, remained active in the drafting of the new law.[50]

In November 1776, Sartine sent a letter to all *intendants* of France requesting information about the number of blacks in the region, whether they were slave or free, the date of their arrival in the region, their age, the number of blacks who have been freed, passed by testament, exchanged, or sold, and, finally, "those who have married since their arrival in the kingdom."[51] This request for information was reissued in May and June of 1777.[52]

The information was not readily forthcoming. For example, Chardon chastised the subdelegate of Dijon: "You have indicated, sir, that all the negroes in your subdelegation have been declared free by their masters. This simple declaration that they have made is not sufficient. It is necessary to have precise information in this matter."[53] The subdelegates of Mâcon and Seurre were similarly reprimanded.[54] These letters are evidence of what would become an ongoing tension between Paris and the provinces, particularly those without ports, the latter of whom did not appear to take the problem of blacks very seriously.

Over the course of 1776 and 1777, the commission sought to draft legislation that would stem the flow of blacks to France. One anonymous commissioner thought that the process of drafting new regulations would be "very simple."[55] His fourteen-point plan began with an absolute prohibition against the arrival of blacks [*nègres*] to the kingdom. The penalty for such intrusion would be their return to the colonies (though one gets the impression that exceptions might be possible, depending on the black's status or condition [*"sort"*]).[56] The proposal suggests the establishment of *dépots* in the ports wherein colonists who, by necessity, brought their black servants to France (for the lack of white domestics in the colonies was deemed a real problem), could leave them for immediate return on the next available ship.[57] The cost of returning the black to the colonies would be born by the colonist, who, as a prerequisite, would be required to leave a deposit with the colonial authorities prior to departure. In his proposal, the commissioner further recommended that all blacks currently in France be accounted for, including their place of residence, or origin, and of arrival in France.

Significantly, the proposal never uses the word *slave* (*esclave*) to describe the people who are to be registered and regulated, for, in the words of the proposal, "Every slave who touches the soil of France is free. This is the principle." Yet, continues the commissioner:

> Some have demanded their freedom in court and it has been declared to belong to them. Some, staying in ignorance or inaction, return with their masters and in America find themselves once again in the same state of slavery. To end this difference, and favor the freedom of those temperaments which do not harm the masters who have detained their negroes in France, it seems appropriate to set a period of two months counting, for example, from the date of publication. The court will have these two months to decide the status of all.[58]

Those who arrive after the law's publication would, according to the commissioner's plan, be immediately returned to the colonies. Regarding those blacks already in France, their masters would be permitted to declare them. "[The masters] will certainly not claim those who have obtained their liberty [in court]," reasoned the commissioner. In this way, free blacks would be winnowed from the enslaved and permitted to stay in France because, "having been acclimatized to France, and accustomed to the mores of the country, they can only carry a spirit of insubordination and disorder, which could corrupt the subordination necessary for the maintenance of others."[59]

The ultimate aim of the proposal is spelled out in the next-to-last provision: "In the end, the race of negroes will be extinguished in the kingdom as soon as the transport of them is forbidden."[60] Noting that it is impossible to prevent blacks from marrying one another, the commissioner nevertheless suggests that, "one can render the act of marriage difficult, without however invoking the power of the king to render them null." Resorting to oblique bureaucratic double-speak, the author continues: "By these 'difficulties' they will be extinguished."[61]

This document echoes the racist sentiments expressed in Poncet de la Grave's 1762 report and makes clear the government's intent to cleanse France of blacks, without, it should be noted, resorting to extermination. By preventing the arrival of new blacks, the French administration hoped that those already in France would die out or perhaps be absorbed over several generations.

While members of the commission worked to draft the new edict, Poncet de la Grave consulted the records of the clerk of the Admiralty to determine how many blacks were registered as living in Paris. He must have been shocked, or at least annoyed, to discover that since the massive registration drive following the Admiralty ordinance of 1762, the number of blacks registering in Paris had slowed to a trickle. Indeed, since 1770, no more than six blacks had registered with the Paris clerk of the Admiralty in any given year (this despite the fact that an average of nine petitions for freedom were presented to the court each year).

On April 16, 1777, Poncet de la Grave proposed to the Admiralty of France an ordinance very similar to that issued in 1762. In anticipation of the king's forthcoming "wise law," which would "prohibit the great quantity of negroes in these states and especially the capital," Poncet de la Grave's proposed ordinance required all subjects with blacks in their service to register them with the nearest clerk of the Admiralty or face a penalty of 100 *livres*. Blacks "in service to no one" were similarly enjoined to register themselves, though no penalty was proposed. The officers of the Admiralty ratified Poncet de la Grave's ordinance, ordering that it be "published and posted" in the city and suburbs of Paris. Similar measures were taken by the Admiralties situated in Bordeaux and Rouen.[62]

The ordinance was moderately effective. Within the four weeks prescribed by the law, 121 blacks were registered with the Paris Admiralty, thirty-four of whom claimed to be freedmen or free by birth.[63] Even after the prescribed time elapsed, blacks and masters continued to make their declarations. On July 7, the officers of the Admiralty officially extended the period of registration for another four weeks (six weeks outside Paris), but raised the penalty for noncompliance to 300 *livres* for masters and imprisonment for free blacks. This added sixty-eight blacks to the registers between May 17 and August 8, bringing the total to 189.[64]

A final draft of the *Declaration pour la police des noirs* was presented to the Paris parlement's De Lamoignon on August 7, 1777. It included virtually all the suggestions in the anonymous commissioner's proposal, including the prohibition on new arrivals, the establishment of port *dépots,* the registration of blacks already resident in France, and a ban on marriages between whites and "blacks, mulattoes, and other people of color."[65]

Chardon, of the legislative commission, went through the proposed legislation point by point with Lamoignon to ensure its approval by the high court. The judge approved all but article 13, prohibiting interracial marriage. Sartine instructed Chardon to consult with the abbot Despagnac who concurred with Lamoignon in his objection to the article.

Chardon suggested to Joly de Fleury that the article be rephrased following English and Spanish law to prohibit the offspring of interracial
marriages from holding public office until the fourth generation, but the
commissioners apparently decided to eliminate the article altogether
because it was not in the final version presented to Louis XVI for his
signature on August 9, 1777.[66]

Conclusion

When Sartine presented the final draft of the *Déclaration pour la police
des noirs* to the king at Versailles for his signature on August 9, 1777, he
sought to justify its necessity in a number of ways. First, he recounted
the lack of registration of earlier laws by the Parlement of Paris and the
proliferation of lawsuits.[67] These lawsuits, noted Sartine, are publicized
by posters and *mémoires,* giving blacks the notion that they are equal to
"the superior beings they were destined to serve."[68] What is more,
some judges were helping slaves to escape from their masters, or they
"detain them in prison, prohibiting the jailers from releasing them,
under the pain of exemplary punishment."[69]

Sartine went on to describe a veritable onslaught of blacks in the
kingdom, reminiscent of Poncet de la Grave's 1762 "deluge." The
familiar complaints against sexual license and racial intermixing are
amplified by political alarm, generated by the recent slave uprisings in
Dutch Guiana (1764 and 1776):

> [In the kingdom] their marriages to Europeans are encouraged; the public
> houses are infected; the colors mingle together; the blood degenerates. A
> prodigious quantity of slaves [who are] removed from cultivation in our
> colonies are brought to France only to flatter the vanity of their masters and of
> these same slaves. If they return to America, they carry with them the spirit
> of liberty, of independence and of equality that they communicate to the
> others; destroy the bonds of discipline and subordination and thereby prepare
> a revolution, of which the colonies of our neighbors have already furnished
> some examples, and which the most alert vigilence will not be enough to
> prevent.[70]

Sartine's letter describes a chaotic world where traditional order is
overturned: blacks and whites mix and slaves escape their subordination. Given the fact that British colonies in North America had only
recently declared their independence from England, Sartine may have

also been concerned about the loyalty of French colonists in the Caribbean.

Sartine concluded that the former justifications for bringing blacks to France were no longer relevant:

> They are better raised in the principles of Religion which are brought to them in the colonies than in France where they are moreover surrendered to laziness and libertinage. The object of learning a trade in France doesn't exist anymore. The number of artisans of this class has grown perhaps too great in the colonies, and it is desirable that the trades there be exclusively in the hands of whites.[71]

Instead, argued Sartine, a new law must be put forward that would prevent the current "abuses," prohibiting the arrival of blacks in France altogether. At the same time, it would create undue hardship for the colonists to prevent them from bringing servants with them on the ocean passage.

Returning to the problem of parlementary registration, Sartine noted that the terms *libre* and *esclave* had been circumvented in the text of the law: "It is not possible . . . to use the word 'slave' in the law. Therefore in the bill that I put before your Majesty's eyes we have substituted that of 'domestic.' "[72] To prevent masters from selling, trading, or disposing their slaves by testament in France, the bill's framers adopted the wording, "cannot change status [*état*]." "The Parlement cannot refuse to accept these terms," noted Sartine, because: "in the *lettres patentes* that your Majesty addressed the third of last September to the Parlement of Paris, and which were registered there, it said expressly that the blacks would live in the same condition where they were before."[73] Confident that the commission had at last hit on a solution that would solve the problem of blacks and slavery in France, the minister of the marine presented the *Déclaration pour la police des noirs* to Louis XVI, who signed it on August 9, 1777.

8

Erosion of the
Police des Noirs

Almost as soon as the *Police des Noirs* was signed into law, it ran into obstacles. One of the most extensive critiques of the new law was a report by Le Moyne, commander of the marine in Bordeaux, to Chardon, head of the commission who drafted the law and was now in charge of implementing it.[1] Sympathetic to the concerns of French colonists, Le Moyne challenged the fundamental basis of the law: the exclusion of individuals from France on the basis of race. He objected to the way that the *Police des Noirs* lumped together blacks free by birth, freedmen, and slaves, without regard to wealth or gradation of skin color. Pointing out that many successful colonists had through years of intermarriage made it possible to "all but forget their origin," Le Moyne drew attention to the fact that many now owned property in Europe, sending their children to France to be educated. "Is it prudent to bring them closer to this kind of slavery?" he wondered.[2] In response to Le Moyne's suggestions for improving the law (which, taken together, would have created vast loopholes, severely undermining the law's effectiveness), Chardon gently but firmly turned down the commander's proposals, reminding him that all of its provisions must be strictly enforced.[3]

As we shall see, Sartine and his subordinate Chardon ran into more than mere criticism as they attempted to implement the provisions of the *Police des Noirs*. Numerous efforts to shore up and extend the *Police des Noirs* during the decade prior to the Revolution ultimately failed because of provincial resistance, professional rivalry, and ineptitude.

Implementation and Resistance

Because their lack of registration had impeded the enforcement of the laws of 1716 and 1738, Sartine made it his first order of business to make sure that the *Police des Noirs* was registered by the sovereign courts of France. The Parlement of Paris complied on August 27, 1777, followed by Corsica, Lorraine, and Toulouse over the next few months.[4] The Admiralty Court of France registered the *Police des Noirs* on September 5, 1777.[5]

Not content with the usual publication of the new law, Sartine instructed Joly de Fleury to take extra precautions to publicize the *Police des Noirs* in Paris:

> The declaration concerning the blacks, *monsieur,* which has been registered yesterday, particularly interests a group of people who are not in a position to purchase [a printed copy of the law] and for whom it is nevertheless important that [the law] be known. I beg you to please give your orders that it be not only cried [announced by a *crieur* in a loud voice] in the streets in the ordinary way, but also that it be posted with placards in the most prominent streets and places in the city, in a large enough number that it can be known by all the people.[6]

Similarly, Sartine's subordinate, Chardon, who apparently was delegated to supervise the enforcement of the *Police des Noirs,* requested all colonial administrators to post copies of the new law so that "no one can pretend to be ignorant of it."[7] In his zeal to enforce the law, Chardon warned colonial officials that subterfuge, such as entering the names of blacks on the ships' mortuary lists in order to receive the return of a deposit, would be detected and dealt with severely.[8] Sartine and Chardon urged administrators in France and the colonies to keep them informed of the names and descriptions of all blacks who traveled to or lived in France and to enforce the other provisions of the law diligently.[9]

Yet at virtually the same time that naval administrators were warning their subordinates to strictly enforce the *Police des Noirs,* a new act lessened its severity. The *arrêt du conseil* of September 7, 1777, extended by two months the period of time during which masters who had registered their slaves could retain them in France.[10]

Judging by the marked increase in the registration of blacks, this one aspect of the law was somewhat effective, at least in Paris. In addition to the 189 declarations made in response to the Admiralty ordinances of

April 16 and July 7, the *Police des Noirs* brought in 125 new declarations in Paris during the first month of its enforcement.[11] Subsequent renewals requiring registered blacks to carry *cartouches,* or identification cards, would similarly inflate the numbers of declarations in 1778 and 1783. As a result of the *Police des Noirs* and its subsequent renewals, 765 persons of color registered with the clerk of the Admiralty of France in Paris between 1777 and 1789.[12] This nearly fivefold increase over the number of Parisian registrants since 1762 is probably not attributable solely to the government's improved efforts to enforce the *Police des Noirs.* It appears that the number of blacks in France was, indeed, on the rise.

Shortly after the *Police des Noirs* was put into effect, however, a power struggle ensued between Poncet de la Grave, *procureur du roi* to the Admiralty of France, and Lenoir, Sartine's successor as *lieutenant général* of the police of Paris. Since 1762 Poncet de la Grave had been sounding the alarm against interracial liaisons. In the *Police des Noirs* he believed he had finally found a weapon against the black prostitutes who so unnerved him. Chardon's instructions to Poncet de la Grave regarding the enforcement of the law in Paris emphasized that the *procureur du roi* required specific, individualized permission for each black that he wished to arrest, obtainable solely through Lenoir.[13] Poncet de la Grave then turned to Lenoir, but he was slow to respond. Poncet de la Grave appealed to Chardon for *ordres du roi* permitting him to arrest the women in question. At the same time, he suggested that he be given blank orders from the king so that he could fill them out himself when colonists requested permission to take their black servants back to the colonies.[14] Chardon sharply reprimanded Poncet de la Grave, reminding him that all *ordres du roi,* whether authorizing arrests or permission to send blacks back to the colonies, would come through Lenoir: "Your place as *procureur* of his majesty at the seat of the Admiralty of France is a place of magistracy!," not, by implication, chief of police.[15]

Yet Poncet de la Grave was unable to let the matter rest. Chardon agreed to have blacks arrested at the *procureur*'s request but insisted that they should be conducted immediately to the Châtelet prison where he would have to request permission to interrogate them.[16] Poncet de la Grave ordered the arrest of two black women in their late twenties, Marie Louis Latour, called L'Espere, and Marie Françoise La Perle, called Fauchonette. In mid-December he arranged to interrogate them in the presence of the Admiralty clerk, Bottée.[17] His summaries of the interrogations show that he was impressed by the character of the first woman, Latour, who "is of a sweet character, one might even say honest."[18] The second woman, referred to as "Fauchonette," made a much less favorable impression: "She is of a very determined and insolent character declaring that she cannot live except by prostitution. We believe her to be infected by venereal disease which has determined us to send her to the hospital so that she can be cured."[19] Poncet de la Grave allowed both women to sell or collect their belongings and then ordered that they be shipped back to the colonies via the depot in Le Havre.[20]

Within a few days, Poncet de la Grave met with Lieutenant General of Police Lenoir and Chardon to discuss the matter. The meeting seems to have gone badly for Poncet de la Grave. He wrote a lengthy, outraged letter to Chardon, complaining that his authority to supervise the arrest and expulsion of blacks was being stripped away. To justify his position, he claimed that the matter was of utmost urgency for the public health. Linking blacks with the spread of venereal disease, Poncet de la Grave urged their complete removal from the kingdom:

> By sending the blacks back to the colonies in the greatest number possible it is certain . . . that the illness/evil [*mal*] would be diminished; by preventing the marriages between blacks and whites, the intercourse [*communication*] is destroyed; by removing the public women, the monsters that take our youth and infect it with the illness that is carried into families, are extinguished.[21]

By linking blacks with venereal disease, Poncet de la Grave confused the literal notion of quarantine against disease with the metaphorical quarantine of the "white nation" from contamination by blacks.[22]

Yet Poncet de la Grave's pleas fell on deaf ears.[23] Chardon wrote to Lenoir countermanding Poncet de la Grave's orders that the women be sent back to the colonies via Le Havre.[24] He attacked Poncet de la Grave's reliance on the king's orders and interrogation of the women in presence of the Admiralty's clerk as "expensive." Because the women were guilty only of "libertinism," Chardon ordered that Fauchonette be confined to the hospital for three months and that La Tour be freed after a month in prison. As for Poncet de la Grave's requests for permission to arrest and interrogate all black prostitutes and vagabonds, "His Majesty . . . has not judged it appropriate to welcome these demands."

To preclude Poncet de la Grave's future demands, Chardon ruled that his authority under the *Police des Noirs* was limited to the arrest of blacks who arrived in France since the law's publication. Chardon would not use the law to support Poncet de la Grave's plans to round up wayward blacks and return them to the colonies.

There were other signs that the measure was not being enforced as strictly as the *procureur* had hoped. In response to Poncet de la Grave's request for instructions regarding princes of the blood who violated the *Police des Noirs,* Chardon ordered that he be informed before any action was taken against the royal family.[25] At the same time, Chardon chastised Poncet de la Grave for the inadequacy of the declarations collected by the clerk of the Admiralty in Paris: "At the very least it was to be hoped that the clerk would take greater care in the transcription of the declarations. The better part of the proper names are disfigured or truncated; the name, quality and address, of proxies who have made the declarations is often omitted; there are even several free blacks for whom the address and status have not been reported."[26] The clerk of the Paris Admiralty, Bottée, was further upbraided for "refusing to accept declarations that had been drawn up with the understandings that the parties requested." Poncet de la Grave excused the clerk, "a very honest man," because of his "illness."[27]

One of the strongest forms of resistance against the *Police des Noirs* came from the officers of the Admiralty in all parts of France who objected to the provision of the *Police des Noirs* that permitted blacks and their masters to make their declarations free of charge. Poncet de la Grave led the resistance on this measure in his early list of grievances, coming back to it again and again: "This is to attack, they say, the property of the officers and the fact is true, notably in Paris, [where it] causes considerable damage to the offices of lieutenant general and *procureur général.*"[28]

Beyond Paris, the effort to register blacks met with stronger resistance. Le Moyne, in Bordeaux, wrote to Chardon that "this declaration made the strongest sensation at first, but today things appear much calmer, seeing that one cannot put into execution any of its points, excepting a few declarations that the most timid have made."[29] In November 1777 Chardon wrote to the administrators of various regions of France, requesting their tallies of blacks (though had they been following the letter of the *Police des Noirs,* such a prompting would not have been necessary).[30]

Meanwhile, Chardon began supervising the establishment of the port depots so necessary to the enactment of the *Police des Noirs*. Le Moyne, in his critique of the law, had objected strenuously to the whole notion of depots. In Bordeaux, he wrote, the only place to retain blacks is a jail: "a frightful abode where the slave will be exposed to all the horrors of imprisonment, to all the maladies that derive from having little cleanliness and bad nourishment. He will be mixed in with bandits, scoundrels capable of inspiring in him the most hideous crimes and indicating the means to practice them."[31] Le Moyne expressed concern that favorite slaves would be exposed to disease in the jails. Grasping for an analogy that would make sense to a Parisian, La Moyne wrote: "There are slaves who can be valued at more than 10,000 *livres*; there are masters who have refused 20,000 *livres* for certain ones. What man would want to place his favorite horse that he had bought at a considerable price in a depot where any sort of horse would be admitted? The comparison is not misplaced."[32] Yet Le Moyne's complaints fell on deaf ears. Chardon went ahead with plans to identify suitable locations for the depots.

In a questionnaire dated October 2, Chardon requested the *procureurs du roi* of all the admiralty seats in the kingdom to provide very specific information regarding potential sites for the depots, the projected cost of keeping blacks there, provisions for security and treatment in case of illness, and the costs associated with return passage to the colonies. Chardon's comments give a picture of what the best-case scenario for blacks held in the depots might be:

> The intention of the king is that the blacks be locked up and guarded in the depots from the instant of their arrival to that of their embarkation. Nevertheless, His Majesty wishes that they not be treated as criminals, or confused with them. They must be locked in a room which can hold several of them, all the while avoiding that there be too many together, for fear of revolt.[33]

Chardon specified that the depots must contain a mattress, two sheets, a blanket, and a bolster filled with straw, "two blacks to a bed." The food should be healthy, but simple and uniform, "and for which the price must remain the same without exception."

At first, the establishment of depots appeared to go smoothly. By December 11, depots had been established in Dunkerque, Le Havre, St. Malo, Brest, Nantes, La Rochelle, Bordeaux, and Marseille.[34] Mistral, for example, reported to Chardon that the depot of Le Havre had been established in the prison of the arsenal.[35] But almost immediately, problems arose concerning the cost of maintaining the depot. According to Mistral, the arsenal prison was under the jurisdiction of the intendant, but Article 8 of the *Police des Noirs* would not cover this particular cost.[36] He proposed to bill the treasurer for costs incurred by blacks.[37] Chardon responded that the costs were to be paid by the slaveowner's deposit, left in the colonies, a matter between the auditor serving in the colonies and the auditor serving in France:

> His majesty has ordered that these same expenses must be paid upon the mandates of his *procureur* in the seat of the admiralty to which the execution of the law is entrusted and which must necessarily be the answerer [*contradicteur*] of these expenses by which he alone can be the legal witness and stamp the seal of authenticity which he conveys to the treasurer general to have for receiving the reimbursement of his advances. There is, in all that, nothing relative to the functions of your grace.[38]

That would seem to be the end of the matter because Mistral assured Chardon that all was well with the depot in his next letter.[39] At the end of December Chardon sent orders to the *procureur du roi* of Le Havre to pay one M. de Selle for costs arrising from the detention of "a negro belonging to Sr. Chatizel."[40] One wonders whether the man unlucky enough to be held in the arsenal prison of Le Havre received the best of care when no one knew for sure who would pay for his expenses.

Further evidence of the failure of the *Police des Noirs* can be found in the Ordinance of February 23, 1778, which stated that "the captains of merchant ships let all blacks, mulattoes, and other people of color who are on their ship disembark before having made their report to the Admiralties, and . . . the officers of the said [Admiralties] consequently find themselves unable to execute the Declaration of August 9, 1777."[41] The new ordinance ruled that ship captains could not let blacks disembark without making their reports to the clerk of the Admiralty who would, in turn, personally inspect the arrivals to verify the numbers of blacks in the reports. Captains who violated the new ordinance and anyone who received the undeclared blacks were subject to a 500-*livre* fine and prohibited from working for three months.

Resistance to the *Police des Noirs* was not confined within the boundaries of France. D'Argout and De Vaivre, of Cap François and Port au Prince, sought exemptions from the law's requirements. Echoing Le Moyne of Bordeaux, they asked that black wet nurses, governesses, and nurses be permitted to enter France with the colonists in their charge.[42] De Vaivre urged Chardon not to enforce the expulsion of blacks from France in too abrupt a manner: "It would be dangerous for [the colony] to receive into her bosom a multitude of bad subjects, spoiled, corrupted, instructed in more than what is necessary by their stay in Europe. . . . It would would be agreeable, it seems to me, to send them back only little by little."[43] In certain respects the colonists were successful in their requests. Exceptions were granted for wet nurses but not multiple slaves to nurse colonists "even if they are ill . . . , [for] this would open the door to an abundance of abuses."[44] Regarding the return of blacks to the colonies, Chardon had already determined not to interpret the confiscatory powers of the *Police des Noirs* very widely.

Perhaps the most cumbersome aspect of the *Police des Noirs* was the surety system meant to pay for the return of slaves who accompanied their masters to France. According to article 5 of the law, a colonist who wished to bring his servant on the ocean passage had to consign a fee of 1,000 *livres,* which would more than cover the cost of the *depot* and the return voyage to the colonies. We have already seen that the payment at the *depots* did not go smoothly at first. Other problems ensued.

When a colonist returned home and attempted to get the remainder of the 1,000-*livre* deposit, he or she did not always get immediate satisfaction. According to Sartine, the problem was that ship captains and colonists did not bring the appropriate paperwork from the colonies: "But, at the same time, the Treasurer General of the Marine could not send the papers of expenditure for recovery of expenses in the colony to his assistant, since he was not instructed that there was a liquid and consigned sum on which he can have recourse."[45] As for those colonists who now demanded the return of the surplus of their deposit, Sartine had little patience: "It is the universal principle that it falls upon the asker to prove the legitimacy of his request." Sartine proposed certain regulations that would address the confusion, but it was evident that such transatlantic operations were difficult at best.

Identification Cards and Interracial Marriages

Poncet de la Grave was nothing if not determined. Despite his earlier run-ins with Chardon, Poncet de la Grave persisted in his efforts to restrict the activities of blacks in Paris. On December 19, 1777, he wrote to Chardon, proposing that each black in Paris be issued a *cartouche,* or identification card, with the bearer's name, age, and master (that is, the person whom he serves):

He must always carry it with him and present it upon first request by an officer charged with this office. If he cannot produce it, he will be taken prisoner. I will interrogate him. If I recognize him, I will release him where, freed by his master, [he will be sent] to the depot to be returned to the colonies in the first instance. And for the second, the master [will be] condemned to the penalties prescribed by the law.[46]

In a second letter of the same date, Poncet de la Grave reflected on miscegenation in France: "bizarre marriages of black men with white women and white men with negresses, monstrous unions of slave with free, by which are graced creatures of neither one or the other species, forming an oddity which will soon disfigure the children of the state."[47] He proposed, once again, a ban on interracial marriages. Anticipating potentional objections to the ban, Poncet de la Grave argued that he could see no reason why the Church would challenge the proposal as "even amongst whites, marriages with Protestants, Jews, Muslims, etc. are reprobate by this same religion which . . . places no distinction between the children of God." Citing numerous precedents for limiting the choice of marriage partners, Poncet de la Grave offered to write a report that would persuade both parlementary and ecclesiastical officials of the wisdom of such a ban.

In these respects, finally, Poncet de la Grave was successful. On January 11, 1778, the king issued an *arrêt du conseil* requiring all blacks who had registered with the Amiralty to carry identification cards under penalty of being shipped back to the colonies.[48] The ban on interracial marriages was proclaimed on April 5, 1778.[49] Yet, even so, trouble continued to brew between the officers of the Admiralty and Lenoir, the lieutenant general of police.[50]

The conflict erupted in February 1778, when Poncet de la Grave, De la Haye, and others formally protested Lenoir's powers of supervision over the *cartouche* policy. According to the *arrêt du conseil* of January 11, blacks were to report to the clerk of the Admiralty within one month to receive their identification cards. The *cartouches* were to be provided free of charge and signed by the lieutenant general of the Admiralty. Yet it was Lenoir, lieutenant general of the police, who was designated to oversee the *arrêt*'s enforcement.

Poncet de la Grave went over the head of Chardon and submitted a formal complaint to Sartine, minister of the marine.[51] The carefully hand-lettered document listed eight charges against the *arrêt*, but the underlying complaint was that Lenoir, rather than Poncet de la Grave,

was charged with the law's enforcement. Poncet de la Grave waited
about a week and then, perhaps fearing that he had overplayed his hand,
sent a meeker letter to Sartine:

> I hope that in your justice you would write me a letter which can calm my
> fears by assuring me that his majesty's intention in issuing the *arrêt du
> conseil* of January 11 was not to give any superiority to the lieutenant general
> of police either over me or over the court of the Admiralty of France and that
> it has not detracted any of the functions that are attributed to me either by the
> Declaration of August 9, 1777 or the *arrêt* of September 7, 1777, and the
> instructions relative to them.[52]

Sartine responded to this request in a brief letter stating that, although
the enforcement of the *arrêt du conseil* properly belonged under the
supervision of Lenoir as "a matter of territorial police," the law itself
"in no way gave the lieutenant of police authority over the officers of the
Admiralty of France."[53]

   Yet the matter was not allowed to rest. Poncet de la Grave was joined
by other officers of the Admiralty, including *lieutenant général* De la
Haye and *lieutenant particulier* Mantel, in a protest over the January 11
measure.[54] They worried that the form of the certificate lent itself to
forgeries, that cases would be judged in inappropriate tribunals, that
blacks who were arrested without papers would be sent to the colonies
via Le Havre without being questioned by officers of the Admiralty, and
so on. Sartine allowed a month to go by before he responded to the
officers of the Admiralty. He claimed that he had presented their complaints to the king who ordered that the *arrêt du conseil* be carried out as
it was written.[55] Mantel, outraged, retorted that the rights of the Admiralty of France "will soon be demolished, along with its provenance; it
will follow that the property of the offices will be destroyed, and the
exercise of their functions thoroughly useless!"[56] Sartine's final response on the matter is a masterwork of doublespeak. He claims to be
angry that the officers of the Admiralty could have thought that the king
had "doubted their zeal," and assures them that there will be many
occasions to prove their attachment and submission. But Sartine deftly
managed to avoid satisfying their primary complaint: the supervision of
the *cartouches* remained with Sartine's successor, Lenoir.[57]

   The ban on interracial marriages appears to have been less controversial, yet it also suffered from lack of enforcement. Prior to the ban, a
procureur général in the town of Châteauroux wrote to Sartine to re-

quest advice concerning a free black domestic servant who wanted to
marry a white woman:

> A negro, age thirty, as near as it is possible to judge from the papers that he
> carries, obtained his liberty from M. de la Condamine upon the return from
> his voyages in Spanish America. This individual, now a domestic in the
> service of a gentleman of this town, wishes to marry a girl who is pregnant by
> him. One of the priests of this town in the parish where the two parties reside
> raises objections to marrying them. Their complaints have been brought to
> me. I can only approve of this ecclesiastic's motives for refusal. I know well
> that these sorts of marriages are dangerous, that they expose French blood to
> corruption, and it is for these reasons that the king issued his declaration of
> August 9, 1777. I would like to find a positive law which could settle my
> uncertainty, but the research that I have been able to do has not made it
> possible for me to succeed. Article 10 of the Declaration of December 15,
> 1738, . . . reports that the Code Noir prohibits marriages between slaves,
> even with the consent of their masters, but it does not speak of negroes who
> are free.[58]

Sartine decided that the best response was a vague one, stating that "the
king will soon make his intentions known on these marriages between
black men and white women, and that [the *procureur* will be informed
of it."[59] On April 5 Sartine issued instructions to all the bishops of
France outlining the provisions of the marriage ban.[60] According to an
anonymous commentator (probably Joly de Fleury), "this response puts
it neither without nor within and *M. le procureur général* can do
whatever his wisdom and his prudence dictate."[61]

Despite Poncet de la Grave's enthusiasm for the ban on interracial
marriages, no one was ever prosecuted for violating the *arrêt du conseil*
of April 5, 1778, in the Admiralty Court of France. Eight years later,
when a parish priest wrote for instructions regarding a mulatto who
wished to marry a white woman in his parish, the minister of the marine
referred him to the archbishop of his diocese but did not pursue the
matter.[62]

Resumption of Petitions for Freedom

Although Sartine and Chardon appeared to be whittling away at the
authority of the Admiralty of France, officers of the court retained one
area of competence that could not be touched: legal decisions concerning petitions for freedom. The *lettres patentes* of September 3, 1776,

had forbidden the court to entertain such lawsuits until the promulgation of the king's new law. Once the *Police des Noirs* was in effect, instructions from Chardon prohibited the Admiralty Court from resuming hearings on petitions for freedom:

> Article 9, stating that . . . masters . . . cannot keep blacks in their service except with their consent, signifies implicitly that all black slaves will be free on this count alone. The execution of this article, based upon the principles which guide the Parlement of Paris, reconciles it with the property rights of masters but it must no longer be a question of requests for freedom on the part of the blacks. The intention of the king was by this article to prescribe them [i.e., requests for freedom] without exception and to avoid all the inconveniences which result from them; therefore you must not respond to any petition which may be presented to you to this end.[63]

Poncet de la Grave apparently complied with these instructions because there are no petitions for freedom within the Admiralty Court records for the entirety of 1777.

Yet in the spring of 1778, Poncet de la Grave received a petition for freedom and backed the petitioner's request until she received satisfaction a year later. Sartine had given his permission for the court to rule on her case. Once this door was opened, other blacks followed to petition successfully for their freedom. Perhaps this is because Poncet de la Grave, Mantel, and others saw these cases as a way to reassert their authority amidst their challenges to the *arrêt du conseil* of January 11, 1778.

The first and most important case was that of Margueritte Gotton, born a slave in Artibonite Saint Domingue, who left for France with her mistress in 1773.[64] The trip was an ill-fated one. Their ship sank off the coast of England and Gotton's mistress drowned. Gotton managed to survive by clinging to a rock until she was rescued by an English ship. From England Gotton made her way to Rouen, via Le Havre, where M. Brion, brother-in-law to the deceased mistress, lived. Brion took Gotton on as a servant, allegedly at the rate of 150 *livres* per year.

According to Poncet de la Grave's account, the question of Gotton's freedom originally came to court in 1775 when Brion, "content with the services of this negress," arranged to have her freedom confirmed by the Admiralty Court in Paris.[65] Yet Brion's actions may not have been as altruistic as the *procureur* portrayed them. Indeed, a more skeptical reading of Poncet de la Grave's account suggests that Gotton served as Brion's unpaid servant (slave) until D'Anache, the husband of Gotton's deceased mistress, showed up to claim Gotton as property belonging to his drowned wife. Brion backed Gotton's claim to freedom in the Admiralty Court as a way to keep her from D'Anache.[66]

Yet once Gotton's freedom was affirmed by the court, she found herself under no obligation to Brion (Poncet de la Grave claims they had a dispute over wages), and she fled to Paris, hoping to escape the surveillance of D'Anache. On September 25, 1777, Gotton registered herself with the clerk of the Admiralty of France, as required by the *Police des Noirs*. She declared that she presently lived and worked on rue Poissonnière as a seamstress for Dame Dichot.[67]

Two weeks later, D'Anache went to the same clerk and declared Gotton as his slave.[68] Several months went by before D'Anache sought and obtained a king's order permitting him to arrest Gotton and have her returned to Saint Domingue.[69] But someone intervened on behalf of Gotton, and Sartine agreed to suspend the order until the court could reach a decision on her case. On April 1, 1778, Gotton demanded 700 *livres* in damages and interest against the Marquis D'Anache for "disturbing her in the possession and enjoyment of her freedom."[70]

Another year passed before Gotton was successful in the Admiralty Court. In their decision of April 21, 1779, the judges ruled that Gotton was free and that the Marquis D'Anache's declaration to the Admiralty clerk to the contrary was null and void. D'Anache was condemned to pay Gotton 200 *livres* in damages.[71]

In the meantime others came forward to claim their freedom through the Admiralty Court and the court dealt with them exactly as they had with similar requests prior to the *Police des Noirs*. In July 1778, two blacks successfully petitioned for their freedom.[72] Two others followed in June of 1779.[73] During the same period four acts of manumission were accepted by the court.

These nine petitions hardly constitute a landslide, but it is clear that within a few years of the 1777 *Police des Noirs,* business within the Admiralty Court was gradually returning to its earlier routine of granting freedom to petitioners. Although the *lettres patentes* that prepared the way for the *Police des Noirs* had made it clear that the new law's purpose was to eliminate these contests between slave and master, in this respect the law was unsuccessful.

Conclusion

The 1780s were very much like the preceding decades in the sense that the government moved the issue of blacks in France to the back burner only to return to it when it occasionally boiled over. Nobody found a way to remove the pot from the stove.

Sartine was replaced by the Marquis de Castries as minister of the marine in 1780. Shortly thereafter, he became embroiled in a conflict between the Countess of Bethune and one Mme Lafarge Paquot regarding a young black woman named Henriette Lucille. Henriette had been brought to France by Paquot's husband to care for their two small children.[74] Paquot twice attained orders from the king to send Henriette back to Saint Domingue, but the young woman resisted.[75] Henriette was assisted by the Countess of Bethune who intervened on her behalf.[76] Ultimately Paquot had Henriette arrested and their case ended up in the Parisian Admiralty Court.[77]

This case and several others prompted Castries to try and clamp down once again on blacks in France.[78] First, the king issued a new *arrêt du conseil* that prohibited people of color from adopting the titles of *Sieur* and *Dame*.[79] Then, in 1782 De Castries appointed a legislative committee to answer two questions: "What is the present condition of blacks and mulattoes living in France? and "What action should the government take relative to these people?"[80] To these questions he received two contrary responses. The first, apparently by Chardon, insisted that slaves could be legally kept in France if they met two conditions: if they had arrived prior to the August 9, 1777, *Police des Noirs,* and if they had been registered with the Admiralty in accordance with that law. He advised that blacks in France be required to renew their declarations every month and that those who did not do so be confiscated and returned to the colonies. He also recommended that all Admiralty tribunals be directed to refuse all petitions for freedom.[81]

The second response to De Castries's questions came from a legislative committee appointed to review Chardon's suggestions. Although they disagreed with Chardon strongly over whether slavery could be recognized in France, members of the committee agreed on the ultimate goal of ridding France of blacks. The committee refuted Chardon's assertion that French laws recognized instances of slavery, concluding that all blacks presently in France were free. Yet it also recommended that all blacks in France be sent back to the colonies. While committee members acknowledged that a large-scale removal would be dangerous, they advocated a slower method of eliminating blacks from France.[82] It is clear, however, that by 1782 the notion of racial purity was firmly entrenched in the minds of even the staunchest defenders of freedom.

De Castries was apparently not persuaded to take drastic action. He opted instead to promote a renewal of the *arrêt du conseil* requiring blacks to carry identification papers.[83] Once again, those failing to produce the *cartouche* would be arrested and returned to the colonies, via the port *dépots*. Five days later, De Castries sent a letter to all colonial administrators: "There disembark every day, gentlemen, black domestics who are arrested upon their arrival in the port and placed in depots conforming with the Declaration of August 9, 1777. But the masters usually claim that they have no cognizance of this law, nor of the prohibition of bringing them to France."[84] The problem was further augmented by the fact that colonists rarely brought with them proof of the deposit they were supposed to have left in the colonies. Consequently, "the embarassing situation is increased when it is a question to pay the costs of the depot."[85] He ordered administrators to print up new copies of the *Police des Noirs* as handbills and post them throughout the colonies and to enforce its provisions "with scrupulous exactitude."[86] Thus, as with earlier legislation, the *Police des Noirs* was ultimately ineffective in stopping the arrival of black slaves in France. *Plus ça change, plus c'est la même chose.*

Things did change in one respect during the decade before the Revolution. Whereas until the 1780s blacks' petitions for freedom had surpassed the number of manumissions initiated by masters, during this period the Admiralty Court of France accepted fifty-eight acts of liberty as compared with forty-three petitions for freedom by blacks, maybe because masters hoped to retain their servants through good will, rather than by force. Freed slaves with identification papers were more likely to be permitted to stay in France than contraband slaves.

The total number of petitions resumed its steady climb that had been hindered in the 1770s by the cessation of the court during the Maupeou years and the ban on lawsuits for freedom begun in 1776. This is not surprising given the continued arrival of blacks in France, the willingness of the Paris Admiralty Court to ratify their freedom, and the inability or lack of effort on the part of the government to limit them beyond 1777.

It appears, then, that the government was by its own standards not very successful in stemming either the flow of blacks to France or their acquisition of freedom once on French soil. The use of the port depots appears to have been somewhat effective as a way to control the number of slaves who entered France, but even these were plagued by administrative problems, not the least of which was paying for the cost of the slaves' care.

Epilogue

The history of blacks and slavery in France can be seen as a series of governmental attempts to impose clear, unambiguous categories on the constantly shifting and merging realities of eighteenth-century life. Just as Enlightenment scientists such as Linnaeus and Buffon had attempted to apply order and structure to the teeming chaos of the natural world, so did French officials struggle in vain to regulate the boundaries between blacks and whites and freedom and slavery in France.

At first, royal decrees attempted to use slavery as the unambiguous boundary between France and its colonies by upholding the maxim that any slave who sets foot on French soil is free. Pressure from powerful colonial interests, however, persuaded administrators that it would be more practical to allow a limited kind of slavery in France, embodied in the legislation of 1716 and 1738. Yet these efforts were largely ineffectual because wealthy colonists flaunted the laws and because the courts of Paris refused to enforce them.

During the second half of the eighteenth century officials in the French Admiralty and the royal administration hit on a new classification system that they hoped would regulate the boundaries between France and its colonies: the policing of race. This must be seen as one of the latent costs of the evolution of the Freedom Principle in France. Lawyers and administrators were all too ready to make use of the panoply of anti-African and anti-Jewish stereotypes to win cases and set policy. Even so, the government's attempts to keep blacks out of the

French kingdom were undermined by colonists, provincial administrators, and blacks themselves.

Much has already been written about the fate of French slaves and free people of color during the Revolution.[1] The Constituent Assembly, prompted by fear of continued slave uprising in the colonies and activists for the free coloreds, including the organization known as the *Amis des Noirs,* extended the franchise to people of color and ultimately abolished slavery in the colonies.

Other effects of the Revolution on the status of blacks have been less well documented. One of the first casualties of the Revolution was the Admiralty Court of France, which was dismantled by a decree of November 11, 1790.[2] Even so, six blacks won their freedom that year prior to the court's demise, suggesting that blacks would have continued to seek their freedom through the courts into the 1790s had not the institutional means been undone by the Revolution.

Even so, the extension of full citizenship to people of color and the abolition of slavery came gradually and lasted only fleetingly. First, the Constituent Assembly granted the franchise to blacks born of free parents, though not freedmen, on May 15, 1791. On September 28 of the same year, the government codified the unwritten maxim of the realm: "Every individual is free as soon as he is in France."[3] The Constituent Assembly finally extended the franchise to all free people of color on April 24, 1792, and abolished French slavery on February 4, 1794.[4]

Despite the progressive changes of the Revolution, colonial slavery was reintroduced under Napoleon in 1802, though by then France had lost its chief colony, Saint Domingue (later Haiti), to the Revolution of Toussaint L'Ouverture. Soon thereafter the *Police des Noirs* was resuscitated, and an order requiring blacks in France to carry identification papers was renewed.[5] By 1843, a lawyer was arguing for the freedom of his client before the Royal Court of Paris on the grounds that "anyone who touches France is free" and that his client, a native of India, could not be considered a negro slave. He cited the cases of Jean Boucaux, Francisque, Louis, and Roc as precedents.[6] Not until the Revolution of 1848 would slavery finally be abolished universally in the remaining French colonies.

The Revolution affected the fortunes of those who assisted blacks in their claims to freedom through the Admiralty Court of France in Paris. The lawyer Regnaud, for example, who had represented so many blacks in their petitions for freedom during the 1760s, became an ardent royalist despite his opposition to the crown during the Maupeou era. He penned a dramatic account of the king's last days before his surrender to the authorities of Paris on August 10, 1792.[7] Regnaud was rewarded for his loyalty by Louis XVIII, who gave him the title "Regnaud de Paris" in 1814.

Henrion de Pansey, whose eloquent attack on slavery won him accolades in 1770, left his Parisian practice in 1790 to hold several offices in the district of Joinville in Haute-Marne during subsequent phases of the Revolution. He would eventually be named to the *Tribunal de Cassation,* where, according to historian Michael P. Fitzsimmons, "he enjoyed a distinguished career and reaffirmed his reputation as one of the most brilliant jurists in all of France."[8]

Probably the most curious epilogue concerns Guillaume Poncet de la Grave, who deserves most of the credit (or blame) for the series of laws, beginning with the *Police des Noirs,* that began to regulate French citizens solely on the basis of race. In particular, Poncet was particularly disturbed about miscegenation and prostitution, a concern that began as early as 1762 and that culminated in the ban on interracial marriages in 1778.

When the Revolution deprived Poncet de la Grave of his office at the age of sixty-five, he retired to Calais, where he wrote several historical works.[9] He was prompted to enter the public political fray in 1801, however, to comment on a new law that rewarded married citizens for having as many children as possible. His *Considerations on the Celibate* dwelt in great detail on "three appalling vices," illicit love, prostitution, and concubinage, and their deleterious effects on morals and the size of the population, which, Malthus aside, was thought to be waning because of a decade of famine, war, and terror.[10] Poncet supported the new law and severely castigated those men who refused to marry and sire new sons and daughters for the nation.

Poncet's treatise was lampooned in an anonymous critique published by the *Journal de Paris* to which Poncet retaliated in a defense of his earlier work.[11] It appears that he died shortly thereafter. Thus, right up until the end, Poncet de la Grave waged his personal war against licentiousness, although once again it is doubtful that he achieved the results he sought.

As for the futures of the hidden protagonists of this history, the enslaved blacks who won their freedom in the French Admiralty courts, they are harder to discern. Some, such as Gabriel Pampy, appear for a while in the registers generated by the *Police des Noirs*.[12] But most disappear from the official records, whether by accident or by design. Yet, as is evident in the outrage of my French boarding house proprietor, their legacy endures to this day in the national myth of freedom, ''There are no slaves in France.''

Notes

Abbreviations

A.N., Archives Nationales, Paris
B.N., Bibliothèque Nationale, Paris
See the Bibliography for a descrption of the various A.N. series.

Introduction

1. From the outset, the problem of what to call the people who are the subject of this study has been troublesome. The word *nègre,* which was common in the seventeenth and eighteenth centuries, connoted both color and slave status; *noir,* which became more common at the end of the eighteenth century, seems to have referred to people with dark skin, regardless of slave status. I have rejected *African American* because many were not, in fact, American, and some were not even African. Ultimately, the terms *black* and *negro* have seemed the most appropriate, the former primarily in my own analysis and the latter when translating the term *nègre,* as a reminder that eighteenth-century social categories were not precisely the same as our own.

2. [François Gayot de Pitaval], "Liberté reclamée par un nègre, contre son maître qui l'a amené en France," in *Causes célèbres et intéressantes, avec les jugemens qui les ont décidées* (Paris: Jean de Nully, 1747), vol. 13, p. 537.

3. Shelby T. McCloy, *The Negro in France* (Lexington: Univ. of Kentucky Press, 1961), p. 5.

4. Pierre Boulle, "Les Gens de couleur à Paris à la veille de la Révolution," in *L'Image de la Révolution française: Communications présentées lors du Congrès Mondial pour le Bicentenaire de la Révolution,* ed. Michel Vovelle, (Paris: Pergamon, 1989), p. 159. Boulle's *Being Black in Eighteenth-Century France: Non-White Residents According to the Census of 1777* is forthcoming.

5. Léo Elisabeth, "The French Antilles," in *Neither Slave Nor Free: The Freedmen*

of African Descent in the Slave Societies of the New World, ed. David W. Cohen and Jack P. Greene (Baltimore: Johns Hopkins Univ. Press, 1972), pp. 158–59.

6. Seymour Drescher, *Capitalism and Antislavery: British Mobilization in Comparative Perspective* (New York: Oxford University Press, 1987), pp. 27–29; F. O. Shyllon, *Black People in Britain, 1555–1833* (London: Pluto Press, 1984), pp. 93–102; Peter Fryer, *Staying Power: The History of Black People in Britain* (London: Pluto Press, 1984), p. 68; Gretchen Gerzina, *Black England: Life Before Emancipation* (London: John Murray, 1995), p. 5.

7. 2 Rushworth 468 (1569), cited in A. Leon Higginbotham, Jr., *In the Matter of Color: Race and the American Legal Process: The Colonial Period* (New York: Oxford University Press, 1978), p. 321, and *Judicial Cases Concerning American Slavery and the Negro*, ed. Helen Tunnicliff Catterall (Washington, D.C.: Carnegie Institution of Washington, 1926–1937), vol. 1, pp. 1, 9.

8. See Seymour Drescher, "The Long Goodbye: Dutch Capitalism and Antislavery in Comparative Perspective," *American Historical Review* 99, no. 1 (February 1994): 65, and Allison Blakely, *Blacks in the Dutch World: The Evolution of Racial Imagery in a Modern Society* (Bloomington: Indiana Univ. Press, 1993), p. 226.

9. Carol Bauer, "Law, Slavery, and Somerset's Case," Ph.D. thesis, New York University, 1973, pp. 5–25; Higginbotham, *In the Matter of Color*, pp. 320–29; Fryer, *Staying Power*, pp. 113–15. The Somerset case has been the subject of a tremendous amount of historical scrutiny. For a recent overview of the scholarship see William R. Cotter's "The Somerset Case and the Abolition of Slavery in England," *History* (February 1994): 31–56.

10. *Smith v. Brown and Cooper*, 2 Salkeld 666 (1706).

11. On the development of slave case law in England, see Bauer, "Law, Slavery, and Somersett's Case," pp. 5–25; Higginbotham, *In the Matter of Color*, pp. 313–32; Fryer, *Staying Power*, pp. 113–15; Shyllon, *Black People*, pp. 17–38.

12. *Gazatteer*, May 26, 1772, cited in Folorin O. Shyllon, *Black Slaves in Britain* (London: Institute for Race Relations, 1974), pp. 115–17.

13. On the legal status of French slaves, see also Paul Trayer, *Etude historique de la condition légale des esclaves dans les colonies françaises* (Paris: L. Baudoin, 1887); Lucien Peytraud, *L'Esclavage aux Antilles françaises avant 1789, d'après des documents inédits des archives coloniales* (Paris: Librairie Hachette, 1897), Book 2, chap. 8, "Des esclaves amenés en France," pp. 373–99; Auguste Lebeau, *De la condition des gens de couleur libres sous l'ancien régime* (Paris: Guillaumin, 1903); Yvan Debbasch, *Couleur et liberté: Le jeu du critère ethnique dans un ordre juridique esclavagiste* (Paris: Dalloz, 1967); and Pierre Pluchon, *Nègres et Juifs au XVIIIᵉ siècle: Le racisme au siècle des Lumières* (Paris: Tallandier, 1984).

14. Here is another discrepancy between France and England. English courts never awarded back wages because they did not recognize a formal contract in master–slave relations.

15. Once again, more work needs to be done on the Dutch legislation of 1776, its relationship to changing notions of race, and the political and social instututions of the time.

16. Seymour Drescher, "The Ending of the Slave Trade and the Evolution of European Scientific Racism," *Social Science History* 14, no. 3 (Fall 1990): 424.

17. David Brion Davis argues that British racial discourse is a response to the antislavery movement (*The Problem of Slavery in the Age of Revolution* [Ithaca: Cornell Univ. Press, 1975]), whereas I would argue that both are really two sides of the same coin. There is a vast literature on the development of so-called scientific racism in Europe and the United States. See especially, William B. Cohen, *The French Encounter with Africans: White Response to Blacks, 1530–1880* (Bloomington: Indiana Univ. Press, 1980); Philip Curtin, *The Image of Africa: British Ideas and Action, 1780–1850* (Madison: Univ. of Wisconsin Press, 1964); Drescher, "The Ending of the Slave Trade"; and George M. Fredrickson, *The Black Image in the White Mind: The Debate on Afro-American Character and Destiny, 1817–1914* (New York: Harper & Row, 1971). For the earlier period, see Winthrop Jordan, *White over Black: American Attitudes toward the Negro, 1550–1812* (Chapel Hill: Univ. of North Carolina Press, 1968). For a succinct theoretical discussion of how racial attitudes change in response to demographic, economic, and other social forces, see Barbara J. Fields, "Ideology and Race in American History" in *Region, Race and Reconstruction: Essays in Honor of C. Vann Woodward,* ed. J. Morgan Kousser and James M. McPherson (New York: Oxford University Press, 1982).

18. Robert Darnton, *The Great Cat Massacre and Other Episodes in French Cultural History* (New York: Basic Books, 1984), p. 89. For a fuller explication of the anthropological models informing his work, see Darnton's "The Symbolic Element in History," *Journal of Modern History* 58 (1986): 218–34.

19. Paul Gilroy, *The Black Atlantic: Modernity and Double Consciousness* (Cambridge: Harvard Univ. Press, 1993).

20. In addition to Darton's *Cat Massacre,* other examples of the genre of microhistory include Natalie Zemon Davis, *The Return of Martin Guerre* (Cambridge: Harvard Univ. Press, 1983); Carlo Ginzberg, *The Cheese and the Worms: The Cosmos of a Sixteenth-Century Miller,* trans. John and Anne Tedeschi (Baltimore: Johns Hopkins Univ. Press, 1980); Gene Brucker's *Giovanni and Lusanna: Love and Marriage in Renaissance Florence* (Berkeley: Univ. of California Press, 1986); and Judith Brown's *Immodest Acts: Life of a Lesbian Nun in Renaissance Italy* (New York: Oxford Univ. Press, 1985).

21. "Thick description" is Clifford Geertz's term for a similar approach in anthropology (*The Interpretation of Cultures* [New York: Basic Books, 1973]).

22. See Keith Michael Baker, *Inventing the French Revolution: Essays on France's Political Culture in the Eighteenth Century* (Cambridge: Cambridge Univ. Press, 1990), pp. 4–7, and his Introduction to *The Political Culture of the Old Regime,* in *The French Revolution and the Creation of Modern Political Culture,* ed. Keith Michael Baker, Colin Lucas, and François Furet (Oxford: Pergamon Press, 1987), vol. 1, pp. xi–xxiv.

23. See especially David Geggus "Racial Equality, Slavery, and Colonial Secession during the Constituent Assembly," *American Historical Review* 94, no. 5 (December 1989): 1290–1308, and Robin Blackburn, *The Overthrow of Colonial Slavery* (London: Verso, 1988), pp. 161–264.

Chapter 1. Slavery in France

1. Robert Louis Stein, *The French Sugar Business in the Eighteenth Century* (Baton Rouge: Louisiana State Univ. Press, 1988), pp. 4–10.

2. Robert Louis Stein, *The French Slave Trade in the Eighteenth Century: An Old*

144   NOTES TO PAGES 11–12

Regime Business (Madison: Univ. of Wisconsin Press, 1979), p. 11. The Senegal Company was established by the "Suppression de la compagnie des Indes occidentales et
confirmation du contrat relatif à la compagnie du Sénégal" (December 1674), in François-
André Isambert, *Recueil général des anciennes lois françaises depuis l'an 420 jusqu'à la
revolution de 1789* (Paris: Belin-Leprieur, 1830), vol. 19, p. 152. A second ordinance
prohibited colonists from circumventing the Senegal Company and purchasing their slaves
from the American Indians: "Ordonnance qui défend aux habitans des îles de l'Amérique
d'acheter aucuns nègres des Indiens, tant de la Terre-Ferme que des îles Caraïbes, et de les
porter dans les îles françoises de l'Amerique et côte Saint-Domingue, et réserve ce droit à
la compagnie du Sénégal" (Fontainbleau, September 23, 1683), in Isambert, *Recueil,*
vol. 19, p. 434. "Arrêt de conseil" of (September 12, 1684) that transferred privileges
from the Senegal Company to the Guinea Company. The privileges of the Guinea Company were spelled out in "Lettres Patentes sur l'establissement de la compagnie de
Guinée, qui lui donne le commerce exclusif des nègres, de la poudre d'or, etc." (Versailles, January 1685), in Isambert *Recueil,* vol. 19, pp. 483–89.

   3. For the text of and commentary on the Code Noir, see Louis Sala-Molins, *Le Code
Noir, ou le calvaire de Canaan,* 2nd ed. (Paris: Presses Universitaire de France, 1988).

   4. J. Mathorez, *Les Etrangers en France sous l'Ancien Régime: Histoire de la formation de la population française* (Paris: E. Champion, 1919), p. 388. This incident was
cited as precedent in many eighteenth-century cases. See, for example, [Gayot de Pitaval],
"Liberté Reclamée par un Nègre, contre son Maître qui l'a amené en France," in *Causes
célèbres et intéressantes, avec les jugemens qui les ont décidées,* vol. 13 (Paris: Jean de
Nully, 1747), p. 549. Pitaval cites *Journal chronologique et historique* of Don Pierre de
Saint Romual.

   5. La Faille, *Histoire de Toulouse,* cited in Antoine Loysel (also spelled "Loisel"),
*Institutes coutumières d'Antoine Loysel ou Manuel de plusieurs et diverses règles, sen-
tences et proverbes, tant anciens que modernes du droit coutumier et plus ordinaire de
la France,* new ed., ed. M. Dupin and M. Edouard Laboulaye (Paris: Durand, 1846),
vol. 1, p. 40. This reference to La Faille first appeared in the 1783 edition of Loisel's
Institutes Coutumières. For more information on the evolution of commentary on Loisel's
original collection of maxims, see Chapter 2 in this volume.

   6. It is true that during the seventeenth century Louis XIV did much to expand the use
of galley slaves and that these constituted another unfree population having contact with
French shores. An administrator for the Marine dismissed the application of the Freedom
Principle to galley slaves in 1694: "Every man who has touched the soil of the kingdom
once is free, and one is not exempt from following this law except [in the case of] the Turks
and Moors who are sent to Marseille for service in the galleys, because, before arriving
there, they are purchased in foreign countries where this kind of commerce is established"
(A.N., B⁶ 26, fol. 431, October 20, 1694, cited in André Zysberg, *Les Galériens: Vies et
destins de 60,000 forçats sur les galères de France, 1680–1748* [Paris: Seuil, 1987],
p. 59). It is not clear why this exemption did not apply to slaves from the French colonies
that also permitted slavery. One hypothesis is that their enslavement was justified on
religious grounds (galley slaves were understood to be Muslims and pagans). See Paul W.
Bamford, *Fighting Ships and Prisons: The Mediterranean Galleys of France in the Age of
Louis XIV* (Minneapolis: Univ. of Minnesota Press, 1973). On the other hand, the administrator's thinking may be a foreshadowing of the rationale behind the royal legislation of

1716 and 1738, namely, people who were made slaves outside of France were subject to those foreign laws and could therefore be held temporarily as slaves while visiting the kingdom. It is also clear, however, that such an exception was a "slippery slope" that undermined the Freedom Principle in its most absolute formulation.

7. Pontchartrain to d'Esragny, October 4, 1691 (A.N., Colonies B 14, fol. 312). All translations from the French are by the author unless otherwise indicated.

8. De Goimpy to Pontchartrain, July 2, 1692 (A.N., Colonies, C^3, 7, cited in Peytraud, *L'Esclavage aux Antilles françaises*, p. 375).

9. "Ordonnance du Roi, qui condamne les Capitaines de Navire à payer les Nègres trouvés à leur Bord" (April 28, 1694), in *Loix et constitutions des colonies françoises de l'Amérique sous le vent*, 6 vol., ed. M. L. E. Moreau de Saint-Méry, (Paris: Chez l'auteur, 1784–1790), vol. 1, p. 524.

10. Pontchartrain to Robert, October 12, 1696 (A.N., Colonies, F 249, fol. 818, cited in Peytraud, *L'Esclavage aux Antilles françaises*, p. 376).

11. I use the term *Freedom Principle* to refer to the tenet that any slave who sets foot on French soil is free. Eighteenth-century lawyers argued that this principle was a maxim of French law, but as I show in Chapter 2, the Freedom Principle is an amalgam of several historical traditions.

12. "Extrait de la Lettre du Ministre à M. Ducasse, concernant les Nègres amenés en France, et la liberté à donner aux Mulâtres du 5 Février 1698" in Moreau de Saint-Méry, *Loix et constitutions*, vol. 1, p. 579.

13. Minister to Ducasse, March 11, 1699, in Moreau de Saint-Méry, *Loix et Constitutions*, vol. 1, p. 629.

14. The distinction that Mithon apparently wanted to make was between someone born of a free mother (*né libre*) and someone born to a slave woman but later freed (*affranchi*). One can infer that freedmen (*affranchis*) enjoyed fewer rights than the freeborn and may have owed certain obligations to their former masters, up to a lifetime of service. The presumed advantage in such a case would be that one's children would be recognized as freeborn.

15. Mithon to Pontchartrain, November 20, 1704 (A.N., Colonies, C^8A 15). According to Mithon, Louis presented him with a petition requesting recognition of his freedom "by privilege of the kingdom of France" in February 1704. The lieutenant general told Mithon to delay judgment on the matter until he heard the orders of the minister of the marine. Mithon acquiesced but, despite a lack of instructions in the minister's recent letters, he was forced into a decision when Sr. Benoist, who claimed to be Louis's master, attempted to confiscate Louis and sell him to a ship headed for the coast of Spain. Mithon ruled that Louis was free, yet Benoist continued to beat Louis and threatened to bring the matter before the colonial council to overturn Mithon's decision. Mithon requested that the minister reprimand Benoist "as he merits it."

16. Ibid.

17. "Lettre du Ministre sur les Nègres amenés en France du 10 Juin 1707," in Moreau de Saint-Mery, vol. 2, p. 99.

18. The jurisdiction of the Admiralty Courts is a complex subject, treated thoroughly by Henri-François Buffet in *Guide des recherches dans les fonds judiciaires de l'Ancien Régime*, (Paris: Imprimerie Nationale, 1958), pp. 255–82.

19. On the importance of convents as places of protection for women, see Olwen

Hufton and Frank Tallett, "Communities of Women, the Religious Life, and Public Services in Eighteenth-Century France," in *Connecting Spheres: Women in the Western World, 1500 to the Present,* ed. Marilyn J. Boxer and Jean H. Quaetaert (New York: Oxford Univ. Press, 1987).

20. Such a declaration would be required by later legislation (1716, 1738, and 1777) but was not a part of statutory law at this stage.

21. [Gérard Mellier], "Réponse au Mémoire presenté à Nosseigneurs du Conseil Royal de la Marine, Concernant les Negres Eclaves que les officiers & habitans des Colonies françoises de l'Amerique amenent en france pour leur service," Archives Départmentales de la Loire-Atlantique, Nantes C742, no. 12.

22. The Duke of Maine and Louis Alexandre de Bourbon, Count of Toulouse, were both sons of Louis XIV by his mistress Mme. de Montespan.

23. "Edict of October, 1716," in Isambert, *Recueil,* vol. 21, p. 123.

24. Ibid., pp. 123–24.

25. Ibid., p. 124.

26. Ibid., pp. 125–26.

27. Article 7 held that "Slaves who come to France will not be able to marry without their masters' consent, and in the case where consent is given, the said slaves will be and remain free by virtue of the said consent" (Isambert, *Recueil,* vol. 21, pp. 124–25). This stipulation would form the grounds of an important case in 1738 when the slave Jean Boucaux married a free French woman without his master's consent (see Chapter 2).

28. Code Noir, article 31, in Isambert, *Recueil,* vol. 19, p. 499.

29. The *parquet* was the ensemble of the king's representatives in the court, known as the *gens du roi,* and the *greffe,* or clerk's office. The *gens du roi* included *procureur général,* the *avocat général,* and their assistants. On the organization of the Parlement of Paris, see Monique Langlois, "Parlement de Paris," in *Guide des recherches dans les fonds judiciaires de l'ancien régime* (Paris: Imprimerie Nationale, 1958), pp. 65–80.

30. On parlementary procedure during the eighteenth century, see William Doyle, "The Parlements of France and the Breakdown of the Old Regime, 1771–1788," *French Historical Studies* 6 (1970): 415–58, and Bailey Stone, *The French Parlements and the Crisis of the Old Regime* (Chapel Hill: Univ. of North Carolina Press, 1986), pp. 20–21. On the different roles played by the *Lit de Justice* assembly in the sixteenth through the early eighteenth centuries, see Sarah Hanley, *The Lit de Justice of the Kings of France: Constitutional Ideology in Legend, Ritual, and Discourse* (Princeton: Princeton Univ. Press, 1983).

31. See J. H. Shennan, "The Parlement in the Eighteenth Century" (chap. 9), in *The Parlement of Paris* (Ithaca: Cornell Univ. Press, 1968), pp. 285–325.

32. The question of which parlements did register the Edict of October, 1716, and the later Declaration of December 15, 1738 (see Chapter 2 in this volume) has been a difficult one to resolve with certainty. Pierre Pluchon writes that both ordinances were registered by the courts of Bordeaux, Rennes, Rouen, Dijon, Grenoble, Besançon, and Metz but not the courts of Aix, Toulouse, Pau, Douai, and Paris, though he offers no citations for this information (*Nègres et juifs au XVIIIe siècle,* p. 247). Isambert records the registration of the Edict of October, 1716, in the following parlements: Paris, December 7; Aix, December 2; Besançon, November 24; Bordeaux, December 1; Dijon, December 7; Grenoble, December 2; Metz, November 26; Rouen, November 3; Conseil Souverain d'Alsace,

November 20 (Isambert, *Recueil*, vol. 21, p. 122). The *Catalogue général des livres imprimés de la Bibliothèque Nationale: Actes royaux*, published under the direction of S. Honoré (Paris: Imprimerie Nationale, 1955), vol. 5, col. 109, lists an undated published version of the Edict of October, 1716, citing its registration by the Parlement of Paris as December 7, 1716. I have located printed copies of the edict that confirm its registration by the Parlements of Dijon and Rennes (A.N., AD $^+$ 738, no. 10, and AD $^+$ 850, no. 25).

Although the Isambert collection and the *Catalogue général* record the Edict of October 1716 as registered by the Parlement of Paris on December 7, 1716, my own research in the parlementary registers indicates that the edict was not registered on that date, nor at any time during the months following the edict's declaration (*Parlement Civil, Registres, Conseil Secret*, November 25, 1716–October 23, 1717 [A.N., X1ᴬ 8436]). Nor do the registers of the Admiralty of France, whose jurisdiction coincided with that of the Parlement of Paris and who ruled on colonial matters, including slavery, indicate its registration (*Registres d'Enregistrement, Amirauté de France*, May 1714–December 1724 [A.N., Z¹ D39]).

Later remarks by attorneys and other officials make it clear that the law was never registered by the Parlement of Paris. See, for example, le Clerc du Brillet, the Procureur du Roi, in the case of *Jean Boucaux v. Sr. Verdelin*, quoted in [Gayot de Pitaval], "Liberté reclamée par un nègre, contre son maître qui l'a amené en France," in *Causes célèbres*, vol. 13, p. 553. Poncet de la Grave refers to this law as "unregistered" in "5 Avril 1762: Sentence de règlement rendue en l'admirauté de la France concernant les déclarations à passer pour les Nègres et Mulatres" (A.N., Z¹ D139). J. B. Denisart believed that the Edict of 1716 was registered by the Parlements of Dijon and Grenoble, but certainly not Paris (see his article, "Nègres," in *Collection de décisions nouvelles relatives à la jurisprudence actuelle*, new ed., 4 vols., [Paris, 1775], vol. 3, pp. 312–13).

Antoine de Sartine, minister of the marine and a principle drafter of the 1777 *Police des Noirs*, noted that the Edict of 1716 and the later Declaration of December 15, 1738, were both registered by the Parlements of Bordeaux, Rennes, and Rouen, but "the Parlement of Paris and other tribunals completely refused this" (B.N., MSS, fonds français, 13357, p. 18).

Until stronger evidence to the contrary is found, it must be supposed that the Edict of October 1716 was never registered by the Parlement of Paris. Moreover, this was the operating assumption of most eighteenth-century jurists.

33. The Joly de Fleury family was one of the most important legal dynasties in eighteenth–century France. Two of its members were involved to various degrees in determining the status of slaves in Paris. Guillaume François Joly de Fleury (1675–1756) was responsible for deciding, along with De Chauvelin, that the Parlement of Paris would not register the Edict of 1716. One of his sons, probably Jean Omer (1715–1810), wrote down his father's account of the edict's lack of registration in 1756, probably as he consulted with the lawyer Collet over which of the Admiralty cases to bring before the Parlement of Paris. On the Joly de Fleury family, see A. Molinier, *Inventaire sommaire de la collection Joly de Fleury* (Paris: Picard, 1881); Jean François Michaud's *Biographie universelle ancienne et moderne*, repr. (Graz, Austria: Akademische Druck– u. Verlags-anstalt, 1968); and Paul Bisson de Barthélemy, *Les Joly de Fleury: Procureurs généraux au Parlement de Paris au XVIIIᵉ siècle* (Paris: Société d'édition d'enseignement supérieur, 1964).

34. [Jean Omer?] Joly de Fleury, "Projet de lettres que M.M. Père m'avait donné pour repondre au G. de Sceau," B.N., MSS Joly de Fleury, vol. 315, fol. 103. The undated draft is filed with a cover sheet bearing the date of January 18, 1756.

35. Pierre Lemerre (also spelled "Le Maire"), father and son, both worked as barristers for the clergy and at parlement (see Michaud, *Biographie universelle,* vol. 24, pp. 82–83).

36. See, for example, David Brion Davis, *The Problem of Slavery in Western Culture,* (Ithaca: Cornell Univ. Press, 1966), pp. 84–111.

37. The relationship between sinner and slave was especially important in the medieval writings of Augustine and Thomas Aquinas (see Marc Bloch, *Slavery and Serfdom in the Middle Ages,* trans. William R. Beer, [Berkeley: Univ. California Press, 1975], p. 12, and Henri Bresc, "L'Etat, l'église, et les esclaves," in *Normes et pouvoir à la fin du moyen âge: Actes du colloque en études médiévales au Québec et en Ontario, May 16–17, 1989,* ed. Marie-Claude Déprez-Masson, [Quebec: CERES, 1989], pp. 37–38).

38. The Christian notion of equality before God did not *necessarily* lead to the conclusion that slavery or other earthly forms of inequality were wrong and should be abolished. Instead, most early Christians saw equality as a spiritual matter, ensuring that all Christians would be judged equally at the gates of heaven.

39. "Code Noir," in Isambert, *Recueil,* vol. 19, pp. 494–95. If these aspects of the Code Noir appear as mere cynical expansions of the power of Catholics over nonbelievers, it should be noted that the Code Noir also sought to protect slaves from the worst abuses by their masters. For example, slaves were not to be worked on Sundays or feast days and certain minimum levels of food were established that could not be supplanted by liquor (Articles 6, 22, and 23). The code discouraged masters' concubinage with slaves in favor of legitimate marriage and required masters to support slaves in their old age. In general, many believe that the Code Noir fell somewhere in between the most severe antislave laws of the English colonies and the more favorable slave laws of the Iberians (see, for example, Davis, *Slavery in Western Culture,* p. 54).

This is not to say that the French were in practice more accommodating or less cruel than their slaveowning counterparts in North and South America. Laws are made to regulate behavior; the very fact of the laws' existence indicates that the authorities felt that the behavior warranted regulation in the first place. Furthermore, because of the distance between the metropolis and colonies and the time it took for correspondence to travel between them, the colonies operated for the most part independently of royal control, especially in regard to master–slave relations.

40. The following discussion is based primarily on J. H. Shennan's account in *The Parlement of Paris,* pp. 293–96.

41. Hardy finds evidence that Jansenism had made significant inroads among the *parlementaires* as well, (*Parlement of Paris,* p. 54).

42. Dale Van Kley, *The Jansenists and the Expulsion of the Jesuits from France, 1757–1765* (New Haven: Yale Univ. Press, 1975), pp. 9–11.

43. Pierre Lemerre, *Mémoire dans lequel on examine si l'appel interjeté au futur Concile général de la Constitution Unigenitus, par quatre évèques de France, auquel plusieurs facultés et un grand nombre de chanoines et de curés ont adhéré, est légitime et canonique, et quels sont les effets de cet appel* (Paris, 1717), and *Mémoires composés par les plus célèbres jurisconsultes et théologiens de France, sur la demande des commis-*

saires du conseil de Régence, touchant les moyens de se pouvoir contre le refus injuste que faisait la Cour de Rome d'accorder des bulles aux évèques et abbés, nommé par le Cour de France (Paris, 1718).

44. Michaud, *Biographie universelle,* vol. 24, p. 82.

45. François Bluche, *Les Magistrats du parlement de Paris au XVIIIe siècle, 1715–1771* (Paris: Les Belles Lettres, 1960), pp. 242–69.

46. M. Le Maire [sic], fils, "Observations sur la liberté que l'on pretend être acquise en france par la seule entrée dans le Royaume" (B.N., MSS Joly de Fleury, vol. 315, fol. 115v). Joly de Fleury notes that this manuscript is a copy of the original containing "many errors by the copyist" (Joly de Fleury, "Projet de lettres," B.N., MSS Joly de Fleury, vol. 315, fol. 103).

47. Le Maistre, in the eighteenth of his *Plaidoyers,* pp. 343–44, cited in Lemerre's "Observations," fol. 125. Antoine Le Maistre, "une des gloires du barreau français," experienced a profound epiphany at the age of twenty-nine and retired from the law into religious retreat at the Port Royal Abbey (Michaud, *Biographie universelle,* vol. 24, pp. 65–66).

48. Antoine Le Maistre, *Apologie pour feu monsieur l'Abbé de St. Cyran: contre l'extrait d'une information prétendue que l'on fit courir contre lui l'an 1638, & que les Jesuits ont fait imprimer depuis quelques mois, à la teste d'un libelle diffamatoire intitulé, Sommaire de la Théologie de l'Abbé de Saint Cyran, & du sieur Arnauld,* 2nd ed. (n.p, 1644).

49. Historians' attempts to identify Jansenists and their influence on eighteenth-century parlementary politics are notoriously difficult because Jansenism was outlawed and consequently its followers tended to keep their faith a secret. (See, for example, Bluche, *Les Magistrats du Parlement de Paris au XVIIe siècle, 1715–1771,* pp. 242–69, and Dale Van Kley, *The Jansenists and the Expulsion of the Jesuits* pp. 42–54.) The reason why I raise the possibility of Jansenist influence on the courts' lack of registration of royal slavery legislation is that the tactic of nonregistration was a fundamental part of the explosive *Unigenitus* conflict and judicial conflicts over slavery tended to erupt during the periods when Jansenists were highly mobilized, that is, 1716, the 1750s, and during the Maupeou crisis.

50. "Sur ce mémoire [i.e., the report composed by Lemerre] le parquet composé alors de M. le Chancelier de Chauvelin et de mon père ne crurent pas que la Déclaration dût être adoptée. Mon père est rendu compte à M. le Compte de Thoulouse qui n'insista pas. Il ne se souvient pas si on en parla au Premier Président ou si le Parquet prit la chose sur lui seul. A l'égard de la Déclaration de 1738: il n'en a eû aucune connaissance," Joly de Fleury, "Projet de lettres," B.N., MSS Joly de Fleury, vol. 315, fol. 103–03^v.

If there is any doubt regarding the Joly de Fleurys' account of the edict's lack of registration, it is because it was written so many years after the fact and is full of ambiguities. The account was set down by Guillaume François Joly de Fleury's son in January 1756, forty years after the events transpired and just two months before the octogenarian died. The account hinges on a copy of Lemerre's "Observations," the original of which has not been found (the younger Joly de Fleury remarks that this copy is full of copyist's errors). The passage that I cited at the beginning of this note refers to a "Declaration" that was not adopted; but the legislation of 1716 was an edict, not a declaration. Perhaps this is just sloppiness on the part of the younger Joly de Fleury or the result the aging man's defective memory. On the other hand, perhaps these inconsistencies are evidence of a plot, hatched by the younger Joly de Fleury in 1756, to concoct a legitimate history to the lack of registration of the Edict of 1716. If this is the case, one would need to find a motive for the younger Joly de Fleury's misinformation campaign.

Another hypothesis as to why the Parlement of Paris did not register the law is that the Edict of 1716 was seen as pertinent only to French slave colonies and the parlements whose jurisdiction included ports where slaves might disembark in France (e.g., Rennes or Bordeaux). In this view, the Edict of 1716 was never presented to the Parlement of Paris for registration and consequently remained unregistered for that region. There are two flaws in this hypothesis, however. First, several port cities including Dunkerque, Calais, and La Rochelle fell within the appellate jurisdiction of the Parlement of Paris. Second, the landlocked Parlement of Dijon is known to have registered the law. It seems unlikely that the government would have sought registration in Dijon and not in Paris.

In sum, the Joly de Fleury account, though flawed, is the best available and, in my view, fairly plausible.

Chapter 2. The Case of *Jean Boucaux v. Verdelin*

1. Sentence of August 9, 1734 (A.N., Z^{1}D 127).

2. "Extrait des registres du greffe de l'amirauté," August 23, 1736 (A.N., Z^{1}D 127).

3. Article 5 of the Edict of 1716 held that slaves could not "claim their freedom on the grounds of having arrived in the kingdom" but did not explicitly address the situation of slaves who sought employment elsewhere. Article 3 required slave owners to declare their slaves at the port of entry but made no provisions regarding the declarations at the Admiralty of France in Paris.

4. Mallet, *Mémoire pour Jean Boucaux, Nègre, Demandeur. Contre le Sieur Verdelin, Défendeur* (n.p.: L'Imprimerie de Claude Simon, Père, 1738).

5. [François Gayot de Pitaval], "Liberté reclamée par un nègre contre son maître qui l'a amené en France," in *Causes célèbres et intéressantes avec les jugemens qui les ont decidées,* (Paris: Jean de Nully, 1747), vol. 13, pp. 492–586.

6. On the resurrection and misreading of Salic law, see Sarah Hanley, "The Monarchic State in Early Modern France: Marital Regime Government and Male Right," in *Politics, Ideology, and the Law in Early Modern Europe,* ed. Adrianna E. Bakos (Rochester: Univ. of Rochester Press, 1994), pp. 107–26; Collette Beaune, *The Birth of an Ideology: Myths and Symbols of Nation in Late-Medieval France,* trans. Susan Ross Huston, ed. Frederic L. Cheyette (Berkeley: Univ. of California Press, 1991), pp. 245–65, 345–50; Ralph E. Giesey, "The Juristic Basis of Dynastic Right to the French Throne," *Transactions of the American Philosophical Society* 51, no. 5 (1961): 17–22; Emile Viollet, "Comment les femmes ont été exclues en France de la succession à la couronne," *Mémoires de l'Academie des sciences, inscriptions, et belles lettres* 34 (1894): 125–78; and Sarah Hanley, foreword to *La Loi Salique* (Paris: Côte-femmes éditions, 1994).

7. "Déclaration concernant les nègres esclaves des Colonies," Versailles, December 15, 1738, cited in François André Isambert, *Recueil général des anciennes lois françaises depuis l'an 420 jusqu'à la révolution de 1789* (Paris: Belin-Leprieur, 1830), vol. 22, pp. 112–15.

8. Gayot de Pitaval, "Liberté reclamée," p. 494. The date is listed as 1734 but must be 1724 given the other dates listed in the text.

9. Mallet, *Mémoire pour Jean Boucaux,* p. 5.

10. Gayot de Pitaval, "Liberté reclamée," p. 495.

11. Boucaux's petition is dated June 19, 1738 (A.N., Z¹D 127).

12. Immediately after this ruling, another slave, Catherine Dumoulin, a mulatto from Leogane, petitioned for her freedom in the Admiralty Court of Paris. She argued that because her masters, the Count and Countess de Granville, had not registered her with the Admiralty of Paris for the years 1735 through 1738, she should be recognized as free. The judges ruled that the count and countess should appear before the court within three days and that in the meantime Catherine Dumoulin would receive the king's protection and forbade the count and countess from interfering with the woman's liberty in any way (Petition of Catherine Dumoulin, "fille mulatre," June 26, 1738, and Sentence of the Admiralty Court of France, June 26, 1738 [A.N., Z¹D 127]). As is the case with many future such petitions, there are no further records on this affair within the archives. It seems likely that because the masters did not appear in court to challenge the charges against them, the magistrates' action successfully discouraged the masters from pursuing their former powers over the petitioners.

13. Gayot de Pitaval, "Liberté reclamée," p. 497.

14. Mallet, *Mémoire pour Jean Boucaux,* p. 1; conclusions of le Clerc du Brillet in Gayot de Pitaval, "Liberté reclamée," p. 542.

15. Bodin's most thorough discussion of slavery is contained in his *Six livres de la république,* first published in 1576. A distinct Latin version of the text with numerous emendations was also published by Bodin in 1584. Knolles's 1606 English translation, which I have relied on here, combines the French and Latin versions, and according to editor Kenneth Douglas McRae, "incorporates all material that was unique to either, and where different, strikes a balance or chooses what he thinks is most correct." McRae describes the 1606 edition as "faithfully, and even meticulously, translated" (Jean Bodin, *The Six Bookes of a Commonweale: A Facsimile Reprint of the English Translation of 1606, Corrected and Supplemented in Light of a New Comparison with the French and Latin Texts,* ed. and with an introduction by Kenneth Douglas McRae [Cambridge: Harvard Univ. Press, 1962], p. A38).

16. Jean Bodin, *Six Bookes,* Book 1, chap. V, p. 35.

17. Ibid., p. 34.

18. Mallet probably found this reference in Antoine Loisel's summary on French customary law, *Institutes Coutumières,* notes by Eusèbe de Laurière, 2 vols. (Paris: Nicolas Gosselin, 1710), p. 7, which I discuss later.

19. Mallet, *Mémoire pour Jean Boucaux,* p. 2. I have not been able to find out with certainty what uprising Mallet was referring to. Achille Luchaire's *Louis VI, le gros: Annales des sa vie et son règne, 1081–1137* (Paris: A. Picard, 1890), mentions nothing relevant around 1108. Jacques Dalperrie de Bayac discusses a Norman rebellion circa 1118, but this was of the feudal lords rebelling against Henri Beauclerc and would seem to have no direct relevance to slavery (*Louis VI: La naissance de la France* [Paris: J. C. Lattès, 1983], pp. 215–17).

20. Jean Bodin's view of the termination of European slavery is more cynical. He

points out that slaves were likely to rebel against their masters if promised freedom by their masters' enemies. To forestall such rebellion, says Bodin, Christian princes freed their slaves (*Six Bookes*, p. 39). Bodin also credits Muslims with the practice of freeing slaves who convert to their faith and notes that Christians merely followed suit (p. 40).

21. "It would be childish," Bloch says, "to deny that the idea of the world to come, of its penalties and rewards, had contributed to the inspiration of more than one manumission," Marc Bloch, *Slavery and Serfdom in the Middle Ages*, trans. William R. Beer (Berkeley: Univ. of California Press, 1975), p. 15.

22. Paul Allard, *Esclaves, serfs et mainmortables*, new, rev. ed. (Paris: Sanard & Derangeon, 1894; first published in 1884), p. 174.

23. Marcel Fournier, *Essai sur les formes et les effets de l'affranchissement dans le droit Gallo-franc* (Paris: F. Vieweg, 1885), pp. 6–7. See also his "Les affranchissements du Vᵉ au XIIIᵉ siècle: Influence de l'église, de la royauté et des particuliers sur la condition des affranchis," *Revue historique* 21 (1883), pp. 1–58. One suspects, in reading their exchange, that the virulence with which these two historians disagreed had at least as much to do with the conflicts between republican and clerical factions for control of the French state at the end of the nineteenth century as with the evidence culled from the archives on behalf of each side.

24. For the former, see Charles Parain, *Outils, ethnies et développement historique* (Paris: Editions sociales, 1979). For the latter, see Pierre Dockès, *La libération médiévale* (Paris: Flammarion, 1979), translated by Arthur Goldhammer as *Medieval Slavery and Liberation* (London: Methuen, 1982).

25. Most important among the legal historians is Charles Verlinden, *L'Esclavage dans l'Europe médiévale*, 2 vols. (Brugge: De Tempel, 1955–1957). More recently, see Danielle Anex, *Le Servage au Pays de Vaud (XIIIᵉ – XVIᵉ siècle)* (Lausanne: Bibliothèque historique vaudoise, 1973), p. 42.

26. Pierre Bonnassie, *From Slavery to Feudalism in South-Western Europe*, trans. Jean Birrell (New York: Cambridge Univ. Press, 1991). Bonnassie's introduction to twentieth-century historiography on the transformation of slavery to serfdom in western Europe is both clear and enlightening.

27. *Corvée* is villein labor, that is, labor owed by a serf to a feudal lord. *Mainmorte* (mortmain) is the perpetual ownership of land that cannot be transferred or sold to another; in this context it applies to serfs who remained attached to a piece of property.

28. Mallet, *Mémoire pour Jean Boucaux*, p. 2. Mallet acknowledged that despite Suger's charter, the institution of *mainmorte* persisted in some regions of France into the eighteenth century.

29. On the centuries of confusion regarding the words *Franc* (Frank), *français* (French), *France* (France), and *franche* (free), see Jacques Barzun, *The French Race: Theories of Its Origin and the Social and Political Implications Prior to the Revolution* (New York: Columbia Univ. Press, 1932).

30. Le Clerc du Brillet, cited in Gayot de Pitaval, "Liberté reclamée," p. 548.

31. Boucaux's lawyer, Mallet, was not the first to confuse Louis X's ordinance freeing serfs with the issue of slavery. Jean Bodin confounds the two in his *Six livres* (p. 41), and Antoine Loisel's eighteenth-century editor Eusèbe de Laurière mistakenly argues that the law must have applied to slaves (see later). Still, Bodin's account is once again the more cynical, noting that Louis X issued the ordinance to defray the cost of his wars.

32. Mallet, *Mémoire pour Jean Boucaux*, p. 3. Neither Mallet nor Le Clerc du Brillet cited a case witnessed by Bodin in Toulouse wherein that court supported a slave's claim to freedom against his master, a merchant who was on his way from Spain to Genoa, on the grounds that Emperor Theodosius had granted the privilege to the city that any slave who entered it should be freed. Perhaps the eighteenth-century lawyers omitted the case from their briefs because the merchant circumvented the magistrates' decision by manumitting the slave after making a contract for lifetime service. Or perhaps it was because Bodin cast doubt on the court's basis for freeing the slave, stating that Rome had never granted these privileges to any other city in its empire (Bodin, *Six Bookes*, p. 42).

33. Le Clerc du Brillet in Gayot de Pitaval, "Liberté reclamée," p. 549.

34. Ibid. Belleforet's *Histoire universelle du monde* was issued in Paris in three editions in 1570, 1572, and 1577.

35. Ibid., p. 550.

36. Ibid.

37. Mallet, *Mémoire pour Jean Boucaux*, p. 3.

38. Le Clerc du Brillet in Gayot de Pitaval, "Liberté reclamée," p. 546.

39. Sarah Hanley's *Lit de Justice* shows how constitutional principles (not called fundamental law until the eighteenth century) were spelled out in ritual and discourse during *Lit de Justice* assemblies held in the Parlement of Paris from the early sixteenth century (Princeton: Princeton Univ. Press, 1983). Donald R. Kelley explores how modern historiography developed out of the search for the origins of French political institutions in his *Foundations of Modern Historical Scholarship: Language, Law, and History in the French Renaissance* (New York: Columbia Univ. Press, 1970).

40. Bodin, *Six livres*, Book 1, chap. 8.

41. William Farr Church, *Constitutional Thought in Sixteenth-Century France: A Study of the Evolution of Ideas* (New York: Octagon, 1979), p. 333.

42. "Toutes personnes sont franches en ce roïaume: et sitost qu'un esclave a atteint les marches d'icelui, se faisant baptizer, est affranchi." Antoine Loisel, *Institutes coutumières* (Paris: Abel l'Angelier, 1608), p. 1.

43. "Par la constitution de l'Eglise le Baptesme affranchit, hoc ius Ecclesia statuit, ut seruus Iudaeorum cum fuerit factus Christianus statim a servitude liberetur, nullo pretio dato, dict S. 2.2 de sa Somme, qu. 10, art. 10 in resp. ad quaest," *Institutes coutumières* (Paris: Henry le Gras, 1657), p. 4. The 1665 edition, published in Paris by Michel Bobin and Nicolas le Gras, is identical to that of 1657.

44. François de Launay, *Commentaire sur les Institutes Coutumières de M. Antoine Loisel* (Paris: Chez Antoine Warin & Guillaume Cavelier, 1688), quoted in a review of the same work in *Le Journal des Sçavans* (1688): 390.

45. Antoine Loisel, *Institutes coutumières*, with notes by Eusèbe de Laurière, 2 vols. (Paris: Nicolas Gosselin, 1710), p. 7.

46. These sources included Justinian's code (534), the Church's Council of Mâcon (581), the Council of Meaux (845), and Saint Thomas' *Summary* (previously cited by Challine).

47. Ibid., p. 9.

48. Ibid., p. 10.

49. Tribard's speech for the defense, cited in Gayot de Pitaval, "Liberté reclamée," pp. 520–21. Tribard reaffirms the maxim on pp. 512, 525, and 529.

50. Ibid., p. 512.

51. Ibid., pp. 513–16.

52. Ibid., p. 520.

53. Ibid., p. 537.

54. Le Clerc du Brillet in Gayot de Pitaval, "Liberté reclamée," p. 543.

55. As seen, the *gens du roi* of the Parlement of Paris refused to register the Edict of 1716 on the basis of Lemerre's report. It appears that the Code Noir was not registered by any French parlement because it concerned only the colonies and was never submitted to the French high courts for registration. The last paragraph of the Code Noir reads: "Si donnons en mandemant à nos amés et féaux les gens tenans notre conseil souverain établi à la Martinique, la Guadeloupe et Saint Christophe, que ces présentes ils aient à faire lire, publier, enregistrer, etc . . ." (Isambert, *Recueil,* vol. 19, p. 504).

56. Between 1673 and 1715 all courts were required to register all royal acts before issuing remonstrances (Jean Egret, *Louis XV et l'opposition parlementaire, 1715–1774* [Paris: Armand Colin, 1970], p. 9). The Code Noir appears not to have been sent to any of the parlements of the metropole, however, because it regulated activity only in the colonies.

57. Le Clerc du Brillet in Gayot de Pitaval, "Liberté reclamée," p. 565.

58. Ibid., pp. 572–73.

59. According to Le Clerc du Brillet, the ship that carried Boucaux and Verdelin to France, the *Profond,* moored at the Isle d'Ais near La Rochelle on December 22, 1728. A statement certified by the *écrivain du roi,* dated January 20, 1729, stated that the ship's merchandise had already been unloaded. But the most damaging evidence presented by the *procureur du roi* was that the equipment list recorded that the unloading began April 20, 1728, and ended January 5, 1729. Thus it seemed likely that Verdelin had allowed more than eight days to elapse before he registered Boucaux at the port of entry. The confusion over Verdelin's date of arrival would claim the attention of the king's ministers when they drafted new legislation regarding slaves who traveled to France (see later).

60. Le Clerc du Brillet in Gayot de Pitaval, "Liberté reclamée," p. 577.

61. Ibid., p. 540.

62. Tribard in Gayot de Pitaval, "Liberté reclamée," p. 526.

63. Ibid., p. 529.

64. See Chapter 4 in this volume.

65. Le Clerc du Brillet in Gayot de Pitaval, "Liberté reclamée," p. 583.

66. "Déclaration concernant les nègres esclaves des Colonies," Versailles, December 15, 1738, in Isambert, *Recueil,* vol. 22, pp. 112–15.

67. Ibid., p. 112.

68. Ibid., p. 113.

69. Ibid., p. 114.

70. Ibid., p. 115.

71. A printed copy of the Declaration of 1738 specifically mentions the law's registration by the parlements of Rouen, Rennes, Dijon, Grenoble, Toulouse, Pau, Bordeaux, Metz, and Flandres, the sovereign councils of Alsace and Roussillon, and the "conseils supérieurs des isles et colonies françaises de l'Amérique," pointedly omitting the Parlement of Paris ("Declaration du Roy concernant les Nègres esclaves des colonies" [Paris, Imprimerie Royale, 1740], A.N., AD+ 850, no. 24). Later commentators are unanimous

in their conviction that the Declaration of 1738 was never registered in Paris; unfortunately, no evidence has been forthcoming to explain why or how the Parlement of Paris neglected to register the law. On the law's lack of registration in the Parlement of Paris, see Denisart, *Collection de décisions nouvelles relative à la jurisprudence actuelle* (Paris, 1775), vol. 3, p. 406; Poncet de la Grave in De la Haye, "Sentence de règlement rendue en l'admirauté de la France concernant les déclarations a passer pour les Nègres et Mulatres," April 5, 1762, fol. 2ᵛ (A.N., Z¹ D139); and Minister of the Marine Antoine de Sartine, "Rapport au Conseil des Dépêches, par M. de Sartine, du Projet de Déclaration sur la Police des Noirs, du Août 1777," B.N., MS français, 13357: "Recueil des pièces relatives à la législation sur la police des noirs," p. 18.

72. "Registre pour servir à l'enregistrement des déclarations qui se font au sujet des noirs amenés des colonies en France" (A.N., Z¹D 139). This apparent inconsistancy is easy to explain. The admiralty clerk charged a fee for registering the declarations; it was therefore profitable for the clerk to assist any slaveowner who wanted to make such a declaration. For example, see the "Extrait des Registres des Greffes de l'amirauté Generalle de france," (The Beinecke Lesser Antilles Collection at Hamilton College, Hamilton, N.Y.) in which the master of La Violette is recorded as having paid 10 *deniers* for the registration of his slave. Furthermore, to refuse a master's declaration would have required that the Admiralty clerk take a controversial position. Political grandstanding might have appealed to lawyers and judges but could be dangerous to an administrator who depended on political favor for his office. Accepting slave declarations was the path of least resistance.

73. "Arrêt qui évoque au Conseil du roi l'appel interjeté par Bernard de Verdelin, maréchal général des logis, d'une sentence obtenue contre lui à la Table de Marbre de Paris, par Jean Boucault, nègre esclave, et qui en interdit l'exécution (nᵒ 10), 12 septembre, 1738" (A.N., Colonies, A³, fol. 71).

74. King's Order, April 25, 1739 (A.N., Colonies F³ 79, Collection Moreau de Saint-Méry, fol. 26).

75. Maurepas to M. Le Clerc du Brillet, April 25, 1739 (A.N., Colonies F³ 79, Collection Moreau de Saint-Méry, fol. 27).

Chapter 3. The Impact of the Declaration of 1738

1. Catin to Maurepas, August 15, 1747 (A.N., Marine, B³ 455, fol. 136). I have inserted punctuation where appropriate.

2. The underscoring beneath the sentence, "*sitot que ju quitté mon Maistre je fut trouvé led. Terrien je luy donné cette somme de neuf cents livres,*" is in slightly darker ink than that of the text and matches Maurepas's marginalia.

3. Catin to Maurepas, August 15, 1747 (A.N., Marine, B³ 455 f. 136).

4. Ibid.

5. Maurepas's letter was written on August 31, 1747, according to Millain's response (Millain to Maurepas, September 12, 1747 [ibid., fol. 130]).

6. "Mémoire apologétique pour la justification du Sieur Terrien, avocat au parlement de Bretagne, militant à Nantes contre les fausses accusations intentées contre luy de Monseigneur le comte de Maurepas par Morgan sous le nom de Catherine négresse," n.d. (ibid., fol. 132).

7. This was after the Declaration of 1738 changed the penalties for noncompliance. See Chapter 2.

8. The duc de Penthièvre, a prince of the blood, was the Admiral of France and consequently had some authority over this dispute because it related indirectly to the colonies.

9. "Mémoire apologétique," fol. 132.

10. Ibid., fol. 133.

11. Ibid., fol. 134.

12. Ibid.

13. Ibid., fol. 134^v.

14. Maurepas to Maillart, intendant of the Leeward Islands [Iles sous le vent], June 7, 1747 (A.N., Colonies, F^3 90, fol. 65).

15. See Chapter 1 in this volume.

16. Millain to Maurepas, September 12, 1747 (A.N., Marine, B^3 455 fol. 130).

17. Millain to Maurepas, September 12, 1747 (Ibid., fol. 138).

18. "Ordre du Roi qui confirme une sentence de l'amirauté de Nantes portant confiscation au profit du Roi d'une négresse et ses deux enfants," June 25, 1747 (A.N., Colonies F^3 90, fol. 66).

19. Maurepas to Maillart, June 7, 1747 (ibid., fol. 65).

20. Cissie Fairchilds argues that corporal punishment was an accepted fact of daily life for servants until around 1750 when attitudes bagan to change and servants no longer accepted routine beatings (*Domestic Enemies: Servants and Their Masters in Old Regime France* [Baltimore: Johns Hopkins Univ. Press, 1984], pp. 124–25). During the sixteenth century this acceptance of limited domestic abuse encompassed wives as well as servants. See Natalie Z. Davis, *Fiction in the Archives: Pardon Tales and Their Tellers in Sixteenth-Century France* (Stanford: Stanford Univ. Press, 1987), p. 81.

21. The Admiralty Court of France heard cases in the first instance arising within its own jurisdiction (including Paris and Versailles). The Admiralty Court of France also heard appeals from the local admiralty seats of Calais, Boulogne, Abbeville, Ault, Saint-Valéry-sur-Somme, and Eu in the North, and Sables-d'Olonne on the Atlantic coast. The court's sentences involving over 150 *livres* could be appealed to the Parlement of Paris (Buffet, "Amirauté de France," p. 262).

22. The term *nègres* carried connotations both of color and of slave status (see discussion in Chapter 4 in this volume).

23. Barentin, intendant of La Rochelle, to Maurepas, September 22, 1741 (A.N., Marine, B^3 405, fol. 267). Barentin's letter refers to an *ordre du roi* accompanying the minister's letter of August 31, 1741.

24. Throughout his correspondence, Barentin used the term *nègre* to refer to all individuals who might be expelled from France. Yet he sought exceptions for those who were free (*libre*), suggesting that in the minds of the inhabitants and administrators of La Rochelle, there was a distinction between free blacks and the enslaved. Nevertheless, Barentin shied away from using the word *esclave* in his correspondance, and most *nègres* were presumed unfree.

25. Barentin to Maurepas, September 22, 1741 (fol. 267). In a later letter (December 10, 1741), Barentin offered the following head counts: In La Rochelle: 31 *nègres*, 7 *négresses*, 8 *négrillons*, and 0 *négrittes*. In Rochefort: 23 *nègres*, 9 *négresses*, 3 *mulâtres*,

and 4 *mulâtresses* (including one "*mulâtre sauvage*") (A.N., Marine B³ 405, fols. 278–80).

26. Barentin to Maurepas, two letters dated December 10, 1741 (A.N., Marine B³ 405, fols. 274 and 276).

27. Barentin to Maurepas, December 19, 1741 (ibid., fol. 282), and "Extrait du testament du feu S. Nicolas Rigault" (ibid., fol. 284).

28. Maurepas to Bellamy, November 15, 1747, (A.N., Colonies, F³ 90, fol. 68).

29. Choiseul to Bois de la Motte and de Lalanne, May 11, 1752 (A.N., Colonies B95, p. 35).

30. Ibid.

31. In their response of July 28, 1752, Bompar and Hurson, colonial administrators of Martinique indicate that it was the particular case of one Mademoiselle Cruzot who had not paid the required security deposit to the treasurer of the Admiralty that attracted the Minister's attention (A.N., Col. F³ 90, fol. 69).

32. Ibid.

33. "Registres pour servir à l'enregistrement des déclarations qui se font au sujet des noirs amenés des colonies en France, 1739–1790" (A.N., Z¹D 139). As noted in the previous chapter, this was probably because the Admiralty clerk, as distinct from the judges of the court, had strong incentives for accepting the declarations.

34. Statement by Bottée, clerk of the Admiralty of France, October 7, 1752; Petition of Jean Baptiste, *nègre,* November 8, 1752; and Sentence of the Admiralty Court of France, November 13, 1752 (A.N., Z¹D 129).

35. "Declaration concernant les nègres esclaves des Colonies," in François André Isambert, *Recueil général des anciennes lois françaises depuis l'an 420 jusqu'à la révolution de 1789* (Paris: Belin-Leprieur, 1830), vol. 22, p. 113.

36. Notarized statement by Nicolas du Chardonet, notary of the Chatelet of Paris, May 6, 1754 (A.N., Z¹D 129). It appears that the beneficiary of François Durant's culinary expertise was to be the same Jesuit Père de la Valette whose corruption in Martinique would become the basis for the anti-Jesuit court cases of 1760 and 1761. On the La Valette affair, see Dale Van Kley, *The Jansenists and the Expulsion of the Jesuits from France, 1757–1765* (New Haven: Yale Univ. Press, 1975) pp. 90–107.

37. Article 11 of the Declaration of December 15, 1738, in Isambert, *Recueil,* vol. 22, p. 115.

38. A fifth case was represented by Claude Hector Michel Thomason. The records concerning all of these cases may be found chronologically in A.N., Z¹D 130.

39. For the Parlement of Paris's test case, see Chapter 4 in this volume.

40. According to historian Michael Fitzsimmons, one Claude Nicolas Collet was inscribed in the Order of the Barristers of Paris on April 20, 1752, and was executed during the Terror in Lyon (*The Parisian Order of the Barristers and the French Revolution* [Cambridge: Harvard Univ. Press, 1987], pp. 108 and 203–18). It is difficult to know whether this is the same lawyer Collet who represented many of the early slave petitions in the 1750s and 1760s, although the dates of his inscription correspond nicely. Claude Nicolas Collet's relationship to Bon Antoine Joseph Collet (see later) is unknown.

41. The clerk's statement that Françoise, known as Fauchon, was not registered with the Admiralty at Le Havre, is dated January 13, 1755, indicating that Collet began

preparing his case at this time (A.N., Z^{1}D 130). Françoise's was the third petition set
before the court in the summer of 1755.

42. Petition for Corinne, July 2, 1755 (A.N., Z^{1}D 130).

43. The petition states that the clerk provided a statement to that effect on June 25, 1755.

44. "Nous avons donné deffaut et pr. le proffit ordonnons que les loix et ord^{nes} du
royaume seront executées selon leur forme et teneur en consequence declarons la partie de
Mallet libre et hors d'esclavage ou elle est née; ordonnons que comme libre elle pourra
demeurer ou elle jugera apropos; faisons deffenses aux defaillans et a tous autres d'attenter
à la personne de la partie de Mallet; condamnons à rendre à lade. partie de Mallet ses habits
et linges faisant à son usage et à luy payer la somme de 500 *livres* pour ses gages et aux
depens," Sentence of the Admiralty Court of France, October 1, 1755 (A.N., Z^{1}D 24).

45. They were Louise, Marie Jeanne, Françoise (Fauchon), Michel Morin, and Jacques
Pierre. Provisional sentences awarding their freedom can be found in the records of the
Admiralty Court, A.N., Z^{1}D 130, under the following dates: July 7, July 14, July 30,
August 1. In each case, the court granted permission for a subsequent audience wherein a
slaveowner might challenge the provisional sentence, but it seems that none of the masters
took advantage of this option.

46. Collet continued to bring these cases before the court into the next decade, resulting
in the freedom of twelve slaves.

47. "Arrêt qui évoque an Conseil du roi aussi bien la demande présenté au siège
général de l'Amirauté à Paris par les négresses esclaves Fanchon, Louison, Marianne, et
Corine, en vue d' être déclarées libres, que toutes autres demandes et procédures portées
en cette amirauté: défense est faite aux officiers du siège d'en connaître, sous peine de
nullité," January 17, 1756, cited in Odile Krakovitch, *Arrêts, déclarations, édits et
ordonnances concernant les colonies, 1666–1779* (Paris: Archives Nationales, 1993),
p. 63. This very personal practice of meting out justice on a case-by-case basis seems to
have been the preferred administrative style of Louis XV (Dale Van Kley, *The Damiens
Affair and the Unraveling of the Ancien Régime, 1750–1770* [Princeton: Princeton Univ.
Press, 1984], p. 117).

48. Machaud to Guillaume François Louis Joly de Fleury, January 18, 1756, B.N.,
MS. Joly de Fleury, vol. 315, fol. 135–135^v.

49. Ibid., pp. 135^v–136.

Chapter 4. Notions of Race in the Eighteenth Century

1. All of the specifics in this case come from the following document, unless otherwise indicated: Joly de Fleury, de la Roue, and Collet, *Mémoire signifié pour le nommé
Francisque, Indien de Nation, Néophyte de l'Eglise Romaine, Intimé; contre le Sieur
Allain-François-Ignace Brignon, se disant Ecuyer, Appellant* (Paris: P. G. Simon, Imprimeur du Parlement, 1759), hereafter cited as *Mémoire pour Francisque.*

2. See T. B. Howell, *A Complete Collection of State Trials* (London: Hurst, Rees,
Orme and Brown, 1814), vol. 20, p. 63.

3. Pierre Boulle's analysis of the French registers of blacks in Paris from 1777 to 1790
shows that the average age at arrival in France for blacks who arrived prior to 1777 was
between 10 and 14 years old, "Les gens de couleur à Paris à la veille de la Révolution," in

L'Image de la Révolution française: Communications présentées lors du Comgrès Mondial pour le Bicentenaire de la Révolution, ed. Michel Vovelle (Paris: Pergamon, 1989), p. 161. Boulle's forthcoming book on the registers of blacks throughout France will help to show whether the figures for Paris were skewed by the demand for domestic labor.

4. See Chapter 5 in this volume.

5. *Mémoire pour Francisque*, p. 3.

6. A footnote in the *Mémoire pour Francisque* states that a rupee is a piece of gold, the equivalent of between 28 and 42 French *sous* at the time.

7. Archives Départmentales d'Ille-et-Vilaine, Rennes, 9B8, fol. 39^v. The boys, André and François, were registered by Hélène Gallicet, widow of Alain Brignon, and mother of Alain Brignon, fils, on April 1, 1750. They were re-registered there by Brignon's surrogates on April 1 and June 2, 1751 (fol. 43), May 17, 1752 (fol. 48^v), October 15, 1756 (fol. 64^v), and September 24, 1757 (fol. 78). Brignon also apparently owned three other slaves: Philippe (of Mozambique), (Louis of Mako, or Macoco), and Antoine (of Pondichéry) (Archives Départementales d' Ille-et-Vilaine 9B8, Rennes, fols. 41, 43, and 48^v). I am indebted to Pierre Boulle for these references.

8. *Mémoire pour Francisque*, p. 4. On the use of black servants as status symbols in Europe, see Hans Werner Debrunner, *Presence and Prestige: Africans in Europe: A History of Africans in Europe before 1918* (Basel: Basler Afrika Bibliographien, 1979), pp. 33, 91–100, as well as Shyllon, *Black Slaves*, p. 11 and *Black People*, pp. 10–12; and Shelby T. McCloy, *The Negro in France* (Lexington: Univ. of Kentucky Press, 1975), p. 34.

9. Ibid., p. 6.

10. Ibid. Strangely enough, the records concerning this case are not in the Paris Admiralty court records for the period (A.N., Z^{1}D 24 or Z^{1}D 130). One possibility is that they were removed by Francisque's lawyers in preparation for their case before the high court.

11. I have not found the judicial records concerning the case in the Archives Nationales, but the publication date of the *Mémoire pour Francisque* is 1759.

12. Collet had represented the following slaves to date: Corinne, Louise, Marie Jeanne, Michel Morin and Jacques Pierre (1755), Pierre Zamor, dit Auguste (1757), Hyppolite Mathieu and Thomas Thelemaque (1758) (A.N., Z^{1}D 130).

13. Cited in Simone Delesalle and Lucette Valensi, "Le Mot 'nègre' dans les dictionnaires français d'ancien régime: histoire et lexicographie," *Langue française* 15 (1972): 84.

14. "Esclaves noirs qu'on tire de la côte de l'Afrique pour la culture du païs, & dans la Terre firme pour travailler aux mines & aux sucreries," Pierre Richelet, *Dictionnaire de la langue française, ancienne et moderne*, 3 vols. (Lyon: Chez les Bruyset, 1728), vol. 2, p. 72.

15. "NEGRES. Peuples d'Afrique, dont le Païs a son étendue des deux côtés du fleuve Niger. . . . Les Européens font depuis quelques siècles commerce de ces malheureux esclaves. . . . ," Jacques Savary des Bruslons, *Dictionnaire universel de commerce: Contenant tout ce qui concerne le commerce qui se fait dans les quatre parties du monde* (Paris, 1723), cited in Delesalle and Valensi, "Le Mot 'nègre,'" p. 88. Savary's *Dictionnaire* was first published posthumously in Paris (1723–1730) by the author's brother. Later Parisian editions include those of 1741, 1748, and 1784–1789. Additional French-language editions were published in Amsterdam (1723–1732), Geneva (1742 and 1750),

Copenhagen (1759–1765; 1761–1762), and Liège (1770). I have consulted the 1759–1765 edition whose entry for *nègre* is identical with the 1723 text.

16. "Nègre, s.m. Mot tiré du latin Niger, qui signifie noir. L'usage a fait donner ce nom en général à toutes créatures humaines qui ont la peau noire; mais on le donne particulièrement à ces malheureux habitans de diverses parties de l'Afrique que les Européens achètent pour le service de leurs colonies. Les Physiciens ont fait de grandes recherches sur l'origine de la noirceur dans un grand nombre de Nations," Abbé Prévost d'Exiles, *Manuel lexique, ou dictionnaire portatif des mots français dont la signification n'est pas familière à tout le monde* (1750), cited in Delesalle and Valensi, "Le Mot 'nègre,'" p. 100.

17. For example, Trévoux's *Dictionnaire universel* . . . (editions of 1728, 1732, and 1740) offers the following geographical description (cited in Delesalle and Valensi, "Le Mot 'nègre,'" pp. 93–94): "*Nègre, esse.* s.m. et f. Nom propre de peuple habitant originaire de Nigritie. *Aethiopie, Niger, Nigra, Nigrita.* Le nom de *Nègre* n'est pas aujourd'hui synonyme d'Ethiopien, comme il le pourrait être en parlant de l'antiquité. L'Éthiopie ne s'etend pas autant que la Nigritie. Nous n'appelons Éthiopiens que les peuples qui sont au midi de l'Égypte, et au Levant des *Nègres*. . . . Au Pérou, il est expréssément défendu aux Noirs et aux Négresses d'avoir aucune communication personelle avec les Indiens et les Indiennes."

18. *Mémoire pour Francisque,* p. 26.

19. Ibid., p. 28.

20. Ibid., p. 27.

21. Ibid., p. 25.

22. Winthrop Jordan, *White over Black: American Attitudes toward the Negro, 1550–1812* (Chapel Hill: Univ. of North Carolina Press, 1968), pp. 7–11, and William B. Cohen, *The French Encounter with Africans: White Response to Blacks, 1530–1880* (Bloomington: Indiana Univ. Press, 1980), pp. 7–8, 13–15.

23. Over 2,000 works on world geography were published in France during the sixteenth and seventeenth centuries. Of these, 8 percent dealt with Africa and approximately one-quarter dealt with the Asian continent (Jean Meyer, *Les Européens et les autres de Cortès à Washington* [Paris: A. Colin, 1975], p. 6).

24. *Histoire générale des voyages,* (Paris: Didot, 1746), vol. 1, pp. 25, 232, 264, and 346; vol. 2, pp. 306, 343, and 504. Beginning with the French translation of John Greene's successful English compilation, *A New General Collection of Voyages and Travels* (London: T. Astley, 1745–47), Antoine François Prévost, known as Abbé Prévost d'Exiles, and his assistants churned out seventeen volumes of over 600 pages each until his death in 1763. Three additional posthumous works were added to the series by the end of the eighteenth century. The series contained scores of travelogues, arranged geographically, with lavish illustrations and maps. By the time of Francisque's case in 1759, volumes 1 to 15 had been published, covering the East Indies, Africa, Asia, Australia, and the Americas.

25. Ibid., vol. 5, p. 2.

26. Indeed, readers familiar with François Bernier's *Travels in the Mogul Empire, AD 1656–1668* may have already made that association (rev. ed. by Archibald Constable, [Delhi: S. Chand & Co., 1968]). Dedicated to Louis XIV, the work recounts the court intrigues of the powerful Mogol emperors Akbar, Shah Jahan, and Aurangzeb. Bernier's

account portrays the emperors' powers as equal to, if not greater than, those of the great Sun King himself. Incidentally, Bernier links lightness of skin with the power to rule in India: "To be considered a Mogol, it is enough if a foreigner have a white face and profess Mahometanism; in contradistinction to the Christians of Europe, who are called Franguis, and to the Hindus [*Indous*], whose complexion is brown, and who are called Gentiles" (*Travels in the Mogul Empire*, p. 3. The linkage between light skin and the ruling order is reiterated in another, lengthier, passage regarding the people of Kashmir, pp. 404–5). Bernier's account enjoyed numerous reprints and translations during the late seventeenth and early eighteenth centuries (e.g., those of Amsterdam in 1699, 1710, and 1724, plus the English translations published in London in 1671 and 1675).

27. *Mémoire pour Francisque*, p. 25.

28. Ibid., p. 26.

29. "Three causes, therefore must be admitted, as concurring in the production of those varieties which we have remarked among the different nations of this earth: 1. the influence of climate; 2. Food, which has a great dependence on climate; and, 3. Manners, on which climate has, perhaps, a still greater influence," G. L. Leclerc comte de Buffon, *Natural History, General and Particular, by the Count de Buffon*, trans. William Smellie, new ed., (London: T. Cadell and W. Davies, 1812), vol. 3, p. 374. Buffon is one of the first great "armchair anthropologists" who based their generalized theories on centuries of travelogue literature. His footnotes are full of citations to books by Dutch voyagers, Jesuit missionaries, English naturalists, and so on (including Prévost's *Histoire générale des voyages*). Because he has a particular theory to put forward, he can pick and choose the evidence he needs among thousands of accounts. His desire to prove the climatological origins of racial difference led him to distinguish among the peoples of Africa based on skin color and latitudinal habitat.

30. Ibid., pp. 381–82. Perhaps Buffon was influenced by the common prejudice that northern Europeans work harder than their indolent southern neighbors.

31. On the importance of Buffon in the anthropological writings of these and other French Enlightenment thinkers, see Michèle Duchet's *Anthropologie et histoire au siècle des lumières* (Paris: François Maspéro, 1971), pp. 329, 407, and 410. According to Duchet, Voltaire was also influenced by Buffon, if only in taking a strong opposition to him (pp. 294–302).

32. *Mémoire pour Francisque*, p. 26.

33. The translation I have consulted for this discussion is Charles Montesquieu, *The Spirit of the Laws*, trans. and ed. Anne Cohler, Basia Carolyn Miller, and Harold Samuel Stone, Cambridge Texts in the History of Political Thought (Cambridge: Cambridge Univ. Press, 1989). Like Buffon's *Histoire naturelle*, Montesquieu's *Esprit des lois* (1748) makes extensive use of travel literature in this case to compare the various legal practices throughout the world (see Muriel Dodds, *Les Récits de voyages: Sources de L'Esprit des lois de Montesquieu* [Paris: H. Champion, 1929]).

34. Montesquieu, *Spirit of the Laws*, Book 15, chap. 5.

35. Ibid., chaps. 7 and 9.

36. Albert Poirot, "Le milieu socio-professionel des avocats au parlement de Paris à la veille de la Révolution," Thesis of the Ecole des Chartes, 1977, vol. 2, p. 191, cited in David Avrom Bell, "Lawyers and Politics in Eighteenth-Century Paris (1700–1790)," Ph.D. diss., Princeton Univ., 1991, p. 46.

37. Yvan Debbasch, *Couleur et liberté: Le jeu du critère ethnique dans un ordre juridique esclavagiste; Tome I, L'affranchi dans les possessions françaises de la Caraïbe (1635–1833)* (Paris: Dalloz, 1967).

38. Pierre Boulle, "In Defense of Slavery: Eighteenth-Century Opposition to Abolition and the Origins of Racist Ideology in France," in *History from Below,* ed. Frederick Krantz (Oxford: Oxford University Press, 1988), p. 235.

39. As evidenced first here by the arguments put forward by Francique's lawyers, but amplified soon after in numerous public declarations by various government officials, it is clear that prejudice against blacks took on a particularly virulent form in public policy during the second half of the eighteenth century. Earlier legal formulations, such as the edict of 1716 and the declaration of 1738, stressed slave status over skin color. In 1738 a lawyer characterized Boucaux as "a man equal to us," and no one remarked on the skin color of his wife. By the 1750s, however, public utterances on blacks were less enthusiastic, if not downright intolerant. For example, the Paris admiralty court's 1762 ordinance, drafted by Guillaume Poncet de la Grave, abhorred the "disfigurement of the French nation" that would result from blacks increased arrival in France. An official report composed in 1776 urged an absolute ban on the arrival of all blacks in France and the creation of impediments to marriage between blacks by which "the race of negroes will be extinguished [in France]." These proposals culminated in the monumental *Police des Noirs* (1777) and subsequent legislation prohibiting marriages between blacks and whites (1778). All of these examples are discussed in the following chapters of this volume.

40. Boulle, "In Defense of Slavery," p. 237, n. 19 cites Jean Tarrade, *Le Commerce colonial de la France à la fin de l'ancien régime: L'évolution du régime de "l'Exclusif" de 1763 à 1789,* 2 vols. (Paris, 1972).

41. David Eltis, "Europeans and the Rise and Fall of African Slavery in the Americas: An Interpretation," *American Historical Review* 98, no. 5 (December 1993): 1415–1416.

42. It is true that other rationales were put forward: Africans could work in a tropical climate where Europeans could not, African slaves were prisoners of war spared from death by being sold into slavery, and so on.

43. This is true, although Brignon consistantly registered Francisque with the Admiralty in St. Malo throughout the 1750s.

44. *Mémoire pour Francisque,* pp. 31–33.

45. Ibid., p. 24.

46. Francisque's lawyers may not have stressed the fact that the Edict of 1716 and the Declaration of 1738 were unregistered because they were unsure whether the Parlement would accept this argument. Instead they focused on the racial argument (whether an Indian could be considered a *nègre*) and the argument that Brignon had failed to fulfill the requirements of the two laws. Their strategy may have been to test the Parlement with this case in order to cite it as precedent in future cases. (Remember that early modern French courts did not provide rationales with their decisions, so a win on any grounds was still a win and might be cited as precedent.)

47. Nicolas Toussaint Le Moyne Des Essarts, "Un Nègre et une négresse qui réclaiment leur liberté contre un juif," in *Causes célèbres, curieuses et intéressantes de toutes les cours souveraines du royaume avec les jugements qui les ont décidées,* 79 vols. (Paris: P.G. Simon, 1775–1789), vol. 36 (1777), p. 83.

48. Des Essarts, "Un Nègre et une négresse," pp. 80–81 (see my Chapter 7). More

immediately, in 1762 Guillaume Poncet de la Grave, the *procureur général* of the Paris Admiralty Court, blamed the increase in France's black population on the laws' lack of registration (see my Chapter 5).

49. See my Chapter 6.

50. Another example of the contemporaneous hardening of antiblack rhetoric and antislavery sentiment can be found in Corinne's 1755 petition for freedom, which begins, "Disant qu'elle a eu le malheur d'être née dans la nigritie . . . elle y est tombée sous l'esclavage dans l'age de dix ans," (Petition of Corinne, July 2, 1755 [A.N., Z¹D 130]).

51. The *Police des Noirs* legislation required all blacks in France, whether free or in the service of a master, to be registered by the nearest Admiralty clerk. Free blacks, such as Francisque, were enjoined to register themselves (see Chapter 7 in this volume).

52. "François Chavry, dit Francisque," registered at the Admiralty of Paris, July 14, 1777, giving as his address as "chez Madame la Duchess de Ville Roy, rue de l'Université," (A.N., Z¹D 139). He stated to the clerk that he had lived in France for "about twenty years," which diverges from the early Francisque's story by about seven years. François Chavry's declaration that he was "né libre" may be evidence that he is not the same Francisque. Other blacks freed by the courts attributed their freedom to a decision by a tribunal. On the other hand, he may have in fact been "born free" and then sold into slavery by his parents. It is possible that he preferred to style himself as freeborn since the term presumably carried less stigma.

Chapter 5. Crisis: Blacks in the Capital, 1762

1. As noted, this is probably because the Admiralty clerk stood to gain financially by accepting any declarations by slaveowners. Unless the clerk had received specific instructions *not* to accept the declarations, he had no reason to reject them.

2. For the sake of simplicity in this chapter I use the term *blacks* in a general sense to denote all nonwhites. As this chapter makes clear, the French nonwhite population comprised people of many complexions and many heritages.

3. Admiralty of France, *Minutes de Jugements,* March 30, 1762 (A.N., Z¹D 132). The case had apparently been working its way through the courts and various appeals since October 1759. Louis, too, was represented by Collet, the lawyer who represented Francisque in 1759 and most of the slaves who sued for their freedom in the 1750s. Collet was assisted in this case by Bigot, the *lieutenant général honoraire de l'Amirauté,* and Jean de L'Estang de la Ménarderie.

4. This figure comes from the report by De la Haye, "Sentence de règlement rendue en l'admirauté de la France concernant les déclarations a passer pour les Nègres et Mulatres," April 5, 1762 (A.N., Z¹D 139).

5. Poncet de la Grave's *réquisitoire* was quoted at length in De la Haye, "Sentence de règlement." Poncet de la Grave states that the Admiralty based its decision on "la maxime constante que tous les esclaves entrant en France devient libre [sic] de plein droit" (Poncet de la Grave in De la Haye, "Sentence de règlement," pp. 3ʳ⁻ᵛ). This implies that the laws of 1716 and 1738 were not seen as having a bearing on the case.

6. Guillaume Poncet de la Grave was *procureur général* of the Admiralty Court of France in Paris from 1758 until 1783. He seems to have had an important role in shaping government policy toward blacks and slaves, both in the report of 1762, which emphasized

the earlier laws' lack of registration, and in later correspondence with ministers concerning governmental policy.

7. Poncet de la Grave in De la Haye, "Sentence de règlement," p. 2ᵛ.

8. Ibid. This is the only reference to slave auctions in France that I have seen. Until further evidence for such sales comes to light, it is wise to treat this claim with some skepticism. Poncet de la Grave, as we shall see, had a penchant for alarmist rhetoric.

9. Poncet de la Grave in De la Haye, "Sentence de règlement," pp. 2ᵛ–3.

10. Ibid., p. 3.

11. This preoccupation manifests itself in the late 1770s in Poncet de la Grave's obsessive determination to arrest and interrogate black prostitutes (see Chapter 8 in this volume). His later writings also reveal a vivid preoccupation with the control of illicit sexuality, whether in the form of prostitution or miscegenation. See, for example, his *Considérations sur le célibat relativement à la politique, à la population, et aux bonnes mœurs* (Paris: Moutardier, An IX [1801]), esp. chaps. 6 and 7.

12. De la Haye, "Sentence de règlement," p. 4.

13. The original draft of the ordinance can be found in A.N., Z¹D 132. A printed version can be found in A.N. Col. F³ 90, fols. 91–94.

14. Shelby McCloy cites a printed copy of the ordinance in the Archives de la Charente Inférieure, B 5592 (*The Negro in France* [Lexington: Univ. of Kentucky Press, 1961] p. 45).

15. In fact, of the 158 blacks registered in Paris in 1762, 86 were registered in May, and 28 more in June, equalling 114, or 72 percent, within two months of the ordinance (A.N., Z¹D 139).

16. The fact that the Ordinance of 1762 encompassed free blacks as well as slaves no doubt helped to swell the numbers in 1762, but, as I will show, this factor alone cannot account for the vast discrepancy.

17. The fee charged by the Admiralty clerk for the process of registration may have dissuaded many individuals from making their declarations.

18. See Pierre Boulle's forthcoming study, *Being Black in Eighteenth-Century France: Non-White Residents According to the Census of 1777,* which analyzes the declarations of arrival at the various port cities. Many port declarations indicate the intent to seek apprenticeships in Paris, yet few of these blacks were declared in Paris.

19. The declarations of blacks in Paris, including those resulting from the 1762 Admiralty Ordinance, are preserved in registers (A.N., Z¹D 139.)

20. A quantitative study such as this tends to render its subjects anonymous. The names of blacks living in Paris include many of the classical Greek names that were popular for naming slaves in the colonies, such as Cupidon, Narcisse, Pyrame, Polidor, Olympien, Scipion, and Télémaque. Others retained names of their African or Indian heritage: Camba, Conpa, Latchimie, Pedre Alemgirin. Still others were named for flowering plants or other natural features: Jasmin, Amaranthe, Zéphir. Upon baptism, many blacks assumed a Christian name, indistinguishable from the names of whites: Pierre, Louis, Nicole, Thérèze, Jean-Baptiste. Only three blacks were registered in the 1762 accounts with last names (Guillaume Quénet, Hector Férère, André Coffy). Léo Elisabeth notes that beginning in 1752 colonies began to restrict the use of family names to whites only, "The French Antilles," in *Neither Slave Nor Free: The Freedmen of African Descent in the Slave Societies of the New World,* ed. David W. Cohen and Jack P. Greene (Baltimore: Johns Hopkins Univ. Press, 1972), p. 157.

21. The first official census of Paris was not conducted until 1801. Alan Williams describes the growth of the city during the late seventeenth century in *The Police of Paris, 1718–1789* (Baton Rouge: Louisiana State Univ. Press, 1979), pp. 20–22. He estimates the population to be approximately 475,000 to 515,000 in 1684. George Rudé estimates the population of Paris to be around 650,000 in 1789 (including around 100,000 transients), "Paris et Londres au XVIIIᵉ siècle: société et conflits de classes," *Annales Historiques de la Révolution Française* (1973): 481. The pattern seems to be one of steady growth over the course of the eighteenth century.

22. One person's sex was not indicated. For additional tables containing much of the information in this chapter, see my dissertation, " 'There Are No Slaves in France': Law, Culture, and Society in Early Modern France, 1685–1789," Univ. of Iowa, 1993, pp. 350–56, available through University Microfilms, Ann Arbor, MI.

23. David Geggus, "Sex Ratio, Age and Ethnicity in the Atlantic Slave Trade: Data from French Shipping and Plantation Records," *Journal of African History* 30 (1989): 23–25, and Arlette Gautier, "Les esclaves femmes aux Antilles françaises, 1635–1848," *Historical Reflections* 10 (1983): 419. Unfortunately, Méderic Louis Élie Moreau de Saint-Méry, the most thorough chronicler of the demographics of Saint Dominque, the largest of France's slaveholding colonies, does not indicate the sex ratio among slaves or freed people. See his *Description topographique, physique, civile, politique, et historique de la partie française de l'isle Saint-Domingue*, new ed., ed. Blanche Maurel and Etienne Taillemite, 3 vols. (Paris: Société de l'Histoire des Colonies Françaises, 1958), vol. 1, p. 100. Moreau de Saint-Méry, a native of Martinique who later practiced in Saint Domingue and wrote a thorough guide to French colonial law, originally published the *Description* in 1797 and 1798.

24. The following discussion derives mainly from Moreau de Saint-Méry, *Decription*, vol. 1, pp. 75–80, 83–111. For a more extensive analysis of the term *nègre*, see Chapter 4 of this volume.

25. For example, if a man was between 125 and 127 parts white, he would be considered *sang-mêlé*, or mixed blood (Moreau de Saint-Méry, *Description*, vol. 1, p. 100).

26. Moreau de Saint-Méry says that in common usage the term *mulâtre* referred to anyone of mixed lineage: "tout ce qui n'est pas nègre ou blanc" (*Description*, vol. 1, p. 103).

27. Winthrop Jordan notes that the term usually referred to an Indian-Negro mixture, but occasionally Indian-white. "American Chiaro-scuro: The Status and Definition of Mulattoes in the British Colonies," in *Slavery in the New World: A Reader in Comparative History*, ed. Laura Foner and Eugene D. Genovese (Englewood Cliffs, N.J.: Prentice-Hall, 1969), p. 191. See also Elisabeth, "The French Antilles," p. 134.

28. Moreau de Saint-Méry, *Description*, vol. 1, p. 100.

29. Margueritte registered with the admiralty on May 18, 1762 (A.N., Z¹D 139).

30. I have included Indians within the same regional grouping with East Africans because the migration of blacks between these ports was significant.

31. Paul E. Lovejoy, *Transformations in Slavery: A History of Slavery in Africa*, African Studies Series, no. 36 (Cambridge: Cambridge Univ. Press, 1983), p. 60. Philip Curtin's important study suggests that Indian Ocean trade never comprised more than 4 percent of French slave exports from Africa (*The Atlantic Slave Trade: A Census* [Madison: Univ. of Wisconsin Press, 1969], p. 200). Edward Alpers's work on the late-eighteenth-century Portuguese slave trade from Mozambique tends to confirm these lower

estimates (*Ivory and Slaves: Changing Patterns of International Trade in East Central Africa to the Later Nineteenth Century* [Berkeley: Univ. of California Press, 1975], p. 187). Joseph Harris, drawing on an earlier work by Alpers notes that the plantations on the Mascarene Islands created a demand for East African slaves beginning around 1735 (*The African Presence in Asia: Some Consequences of the East African Slave Trade* [Evanston, Ill.: Northwestern University Press, 1971], p. 8).

32. The remaining "probable creole" from West Africa lists his master's colony as Senegal and his natal origin as "Sevveds," January 28, 1762 (A.N., Z¹D 139).

33. Moreau de Saint-Méry, *Description*, vol. 1, p. 59.

34. The mean age was twenty-two. When two ages were given in the registers (e.g., "nine or ten years old"), I have adopted the older of the two.

35. Arlette Farge cites a case wherein two men, one of them a negro, beat a carriage driver with a cane on September 11, 1775 (*Vivre dans la rue à Paris au XVIIIe siècle* [Paris: Editions Gallimard/Julliard, 1979], p. 48). This is the only black I was able to discover in Farge's study of eighteenth-century Paris police reports, but Pierre Pluchon indicates that there is another incident, bringing the total of only two blacks in Farge's work (Pluchon, *Nègres et Juifs au XVIIIe siècle: Le racisme au siècle des Lumieres* (Paris: Tallandier, 1984), p. 133; Pluchon does not cite the pages of the incidents involving blacks in Farge's *Vivre dans la rue*).

36. Register of May 15, 1762 (A.N., Z¹D 139).

37. Figures compiled for manumission in the 1830s show women and children being freed in far greater numbers than men in Martinique, Guadeloupe, French Guiana, and Ile de Bourbon (Léo Elisabeth, "The French Antilles," p. 146).

38. The age of majority was established at 30 for males and 25 for females by civil statute in 1556. See François André Isambert, *Recueil général des anciennes lois françaises depuis l'an 420 jusqu'à la révolution de 1789* (Paris: Belin-Leprieur, 1830), vol. 13, pp. 469–71.

39. I have recorded a black as a slave only when the word *esclave* appears in the registers. Other language that appears to suggest this relationship is common, but not definitive, for example: "appartient à" ("belongs to"), "l'a donné à" ("gave him to"). One registration is revealing in this regard: Louis Joseph Meeger registered Gabriel Narcisse as "belonging to" M. le Prince. These words are scratched out and replaced with "being in the service of" M. le Prince, following the act of July 21, 1749, which freed him (registered April 7, 1763, A.N., Z¹D 139).

40. Jacques le Doux, registered May 5, 1762 (A.N., Z¹D 139).

41. For example, Claude Alexandre le Grand, François Polidor, Charlotte, and Arthemise (registered May 5, 1762); St. Louis (registered May 8, 1762); and Louis, dit Paté (registered May 22, 1762 [A.N., Z¹D 139]).

42. For example, Jean Hilaire (registered May 8, 1762); St. Louis, baptized in Paris at St. Jacques du haut pas on July 17, 1749, freed on August 8, 1749 (registered June 3, 1762); and Michel, who was given his freedom by M. de la Care, but who lost the *acte de liberté* (registered June 7, 1762 [A.N., Z¹D 139]). These *actes* were issued either by the former master or by the Admiralty tribunal (see the discussion in Chapter 6 of this volume).

43. Perhaps Thérèze, identified as having been nursed by the same woman as his own daughter, was actually Febvre's daughter. It is also possible that this was the same Jean

Jacques le Febvre who lost his case against Louis, the mulatto, which spawned the registration drive of 1762 (registered May 12, 1762 [A.N., Z¹D 139]).

44. Elizabeth, "The French Antilles," p. 141.

45. Campigny and d'Orgeville to Maurepas, June 29, 1934 (A.N., Colonies C⁸A 47, fol. 82), cited in ibid.

46. The notion that baptism conferred freedom in England and the English colonies persisted through the late seventeenth and early eighteenth centuries. In some instances it was codified (e.g., Jamaica until 1717, and under the rules of the East India Company), whereas in others (e.g., England) it remained only customary (Seymour Drescher, *Capitalism and Anti-Slavery: British Mobilization in Comparative Perspective* [New York: Macmillan, 1986], pp. 32–35). See also Carol Phillips Bauer, "Law, Slavery, and Sommersett's Case in Eighteenth-Century England: A Study of the Legal Status of Freedom," Ph.D. diss., New York Univ., 1973, pp. 12–13; F. O. Shyllon, *Black Slaves in Britain* (London: Institute for Race Relations, 1974), pp. 20, 25; and F. O. Shyllon, *Black People in Britain, 1555–1833* (London: Pluto Press, 1984), pp. 17–20.

47. Registered May 18, 1762 (A.N., Z¹D 139). Margueritte, who was sent by Vincent François Marie Houdayer du Percival to his wife in 1758 to serve as a *femme de chambre*, was baptized in Ile de France. S. du Percival stated that he "regards her as a free person," though whether this was a result of her baptism or not is not clear (May 18, 1762).

48. Registered July 20, 1762 (A.N., Z¹D 139). It is remarkable that Joseph registered himself this way with the Admiralty, apparently without fear of being confiscated and returned to his former master. This is strong evidence that confiscation was totally out of use by 1762 within the jurisdiction of Paris.

49. According to the Admiralty clerk's registers, the following slaves received their freedom from the admiralty: Pierre Fidel (registered May 7, 1762); Louis in August, 1750 (May 14, 1762); François in Paris on May 14, 1759 (registered May 19, 1762); André, dit Lucidor, in Paris on March 26, 1750 (May 24, 1762 [A.N., Z¹D 139]). The statements of Pierre Fidel and François are verified by Admiralty Court records (Pierre Fidel won his freedom in a lawsuit ended on February 13, 1761; François by an *acte de liberté* of April 4, 1759), but the statements of Louis and André, dit Lucidor, are not verified in the Admiralty Court records for those dates (A.N., Z¹D 131). In the last instance, this may be because, as stated in the clerk's register, André, dit Lucidor, "has declared to be free by an act passed before the notaries of this court . . . by Sir Blancheton, counselor to the king." In other words, the seat of the Admiralty provided other avenues to freedom besides its court.

50. Registered June 2, 1762 (A.N., Z¹D 139).

51. Their names are Jerome Richard Konoki, Kenothy, or Koanruly (first registered May 22, 1758, by Sr. Delacroix for Dame Prettsy Irlandoise; again on January 7, 1761, by Dame Irlandoise herself; and he registered himself on May 10, 1762, and signed his name "Koanruly"; perhaps "Kennedy" would be the modern spelling of his name?); Pierre Fidel (signed "Fidelle" on May 7, 1762), Louis Claude, dit Ursule (registered Louis Claude Ursule on May 8, 1762); André, dit Lucidor (signed "Lucidor" on May 24, 1762); Guillaume Quenot (signed "Quenot" on May 25, 1762); Sr. Etienne Douset (signed "Douset" on June 14, 1762); and André Coffy (registered June 18, 1762 [A.N., Z¹D 139]).

52. André Coffy was the tailor, André, dit Lucidor, was a fencing master at the Abbey

St. Martin, Guillaume Quenot was a fencing master "au Grand Courier," and Pierre Fidel was "au service de Madame Desbline." The other two did not specify their trades.

53. Elisabeth, "The French Antilles," p. 158.

54. Only fifteen blacks signed upon registration in Bordeaux between 1740 and 1787 (Elisabeth, "The French Antilles," p. 158). Elisabeth does not indicate the specific decades during which these declarations were made. It would also be useful to know the total number of registrants for this period and a breakdown for the categories of race, sex, age, and origin. On the education of blacks in Paris, see section on "Purpose and Trade" below.

55. This is borne out by the white registrants who declared their blacks as slaves in 1762. Of the twenty-one registrants who were declared as slaves in 1762, only four neglected to mention either instruction in Catholicism or training in a trade as the purposes for bringing the slaves to France.

56. Registers of May 10, 1762; May 13, 1762; and May 12, 1762, respectively (A.N., Z¹D 139).

57. Thirteen declarations did not specify the place of baptism.

58. Dame Marie Anne Godefroy, widow of Sr. Charles Duvivien Bourgogne first registered three blacks in 1756. She reregistered them in compliance with the law in 1757 and 1758. Beginning in 1760, she petitioned the king annually for three years to extend their stay in Paris for continued religious instruction. Dame Godefroy is unusual in her persistent compliance with the letter of the law, though her insistence on six years of religious instruction sheds doubt on her complicity with its spirit (December 16, 1756; December 17, 1757; December 16, 1758; May 5, 1760; February 27, 1761; January 30, 1762 [A.N., Z¹D 139]).

59. Article 3 in Isambert, *Recueil*, vol. 22, p. 113.

60. Marie Pepin and Nicole, both female mulattoes, were brought to Paris by Nicolas le Buisson Moriniere. He explains his purpose for bringing them to France in 1756 in this way: "Sa femme et un enfant agé de deux ans se trouvaient alors éxtrémement malade par le séjour de trente ans que ledit déclarant avait fait à St. Domingue quartier Port-au-Prince et qu'en consequence M. le Vaudreuil alors général lui permit d'ammener avec lui pour le soigner ainsi que sa femme et son enfant les nommées, Pepin, pour apprendre la cuisine sous une cuisinière qu'il avait chez lui, et Nicole, pour apprendre couture chez Mlle la Baume Mlle Couturière à Paris. Il entend les renvoyer au moment de la paix" (register of May 3, 1762). Jean, a negro boy aged 12, was similarly brought from St. Domingue by Louis Fourneau who, "étant depuis longtemps malade il auroit obtenu de M. Bar, Général de ladit Isle la permission de venir en France rétablit sa santé et d'emmener avec lui pour le soigner un jeune négrillon," the aforenamed Jean (register of May 5, 1762). The fourth apprentice was Louis Charles, dit Lamon [sp?], who was apprenticed to the hatmaker, M. Gravems [sp?] (register of July 13, 1762 [A.N., Z¹D 139]).

61. L'Eucille was born an Ibo in today's eastern Nigeria (Register for June 8, 1762 [A.N., Z¹D 139]).

62. François Couy (registered May 5, 1762); André, dit Lucidor (May 24, 1762); Guillaume Quenot (May 25, 1762); and Sr. Etienne Douset (June 14, 1762).

63. The practice of servants living in the homes of their masters is well documented. See Daniel Roche, *The People of Paris: An Essay in Popular Culture in the Eighteenth Century,* trans. Marie Evans with Gwynne Lewis (New York: Berg, 1987), pp. 104–106,

and David Garrioch, *Neighborhood and Community in Paris, 1740–1790,* Cambridge Studies in Early Modern History, (Cambridge: Cambridge Univ. Press, 1986), p. 131.

64. The parishes, *quartiers,* and regions listed in the registers include St. André des Arts, St. Benoît, St. Eustache, St. Germain, St. Germain l'Auxerrois, St. Germain le Viel, St. Honoré, St. Jacques la Boucherie, St. Jacques de l'Hospital, St. Jacques de l'Haut Pas, St. Jean en Grève, St. Louis de Louvre, St. Laurent, la Madeleine, St. Méderic, St. Merri, St. Nicolas des Champs, St. Paul, St. Roch, St. Sulpice, St. Sauveur, St. Séverin, the Marais, the university quarter, the Faubourg St. Germain, Montmartre, Champagne, Mâcon, Rouen, and Versailles.

65. Garrioch, *Neighborhood and Community,* p. 10.

66. The addresses registered for the thirty-four domestic servants (including cooks) include: St. Roch (8), St. Sulpice (4), St. Nicolas des Champs (2), St. André des Arts (2), St. Eustache (2), St. Germain (2), Faubourg St. Germain (2), St. Honoré (1), St. Jean de l'Haut Pas (1), St. Laurent (1), St. Louis de Louvre (1), la Madeleine (1), St. Séverin (1), Mâcon (1), Versailles (1), and four unknown.

67. *Almanach Royal* (Paris, 1762), p. 258.

68. Marie, *mulâtresse,* aged 21, and Augustin, *nègre,* aged 14, lived with their mistress, Madame Elizabeth Hargenvillier in the Marais district (June 7, 1762 [A.N., Z¹D 139]).

69. The word *hôtel* is sometimes used to denote great private houses (e.g., "Hôtel Conti"), but here some (e.g., "Hôtel des deux suites," "Hotel de l'aigle d'or") are clearly inns for travelers.

70. The addresses for the twenty-one self-registrants were located in the following parishes: St. Eustache (3), Faubourg St. Germain (3), St. Roch (3), St. Germain (2), St. Germain l'Auxerrois (1), St. Nicolas des Champs (1), and unknown (8).

71. Addresses given for those among the skilled trades include: St. Eustache (7), St. Nicolas des Champs (2), St. Germain (2), Faubourg St. Germain (1), St. Benoît (1), St. Mederic (1), St. Jacques de l'Hôpital (1), Versailles (1), and unknown (2).

72. "Letter du Ministre aux Administrateurs, qui défend d'accorder aucun passage pour France aux Esclaves et aux nègres libres," June 30, 1763, in Moreau de Saint-Méry, *Loix et constitutions des colonies françoises de l'Amérique sous le vent,* 6 vols. (Paris, 1784–1790), vol. 4, p. 602. The letter cited here was addressed to the administrators of Saint Domingue, but correspondence between the intendant of Metz and the minister of the marine makes it clear that a similar letter circulated within France (see later).

73. Letter from Bernage de Vaux, intendant of Metz, to Choiseul, July 16, 1763, and poster, "Nègres-esclaves" (A.N., Marine, B³ 560, fol. 72–74).

74. "Lettre de Fénélon au ministre," April 11, 1764 (A.N., Col. F³ 90, fol. 107.) The notion that slaves who had experienced life in France and returned to the colonies were responsible for spreading discontent was a common theme in the late eighteenth century. Emilien Petit commented on it in 1777: "I perceive the greatest dangers for the public security and the maintainance of the subordination of the slaves [who] stayed in the colonies when the slaves, returning from France, carry a spirit of equality, that a same service, a same livery, puts between the whites and the blacks a familiarity which lifts the blacks' hearts and degrades the whites in their opinion," (*Traité sur le gouvernement des esclaves,* 2 vols. [Paris, 1777], vol. 2, p. 99). One decade later, Pierre Régis Dessalles, a lawyer who practiced in Martinique, would write: "It is inconceivable how this multitude

of Blacks who has been to France since the peace of 1763 has changed the spirit and the manners of the slaves of our Colonies. The Negroes are no longer what they were thirty or forty years ago; it would seem, in watching them, that they had all read the passage regarding them in [Abbé Raynal's] *Histoire philosophique & politique du commerce des Européens dans les deux Indes,* in which the Author appears to have consulted more the brilliance of his imagination than the lights of reason and a sane politic. The Slaves live no longer but in the ideas of liberty which they try to procure in all manners'' (*Annales du Conseil Souverain de la Martinique,* 2 vols. [Bergerac: chez J. B. Puynesge, 1786], vol. 2, pp. 349–50).

75. Lucien Peytraud, *L'Esclavage aux Antilles françaises avant 1789, d'après des documents inédits des archives coloniales* (Paris: Librairie Hachette, 1897), p. 388.

76. Here are the numbers of blacks registered with the Paris Admiralty in the following years: 1763 (30); 1764 (3); 1765 (19); 1766 (26); 1767 (9); 1768 (9); 1769 (8); 1770 (8); 1771 (2); 1772 (2); 1773 (1); 1774 (8); 1775 (1); 1776 (13) (A.N., Z¹D 139). It should be remembered that the Admiralty ordinance of 1762 required all *blacks* to register, as opposed to *slaves,* and only once, as opposed to annually.

77. See Peytraud on these documents, *L'Esclavage aux Antilles,* pp. 388–89.

78. These orders were issued on March 13 and October 3, 1769, according to Emilien Petit, *Traité sur le gouvernement des esclaves,* 2 vols. (Paris: Knapen, 1777), vol. 2, pp. 99–100.

79. The obvious place to look for evidence to substantiate Poncet de la Grave's claim are the Police records for this period. I have not made a systematic study of them, but it may be significant that those who have studied police files do not note the presence of blacks as an important factor. See, for example, Arlette Farge, *Vivre dans la rue*; Daniel Roche, *The People of Paris*; David Garrioch, *Neighborhood and Community in Paris*; and Allan Williams, *Police of Paris.*

Chapter 6. Antislavery and Antidespotism, 1760–1771

1. Only thirteen slaves had initiated lawsuits for freedom between 1730 and 1759, but seventy-one slaves sought their freedom this way during the 1760s. At the same time, a similar increase in the number of manumissions, or *actes de liberté,* granted by slave-owners occurred during this period. From 1730 to 1760, the court recorded only two such *actes de liberté*; during the 1760s alone, this number increased to eleven.

2. For the sake of simplicity, I have referred to the two parties in this discussion as ''slave'' and ''master,'' although, strictly speaking, neither term is correct because the court uniformly ruled that the petitioner had been free since his or her arrival in France.

3. In the first petitions of the 1760s, domestics requested between 100 and 300 *livres* per year for back wages, but the court only awarded them 100 per annum. After 1762, the going rate was raised to 120 *livres* per year (see the petition of Jean Baptiste, who requested 300 *livres* [December 10, 1762, A.N., Z¹D 132] but was awarded 120 *livres* by the court [Sentence of January 17, 1763, A.N., Z¹D 26]). Pélagie, a negress, sued her mistress Dame Julie D'Uttrousset d'Hericourt, widow of Sir Butler, for 120 *livres* per year plus interest, and 300 *livres* for ''alimentary provision'' while imprisoned at the Châtelet (*Sentence en l'Amirauté,* March 23, 1763 [A.N., Z¹D 132]). Pauline won back wages

(120 *livres* per year) plus 1,200 *livres,* which she had "confided [to her master] at different times in the Ile de France deriving from her savings and the commerce which she had the freedom to do" plus interest and costs (*Sentence contradictoire en l'amirauté,* March 18, 1765 [A.N., Z¹D 132]).

4. See, for example, the sentence for Isabel Flore Durosol, September 10, 1760, which promised safeguard in Guyenne, Bretagne, and Paris (A.N., Z¹D 131).

5. This is based on my examination of the "Minutes de Jugement: Admirauté de France," for the period from 1723 to 1790 (A.N., Z¹D 125–37) and the "Registres d'Audience" from 1761 to 1790 (A.N., Z¹D 26–28).

6. Petitions give the following places of origin: Senegal, Guinea, Martinique, Guadeloupe, Saint Domingue, New Orleans, Pondichéry, Bengal, Bombay, Madagascar, Ile de France, Ile Maurice, England, France, Batavia (in the Dutch Indies), Santo Domingo (in the Spanish Caribbean), and Balasor (in Asia).

7. This figure is based upon 32 petitions dated 1760 to 1769 wherein the length of time in France is mentioned (A.N., Z¹D 131–33). There seems to be no consistant pattern regarding the amount of time a slave spent in France before suing for freedom. Many sued within three years of arrival, but others waited a decade or more.

8. Véronique, a black woman born on a plantation in Saint Domingue, had been brought to France in 1748. She served her mistress until the woman's death in 1761. At some point she married Sr. Pillard, a master surgeon in Rouen. It was his second marriage, after the death of his first wife. Later she "left the service of her husband" and continued to serve in Paris in the capacity of cook but, wishing "to assure the state of freedom which she acquired upon arriving in France," petitioned the court for affirmation of her free status (Petition of Véronique, negress, July 30, 1764 [A.N., Z¹D 132]). Marie Thérèze Urselle had married Pierre Adrien, creole of Saint Domingue in 1754 at the age of ten, but the man she named as her master was Sr. Miton de Senneville (Petition of Marie Thérèze Urselle, September 11, 1766 [A.N., Z¹D 133]).

9. See the petitions of Jean Baptiste (July 22, 1763), André Bordmarc (November 21, 1763), Louis (December 5, 1763), Antoine Thomas (June 6, 1764), and Emmanuel Vettout (June 25, 1764 [A.N., Z¹D 132]).

10. For example, Pierre Louis Hamar and Jean Narcisse (petitions of January 23, 1764 and April 17, 1765, respectively [A.N., Z¹D 132]).

11. Petition of Odissen Postillon, December 16, 1766 (A.N., Z¹D 133). These grounds inferred by implication the validity of either or both the Edict of 1716 and the Declaration of 1738. If the petitioner was demanding freedom on the basis of the latter, the law would have required that he be confiscated by the king and returned to the colonies. Instead, the court awarded him protection in a provisional sentence that was never followed up with an audience. Not surprisingly, this was the lawyer Sasserie's first (and only) venture at a slave's petition.

12. See the petitions for Paul (December 22, 1762) and Odissen Postillon (December 16, 1766 [A.N., Z¹D 132]).

13. For example: "Tout esclave entrant en France est libre" (Petition of Séraphine Bertrand, December 17, 1762, represented by Jean De l'Estang); "Nul n'est esclave en France" (Petition of Paul December 22, 1762, represented by Jean De l'Estang); "Toutte [sic] personnes sont libres en France" (Petition of Victor Goret, July 2, 1766, represented by Pierre Etienne Regnaud [A.N., Z¹D 132 and 133]).

14. "Les suppliants sont libres par les principes constitutifs de la monarchie" (Petition of Remon and Marie Françoise Scipion, April 28, 1766, drafted by Poussavain).

15. "Il n'y a point d'esclave en France aux termes des édits, ordonnances, et déclarations de sa majesté" (Petition of François Gabriel, dit Le Blanc, September 5, 1767). See also, "Aux termes des édits et déclarations de sa majesté il n'y a aucun esclave en France" (Petition of Jean Baptiste Auajou, October 14, 1768); the petition of Favori, May 29, 1769; and the petition of Auguste, October 26, 1769, all drafted by Regnaud (A.N., Z¹D 133).

16. See, for example, the petition of Dodo, October 26, 1767, drafted by the lawyer Chrestien (A.N., Z¹D 133).

17. In at least one instance, a master ignored the court's ruling and forced his former slave to return to the colonies, but the Admiralty's provisional sentence won the petitioner's case in the colonial court and he was returned to France. Charles August petitioned for his freedom on February 4, 1763, and was awarded provisional safeguard of the king and the court. At the Admiralty Court audience of February 11, 1763, the judges decided by default against his master, who apparently did not show up. Finally, on April 22, the court awarded Charles Auguste his freedom and 120 *livres* per year for wages (A.N., Z¹D 132; A.N., Z¹D 26). But in 1765 the court received a packet of documents from the *conseil supérieur* of the Ile de France that stated that Charles Auguste was being returned by boat to France after successfully producing a copy of his provisional sentence awarded by the court (A.N., Z¹D 132).

18. See the *Sentence en l'Amirauté du Palais,* March 23, 1763 (A.N., Z¹D 26; A.N., Z¹D 132).

19. See the sentences of March 28 and June 20 (A.N., Z¹D 26; A.N., Z¹D 132). In a similar countersuit, Peidre won his freedom and the return of his clothes and belongings but no wages (see the sentences of February 22, May 13, and June 28, 1765, A.N., Z¹D 26; A.N., Z¹D 132).

20. A.N., Z¹D 132. Poncet de la Grave also requested that the petitioner be permitted to see "whatever surgeon he chooses."

21. Admiralty Sentence of August 20, 1762 (A.N., Z¹D 26).

22. Petitions of Camille and Marie Anne, December 17, 1762 (A.N., Z¹D 132).

23. Petitions for Louis Patté (February 21, 1763), Marie (July 27, 1763), and Moniche Nannon (August 22, 1763, A.N., Z¹D 132).

24. Petition for Jacques le Doux, dit Hippolite, and Anne Dïaconce, his wife, October 12, 1764 (A.N., Z¹D 132).

25. Petition of Dominique Julien dit Narcisse, November 28, 1766 (A.N., Z¹D 133).

26. See the *Acte de liberté, requête,* and *sentence,* of August 1, 1768 (A.N., Z¹D 133).

27. See, for example, the petitions by Pierre Louis Hamar (January 23, 1764), Hazan (November 26, 1764), Peidre (February 22, 1765), Charles Dominique Lazy (April 5, 1765), and Jean Narcisse (April 17, 1765, A.N., Z¹D 132). Interestingly, if their petitions can be believed, none of these slaves was born into American slavery. Pierre Louis Hamar and Jean Narcisse were born free in Africa; Hazan in Pondicherry, India; Peidre in "Cantorbery des Indes" or "San Fran Conty Bellony" (perhaps in New Zealand?); and Charles Dominique Lazy in Angoulême, France. In each case, they had been sold into slavery and their current masters wished to take them or arrange for them to be taken as slaves to America (Pierre Louis Hamar's master intended to sell him to Americans). It

seems plausible that their masters' plans were prompted by the government's threat of confiscation.

28. David Avrom Bell, *Lawyers and Citizens: The Making of a Political Elite in Old Regime France* (New York: Oxford Univ. Press, 1994), pp. 26–40.

29. David Avrom Bell, "Lawyers and Politics in Eighteenth-Century Paris (1700–1790)," Ph.D. diss., Princeton Univ., 1991, p. 31.

30. Bell, *Lawyers and Citizens,* p. 40.

31. The *peculium,* a tradition dating from ancient Rome, permitted slaves to use property, including cash, which technically belonged to their masters (Alan Watson, *Slave Law in the Americas* (Athens: Univ. of Georgia Press, 1989), p. 24. This tradition was picked up by the French in the Code Noir, which held that "slaves shall not be permitted to own anything that does not belong to their masters; and whatever may come to them through hard work or the liberality of other persons . . . shall be acquired to the full estate of their Masters" (article 28). Article 10 of the Edict of October 1716 further stipulated that if slaves should die while in France, their *peculium* would revert to the master. In the early years of the nineteenth century, a visitor to Louisiana observed, "The law here does not specifically grant to them a *pecula,* but if they take advantage of the hours of the day that are left to them and their Sundays to obtain money of their own it belongs legally to them. It must be admitted that in spite of the sordid interests of the majority of the masters, that the property that a slave requires [sic] on his own, is almost universally respected, and infractions of this custom are rare" (C. C. Robin, *Voyage to Louisiana: An Abridged Translation,* trans. Stuart O. Landry, Jr. [New Orleans: Pelican, 1966], pp. 242–43).

Because the courts of Paris uniformly ruled that slaves were free upon their arrival in France, their free status would presumably enable them to own property outright. I have not seen any instances where this particular issue was addressed directly by the courts, however.

32. Bell, "Lawyers and Politics," pp. 249–50.

33. Ibid., p. 277.

34. On the refusal of the sacraments controversy, see Jean Egret's *Louis XV et l' opposition parlementaire 1715–1774* (Paris: Armand Colin, 1970), chap. 2, and Dale Van Kley, *The Damiens Affair and the Unraveling of the Ancien Régime, 1750–1770* (Princeton: Princeton Univ. Press, 1984), chap. 3.

35. On the mid-1750s rivalry between the *Grand Conseil* and the parlements, see Jean Egret, *Louis XV et l' opposition parlementaire,* pp. 72–76, and Jean Paul Laurent, "Grand Conseil," in *Guide des fonds judiciaires dans l'ancien régime* (Paris: Imprimerie Nationale, 1958), pp. 29–32.

36. Egret (*Louis XV et l' opposition parlementaire,* pp. 140–81) and J. H. Shennan (*The Parlement of Paris* [Ithaca: Cornell Univ. Press, 1968], pp. 316–17) emphasize the unity of the sovereign courts in their opposition to Louis XV. For a different interpretation of this conflict, see Steven L. Kaplan, *Bread, Politics, and Political Economy in the Reign of Louis XV,* 2 vols. (The Hague: Martinus Nijhoff, 1976). Kaplan argues that the liberalization of the grain trade led to panic over rising prices in the mid–1760s. In contrast to Egret and Shennan, Kaplan argues that the grain crisis split the courts and also the *philosophes* in their commitment to liberty in all its forms.

37. Egret, *Louis XV et l' opposition parlementaire,* p. 178.

38. Ibid., p. 190.

39. Ibid., pp. 197–202.

40. On the formation of public opinion under the Maupeou regime, see Shanti Marie Singham, "A Conspiracy of Twenty Million Frenchmen: Public Opinion, Patriotism, and the Assault on Absolutism during the Maupeou Years, 1770–1775," Ph.D. diss., Princeton Univ., 1991. Singham's latest work on Maupeou will soon be published as *Rehearsal for Revolution: The Maupeou Crisis and the Making of Political Consciousness in France, 1771–1775*.

41. Bell, *Lawyers and Citizens*, p. 139.

42. Ibid., p. 144.

43. Bell, *Lawyers and Citizens*, pp. 145–48. The royalists' support for Maupeou is not difficult to understand. "Enlightened" lawyers may have initially been attracted to Maupeou's attempts to bring order to the unwieldy Parisian judicial system while they opposed the *parlementaire*'s Jansenist piety.

44. See Jean-Jacques Rousseau, *Discours sur l'origine et les fondements de l'inégalité parmi les hommes*, intro. by F. C. Greene (Cambridge: Cambridge Univ. Press, 1941). Both this *Second Discourse* (1753) and the first, on whether sciences and the arts have contributed to the purification of morals (1750), were composed as entries to essay contests sponsored by the Académie de Dijon.

45. Jean-Jacques Rousseau, *On the Social Contract*, ed. Roger Masters, trans. Judith R. Masters (New York: St. Martin's Press, 1978), p. 46. The original title was: *Du Contrat social ou principes du droit politique*.

46. Rousseau, *On the Social Contract*, p. 49.

47. Jean-Baptiste Pigalle to Voltaire, July 23, 1763, Letter 10494 in *Voltaire's Correspondence*, ed. Theodore Besterman (Geneva: Institut et Musée Voltaire, 1953), vol. 52, p. 183.

48. Ibid.

49. I have worked with the later edition, Guillaume Thomas Raynal, *Histoire philosophique et politique des établissemens et du commerce des Européens dans les deux Indes*, 5 vols. (Geneva: J. L. Pellet, 1780).

50. Michèle Duchet, *Diderot et l'Histoire des Deux Indes, ou, l'écriture fragmentaire* (Paris: Nizet, 1978), *passim*.

51. See, for example, the passage beginning, "Nous avons vu d'immenses contrées envahies & dévastées; leur innocens & tranquilles habitans, ou massacrés, ou chargés de chaînes" (Raynal, *Histoire des Deux Indes*, vol. 3, p. 91).

52. See the arguments against the enslavement of blacks in the Americas, ibid., pp. 186–205.

53. Ibid., vol. 3, p. 230.

54. Ibid., p. 197.

55. Petition of January 5, 1770 (A.N., Z¹D 134).

56. Poupet's petitions of January 18 and 20 were summarized in the Admiralty's decision of March 2, 1770 (A.N., Z¹D 134).

57. Also cited in the decision of March 2, 1770 (A.N., Z¹D 134).

58. A.N., Z¹D 26.

59. Much of the following information comes from Jean François Michaud's *Biographie universelle ancienne et moderne* (Paris, 1818; reprint Graz, Austria: Akademische Druck- u. Verlaganstatt, 1968) vol. 19, pp. 214–17. After the Maupeou crisis Henrion

published several articles on feudalism (including "Fief" and "Féodalité") in Panckoucke's *Encyclopédie méthodique,* a revised version of Diderot's *Encyclopédie.* (On Panckoucke's encyclopedia, see Robert Darnton, *The Business of Enlightenment: A Publishing History of the Encyclopédie, 1775–1800* [Cambridge: Belknap, 1979], chap. 8). Later, Henrion distanced himself from the Revolution and survived the Terror in retreat in his native Pansey *(Biographie Universelle,* p. 215). He reemerged into public life under Napoleon, who consulted Henrion on matters of state (p. 216).

60. Michaud, *Biographie Universelle,* vol. 19, pp. 214–15. The same account also lists the publication of the *Eloge de Mathieu Molé* in Paris and Geneva in 1771 (p. 215), though I have not been able to find references to it in the catalogue to the Bibliothèque Nationale. Another project developed by Henrion during the Maupeou hiatus was a biography of the abbot Pluche, a cleric accused of Jansenism (Pierre Paul Nicolas Henrion de Pansey, "L'Abbé Pluche," *Galerie françoise* 2:8 [1772]).

61. Pierre Paul Nicolas Henrion de Pensey [sic], *Discours prononcé à la rentrée de la Conférence publique de messieurs les avocats au Parlement de Paris, le 13 janvier 1775* (Lausanne, 1775).

62. Michaud, *Biographie Universelle,* vol. 19, p. 214.

63. Sara Maza, "Le Tribunal de la nation: Les mémoires judiciaires et l'opinion publique à la fin de l'ancien régime," *Annales ESC* (January–February 1987): 73–90. See also Shanti Marie Singham, "'A Conspiracy of Twenty Million Frenchmen': Public Opinion, Patriotism, and the Assault on Absolutism during the Manpesee Years, 1770–1775," Ph.D. diss., Princeton Univ., 1991, p. 62, n. 132, and David Bell, *Lawyers and Citizens,* pp. 83, 87–89.

64. [Pierre Paul Nicolas] Henrion de Pensey [sic], *Mémoire pour un nègre qui réclame sa liberté* (n.p.: L'Imprimerie de J. Th. Hérissant, Imprimeur du Cabinet du Roi, 1770). The *mémoire* is also signed by Poncet de la Grave, *procureur du roi,* and De Fossi, *procureur.*

In one very interesting way, the story of the individual Roc parallels Henrion's history of the spread of slavery in general. Following natural law, all men—like Roc—are born free. The Spaniards are responsible, in Henrion's text, for spreading slavery in the New World. But the French are not innocent and perpetuate the slavery of Africans, just as Roc endures slavery under the French in Louisiana. Both stories culminate in the attempted transference of slavery to France itself.

65. The emphasis on Roc's free birth derives from the natural law argument that all men are born free. Coming from the same source, it also resonates with Rousseau's dictum, "Man is born free and everywhere he is in chains," (*On the Social Contract,* p. 46).

66. According to the *mémoire,* Poupet failed to obtain permission from the governor of Louisiana to transport Roc to France, he did not register Roc upon arrival in Paris, and he neglected to list the slave's name or description (presumably in the registration at La Rochelle) (Henrion, *Mémoire,* p. 22).

67. "It's the spirit of the nation; spirit all the more estimable as the purety of the religion professed in these happy climates seems to animate it. . . . Are you Christian? Every Christian is your brother: as such, you can not obligate another to more than you can demand of yourself. . . . Here is the spirit of Christianity: here is the spirit of France" (Joly de Fleury et al., *Mémoire signifié pour le nommé Francisque, Indien de Nation,*

Néophyte de l'Eglise Romaine, Intimé; contre le Sieur Allain-François-Ignace Brignon, se disant Ecuyer, Appellant (Paris: P. G. Simon, Imprimeur du Parlement, 1759), p. 17.

68. Poncet de la Grave in De la Haye, "Sentence de règlement," p. 1ᵛ.

69. Henrion de Pensey, *Mémoire pour un nègre,* pp. 4–5.

70. Ibid., pp. 6–7.

71. Jean Baptiste Labat, *Nouveau voyage du père Labat en Amérique* (Paris: P. F. Giffart, 1722), vol. 4, p. 114. I have not been able to corroborate this anecdote in any earlier source.

72. The lawyers for both slave and master argued that slavery was necessary for the colonies in *Jean Boucaux v. Sr. Verdelin* (1738) [François Gayot de Pitaval], *Causes célèbres et intéressantes, avec les jugemens qui les ont décidées* (Paris: Jean de Nully, 1747), pp. 521–22, 552–53. Francisque's lawyer did not challenge the necessity of slavery in France's American colonies, since his argument turned on portraying Francisque as a native of a "civilized" country (Joly de Fleury, pp. 26–27). Poncet de la Grave gave credence to the notion of the "necessity" of slavery: "Uniquement destinés à la culture de nos colonies, la necessité les y a introduits, cette même necessité les y conserve, on n'avait jamais pensé qu'ils vinssent[?] trainer leurs chaines dans le sein du Royaume" (Poncet de la Grave in De la Haye, "Sentence de règlement," p. 2ᵛ).

73. Henrion de Pensey, *Mémoire pour un nègre,* p. 27.

74. "Est-ce que la moralité de nos actions varie comme les climats? Est-ce que ce qui est injuste sous une latitude, peut être juste sous un autre?" Henrion de Pensey, *Mémoire pour un nègre,* p. 12.

75. Ibid., p. 28. Edward Derbyshire Seeber has identified an increased French awareness of the Quakers' antislavery efforts in the period immediately prior to the trial of this case (*Anti-Slavery Opinion in France during the Second Half of the Eighteenth Century* [Baltimore: Johns Hopkins Univ. Press, 1937; reprint New York: Greenwood, 1969], pp. 84–89). For example, Anthony Benezet published a French translation of his *Avertisement* [sic] *à la Grande-Bretagne at à ses colonies, ou Tableau abrégé de l'état misérable des nègres esclaves dans les dominations angloises* in 1767. Two other important French works that discussed Quaker antislavery activities appeared in 1769: an article on "L'Affranchisdement des Nègres en Pennsylvanie" in the *Ephémérides du citoyen* and Saint-Lambert's story *Ziméo.*

76. Henrion de Pensey, *Mémoire pour un nègre,* p. 26, n. 1.

77. In addition to Seeber's *Anti-Slavery Opinion in France,* see Russell Parsons Jameson, *Montesquieu et l'esclavage* (Paris: Hachette et cie, 1911). Abbé Raynal's *Histoire philosophique,* which contains many antislavery passages, was first published in Amsterdam in 1770 at the time of Roc's trial.

78. Charles Montesquieu, *The Spirit of the Laws,* p. 246.

79. Ibid.

80. Elsewhere Henrion was more explicit in his references to Montesquieu. At the conclusion of the *mémoire,* Henrion quotes the culmination of Montesquieu's satirical defense of the enslavement of negroes: "Les princes de l'Europe, qui font tant de Conventions inutiles, en feront-ils une enfin en faveur de la miséricorde & de la piété?" Henrion de Pensey, *Mémoire pour un nègre,* p. 28, quoting Montesquieu, *L'Esprit des Lois,* Book 15, chapter 5.

81. Henrion de Pensey, *Mémoire pour un nègre,* p. 15, emphasis in the original.

Henrion's evocation of "liberty seated at the feet of the throne" recalls the sculptor Pigalle's attempts to replace the slaves on the base of kings' statues with imagery more consistent with current political thought.

82. Ibid., p. 16.

83. Ibid., pp. 18–19.

84. Sentence of March 2, 1770 (A.N., Z¹D 26). His wages were set at the rate of 100 *livres* per year.

85. Sentence of April 6, 1770 (A.N., Z¹D 134).

86. Evidence concerning slaves' sources of money to pay lawyers is rare. One petition, dated December 22, 1760, indicates that Jean Baptiste, of New Orleans, was given 48 *livres* by *Monsieur le président* Turgot, which he subsequently put into the hands of Mademoiselle Hanato, a relative of his master. Turgot is likely Anne Robert Jacques Turgot, then *maître des requêtes* of the Parlement of Paris, a frequenter of salons, defender of tolerance, and contributer to the *Encyclopédie*. Turgot would later ascend to Minister of the Marine when Maurepas replaced Maupeou as Chancellor (*Nouvelle biographie générale,* ed. Hoefer, [Paris, 1870], vol. 45, col. 717–31).

87. The case was *Isabel Flore Durosol, ditte Sarah, v. Dame Louise Bignol, Veuve du Sieur Fornet,* sentenced in the third audience before the Admiralty, December 17, 1760 (A.N., Z¹D 25). The slave was represented by the *avocat* Bigot and the *procureur* Collet.

We have already seen how Jean Boucaux's *avocat,* Mallet, assisted Collet in the preparation of Corinne's case in 1755. Between 1755 and 1762, Collet went on to represent or assist in representing thirteen slaves as *procureur* before the Admiralty Court. His last case was that of Louis against his master, Le Febvre, which resulted in the Admiralty ordinance of April 5, 1762. In the *Louis v. Le Febvre* case, Collet was assisted by two other attorneys, Bigot and De L'Estang. Subsequent to this case, De L'Estang represented three slaves, and the *procureur du roi,* Poncet de la Grave represented one, all during the year 1762 (A.N., Z¹D 131–32).

Collet was also Francisque's *procureur* before the Parlement of Paris in 1759, assisted by Joly de Fleury, *avocat général,* and a M. De la Roue, *avocat* (*Mémoire signifié pour le nommé Francisque,* p. 38). David Bell notes that Collet had formerly been a member of the Parisian Order of Barristers from 1729 until 1751 when he was expelled in a "purge of people persuing 'other employment incompatible with the bar' (in this case being a *procureur*)" (David Avrom Bell, letter to author, March 19, 1993).

88. Bell, *Lawyers and Citizens,* pp. 145–47; Shanti Marie Singham, "Rehearsal for Revolution: Political Opposition in France during the Maupeou Years," unpublished paper delivered March 17, 1993, at the Bunting Institute, Radcliffe College.

89. Pierre Etienne Regnaud, *La Journée du 10 Aoust 1792, avec des réflexions tant sur les événements qui l'ont immédiatement précédé et suivie, que sur la Révolution en général* (Paris: Crapart, 1795), pp. 21–61. Regnaud was also, apparently, quite concerned about his place in posterity. Though his massive history of the Maupeou period was never published, his account of the fall of Louis XVI and several other eyewitness accounts of the revolution were. See Pierre Etienne Regnaud, "Histoire des événemens depuis le mois de septembre 1770, concernans les parlemens et les changemens dans l'administration de la justice et dans les loix du royaume," 2 vols., B.N., MSS, fonds français, 13733 and 13734.

90. Michaud, *Biographie universelle,* vol. 35, p. 333.

91. Bell, *Lawyers and Citizens,* pp. 148–55.

92. Pierre Boulle, "La Législation sur les résidents noirs en France au XVIIIe siècle," paper presented at the Collogue international de Port-au-Prince, Haiti, December 4–10, 1989, p. 15, n. 2.

Chapter 7. The *Police des Noirs,* 1776–1777

1. Jean Louis petitioned against his master Sr. de Lombas on August 21, 1775 (A.N., Z¹D 134). The first of three hearings took place on August 23. On September 6, the court awarded Jean Louis his freedom and 700 *livres* for seven years' wages plus 20 *livres,* 16 *sols* for the food that he was required to purchase while detained in prison (A.N., Z¹D 27). The Admiralty Court of France was reestablished by an edict of July 1775, registered by the Parlement of Paris on August 2, 1775 (A.N., Z¹D 134).

2. The court also accepted six acts of enfranchisement in 1775 and four in 1776, for a total of twenty lawsuits for freedom in 1775 and 1776.

3. Nicolas Toussaint Le Moyne Des Essarts, "Un Nègre et une négresse qui réclament leur liberté contre un juif," in *Causes célèbres, curieuses et intéressantes de toutes les cours souveraines du royaume et des jugements qui les ont décidées* (Paris, 1777), pp. 49–110. Des Essarts's account is also reproduced in Pierre Pluchon's *Nègres et Juifs au XVIIIe siècle: Le racisme au siècle des lumières* (Paris: Tallandier, 1984), pp. 18–37. Pampy and Julienne's given names are supplied in the sentence of February 5, 1777 (A.N., Colonies, F¹B 4, fol. 437).

4. See Pluchon, *Nègres et Juifs,* pp. 15–42 and 243–83. It is interesting to note that Des Essarts's account of this case simply refers to the slaveowner as Isaac Mendès, rather than Mendès France. Perhaps this was to emphasize the slave owner's foreignness. Pluchon has demonstrated the rampant anti-Semitism of Des Essarts's account and the origins of anti-Semitism among Enlightenment thinkers (*Nègres et Juifs,* pp. 64–81 and 245–49).

5. Ibid., pp. 39–42.

6. Mendès France arrived with a third slave, Cézar, who disappears shortly from the records. Perhaps he was sold, ran away, or died.

7. Pluchon, *Nègres et Juifs,* pp. 15–16.

8. Des Essarts, "Un Nègre et une négresse," p. 59. This account does not explain why the two were arrested.

9. Ibid., pp. 60–61.

10. Ibid., pp. 56–59 and 61. Des Essarts also emphasizes that Mendès France branded Pampy and Julienne in Saint Domingue to prevent their running away.

11. Henrion de Pensey, *Mémoire pour un nègre,* p. 8.

12. Des Essarts, "Un Nègre et une négresse," pp. 52–53.

13. Henrion de Pensey, *Mémoire pour un nègre,* p. 9; Le Clerc du Brillet in [François Gayot de Pitaval], "Liberté reclamée par un nègre contre son maître qui l'a amené en France," in *Causes célèbres et intéressantes, avec les jugemens qui les ont décidées* (Paris: Jean de Nully, 1747), vol. 13, p. 540.

14. David Bell, "Lawyers and Politics in Eighteenth-Century Paris (1700–1790)," Ph.D. diss., Princeton Univ., 1991, pp. 269–77.

15. Pierre Louis Claude Gin, *De l'éloquence du barreau,* p. 285, quoted in David Bell, "Lawyers and Politics," p. 274.

16. Jean Louis and Louis Camille Crispin of Bengal both won their freedom in separate suits on September 6, 1775 (A.N., Z^{1}D 27, and 134).

17. Antoine Sartine, "Rapport au Conseil des Dépêches, par M. de Sartine, du Projet de Déclaration sur la Police des Noirs, du Août 1777," in B.N., MS français, 13357: "Recueil des pièces relatives à la législation sur la police des noirs," pp. 19–20.

18. *Le Voyageur à Paris*, a travel guide published in Paris in 1789, lists the *Journal des Causes célèbres* as one of the regular publications of the city (reprinted Leuven, Belgium: Bernard Copens, 1989), vol. 2, p. 4.

19. Des Essarts, "Un Nègre et une négresse," pp. 62–64; see also the sentences in A.N., Z^{1}D 134, and Z^{1}D 27. A copy of this sentence can also be found in A.N., Colonies, F^{1}B 4, Dossier 4, fol. 437.

20. De la Haye to M. de Villeneuve, February 7, 1776, (A.N., Colonies, F^{1}B 4, Dossier 4, fols. 433^v–434).

21. See the sentence of February 23, 1778 (A.N., Z^{1}D 134, and Z^1 D27).

22. Des Essarts, "Un Nègre et une négresse," p. 74.

23. Ibid., p. 67 (emphasis in original).

24. It is true that Des Essarts quotes the *defenders* of the Jews of Metz, ostensibly to show that he is not using Mendès France's Judaism against him. Nevertheless, even these passages are inflammatory, such as the following: "On observe, effectivement, . . . que le juif, familiarisé avec le mépris, fait de la bassesse, la voie de sa fortune.

"Incapable de tout ce qui demande de l'énergie, on le trouve rarement dans le crime; on le surprend sans cesse dans la friponnerie.

"Séparé de toutes les propriétés, l'or qui les représente fait sa passion unique.

"Barbare par défiance, il sacrifieroit une réputation, un fortune entière, pour s'assurer la plus chétive somme.

"Sans autre ressource que la ruse, il se fait une étude de l'art de tromper. L'usure, ce monstre qui ouvre les mains de l'avarice même pour l'assouvir davantage . . . qui va partout épiant la foiblesse, le malheur pour leur porter ses perfides secours; ce monstre paroît l'avoit choisi pour son agent" (Des Essarts, "Un Nègre et une négresse," pp. 77–78).

25. Ibid., pp. 71–73.

26. One year later, Pampy registered himself with the Admiralty in accordance with the Admiralty ordinance of April 16, 1777, as a free black, "having received his freedom from a tribunal" (Registration of June 4, 1777 [A.N., Z^{1}D 139]).

27. I have not been able to locate the original *mémoire*, but a letter from Miroménil to Sartine (February 19, 1776) summarizes that document (A.N., Colonies, F^{1}B 4, fols. 440–42). An apparent draft of Poncet de la Grave's report can be found in the same collection (fol. 334).

28. Though De la Haye's request of February 7 was addressed to the minister of the navy, it was acknowledged by Miroménil (A.N., Colonies, F^{1}B 4, fol. 435).

29. A.N., Colonies, F^{1}B 4, fol. 441^v.

30. "Lettre circulaire aux chambres du commerce," March 25, 1776 (A.N., Colonies, F^3 90, fol. 164).

31. One unintended result of Sartine's letter may have been to alert slaveowners who did not wish to return their slaves to the colonies that they should take prompt action. At least one owner apparently decided to manumit his slaves rather than risk their being sent

back to the colonies. André Michaud, a former colonist of Saint Domingue, manumitted Marie Dagué, her mulatto daughter Marie Catherine, and the latter's four children on April 3, 1777. He made sure to mention that Marie Catherine had been brought to France to learn the profession of seamstress, that he would have returned her to the colonies but her poor health and the lack of religion there made it advisable for her to stay in France. The act is reprinted in J.-F. Henry's "Une Mulâtresse de pension à Nantes en 1777," *La Revue du Bas Poitou et des provinces de l'ouest* (May–June 1972): 241–44. Henry misses the significance of the act of manumission, however, which was almost certainly to evade the necessity of returning Marie Catherine to the colonies.

32. Most of the following account of Sartine's career comes from Jacques Michel, *Du Paris de Louis XV à la marine de Louis XVI: L'œuvre de Monsieur de Sartine, vol. 1: La vie de la capitale; vol. 2: La reconquête de la liberté des mers* (Paris: Les Editions de l'Erudite, 1983–84).

33. Jean François Michaud, *Biographie universelle ancienne et moderne* (Paris, 1818; reprint Graz, Austria: Akademische Druck- U. Verlaganstalt, 1968) vol. 38, p. 37.

34. Ibid., pp. 36–37.

35. Shanti Marie Singham, "'A Conspiracy of Twenty Million Frenchmen': Public Opinion, Patriotism, and the Assault on Absolutism during the Maupeou Years, 1770–1775," Ph.D. diss., Princeton Univ., 1991, pp. 162–65.

36. Michel, *L'Œuvre de Monsieur de Sartine,* vol. 2, pp. 19–20.

37. Sartine's biographer does not mention the *Police des Noirs* except in passing (Michel, *L'Œuvre de Monsieur de Sartine,* vol. 1, p. 35).

38. I have found no references to the author of the projected edict, which was apparently circulated anonymously for comment. One likely candidate was Poncet de la Grave as he knew the issue better than most and because the plan bears the signature of so many of his obsessions, including miscegeny and a continued emphasis on religion.

39. De la Rivière's response, dated April 12, 1776, can be found in A.N., Colonies, F^{1}B 4, fols. 414–16. Though the response was not signed, another document (ibid., fol. 344) indicates that De la Rivière was its author. Most likely this is Mercier de la Rivière, an economist, judge, and former intendant of Martinique (Michaud, *Biographie universelle,* vol. 36, p. 87).

40. A.N., Colonies, F^{1}B 4, fol. 414.

41. The *lettres patentes* of September 3, 1776, were registered by the Parlement of Paris on September 6, 1776, according to the document "Recueil des pièces relatives à la législation sur la police des noirs," B.N., MSS fonds français 13357, p. 7.

42. "Arrêt de conseil par lequel le roi nomme une commission pour lui proposer un règlement sur la police des noirs," Versailles, September 8, 1776, in François André Isambert, *Recueil général des anciennes lois françoises depuis l'an 420 jusqu'à la révolution de 1789* (Paris: Belin-Leprieur, 1830), vol. 24, p. 114.

43. Emilien Petit, *Traité sur le gouvernement des esclaves,* part 2 (Paris: Knapen, 1777), pp. 96–97.

44. Isambert, *Recueil,* vol. 24, p. 106.

45. "Recueil des pièces relatives à la législation sur la police des noirs," B.N., MSS, fonds français, 13357, p. 7.

46. Manoeuvrer's petition of October 2, 1776, can be found in A.N., Z^{1}D 134. The

Admiralty Court's registration of the *lettres patentes* is recorded on the same date in the "registre pour l'enregistrement des actes, édits, déclarations, provisions et receptions d'officiers, passeports, et autres enregistremens, commencé le 7 août 1775" (A.N., Z¹D 42).

47. Isambert, *Recueil*, vol. 24, p. 114.

48. B.N., MSS, fonds français, 13357, pp. 11–12. Daniel Marc Antoine Chardon had a varied career as judge and intendant to Corsica and St. Lucia. At the time of his appointment to the commission, he was apparently between posts (*Le Gouvernement et l'administration sous Louis XV; dictionnaire biographique* [Paris: Editions de S.N.R.S., 1978], pp. 62–63).

It is not clear which Joly de Fleury was appointed to the commission. The most likely candidate is Jean Omer, then *président à mortier*, who represented Francisque before the Parlement of Paris in 1758 and thus knew the previous legislation well. It is also possible that his older brother, Guillaume François Louis, the parlement's recently appointed *procureur général*, was the Joly de Fleury family's appointment to the commission.

Similar confusion exists regarding the Taboureau appointment. It could be Louis Gabriel Taboureau Désreaux, then controller general of finances, or his brother Louis Philippe Taboureau de Villepatour, *maréchal de camp* and *inspecteur d'artillerie* (Michaud, *Biographie universelle*, vol. 43, p. 492).

Jean Charles Pierre Lenoir was Sartine's successor as *lieutenant général* of the police of Paris. I have not been able to identify commissioners d'Aguesseau or de Bernage. In January 1777, Taboureau would quit the commission and be replaced by Bertier de Sauvigny (B.N., MSS, fonds français, 13357, p. 15).

49. B.N., MSS, fonds français, 13357, p. 13.

50. See the letter from [Sartine] to Poncet de la Grave, September 6, 1777 (A.N., Colonies, F¹B 4, fol. 39).

51. "Lettre circulaire de M. de Sartine à M.M. les intendants sur le recensement des noirs, le 19 novembre, 1776" (B.N., MSS, fonds français, 13357, p. 14).

52. A.N., Colonies, F¹B 4, fols. 569–95.

53. [Chardon] to M. le subdélégué à Dijon, May 15, 1777 (A.N., Colonies, F¹B 4, fol. 585).

54. [Chardon] to M. le subdélégué à Mâcon, May 15, 1777 (A.N., Colonies, F¹B 4, fols. 586–89).

55. Because the following plan was found within the Joly de Fleury manuscript collection, it seems likely that the plan was drafted by the commissioner from this family. He would have had access to the papers concerning Francisque's case in 1758.

56. See item III, B.N., MS Joly de Fleury, vol. 485, fol. 396.

57. The idea of depots appears to have originated with Poncet de la Grave in his February 1776 *mémoire* to Sartine. Olwen Hufton reports that similar *depots* were established for France's poor in 1764 and 1773 (*The Poor of Eighteenth-Century France* [Oxford: Clarendon Press, 1974], pp. 389–90).

58. B.N., MS Joly de Fleury, vol. 485, fol. 397, item XII.

59. Ibid.

60. Ibid.

61. Ibid.

62. A printed copy of the Admiralty ordinance of April 16, 1777 can be found in A.N., Z¹D 135. Folded inside this document is a hand-written copy of the same text indicating its registration by the *sièges* of Guyenne and Bretagne.

63. A.N., Z¹D 139.

64. Even after the July 7 delay expired, registrations continued to be made at the rate of about two or three per day.

65. B.N., MS Joly de Fleury, vol. 485, fols. 392–95.

66. Ibid., vol. 593, fol. 303.

67. Sartine to Louis XVI, August 9, 1777 (B.N., MSS, fonds français, 13357, p. 18).

68. B.N., MSS, fonds français, 13357, pp. 19–20.

69. "Les détiennent en prison avec deffenses aux concierges de s'en désaisir, sous peine de punition exemplaire," Ibid., p. 20.

70. Ibid., pp. 20–21.

71. Ibid., pp. 21–22. A comparative guide to slave law published while the *Police des Noirs* was being drafted echoed Sartine's disesteem for the traditional justifications for bringing slaves to France: "Experience shows that the Christian intruction is completely neglected, is not supervised by anyone. . . . There is more compliance on the part of some masters to have their slaves learn some trades [but] the number of them is small" (Petit, *Traité sur le gouvernement des esclaves,* vol. 2, pp. 96–97).

72. Sartine to Louis XVI, August 9, 1777 (B.N., MSS, fonds français, 13357, pp. 22–23).

73. "Dans les lettres-patentes que votre Majesté a adressées le trois septembre dernier au Parlement de Paris, et qui y ont été enregistrées, il y ont dit expressément que les noirs demeuront dans le même état où ils étoient avant les demandes qui y'étoient rélatives, et qui ont été suspendues jusqu'à la nouvelle loi, dont il est question aujourd'hui" (ibid., p. 25).

Chapter 8. Erosion of the *Police des Noirs*

1. "Réflexions sur la Déclaration du Roy du 9 aoust 1777—Registrée au Parlement le 27. pour la Police des Noirs par raport à leur residence en europe" (A.N., Colonies F¹B 4, fols. 401–11). The document is anonymous and undated but can be identified by Chardon's reponse to Le Moyne of November 1, 1777 (A.N., Colonies F¹B 4, fol. 607). (Le Moyne is also occasionally spelled "Le Moine.")

2. Ibid., fol. 402ᵛ.

3. "Cette loi au surplus a, non seulement été le résultat d'un long travail de plusieurs magistrats; mais même elle a été communiqué aux administrateurs des colonies. Toutes les dispositions ont été approfondies et discutées avec soin" (Chardon to Le Moyne, November 1, 1777, A.N., Colonies F¹B 4, fol. 607). Le Moyne had suggested exceptions for wet nurses, slaves brought to nurse sick colonists, and the enslaved governesses of small children (thereby, no doubt, enabling white colonists to bring their black mistresses into France). Most important, Le Moyne opposed the depots, which, he felt, exposed slaves to all kinds of risks.

4. François André Isambert records the law's registration at the following courts: Paris (August 27, 1777); Corsica (September 29, 1777); Lorraine (November 20, 1777); Tou-

louse (January 24, 1778) (*Recueil génèral des anciennes lois françoises depuis l'an 420 jusqu'à la révolution de 1789* [Paris: Belin-Leprieur, 1830], vol. 25, p. 84). Méderic Louis Elie Moreau de Saint-Méry notes that the declaration was registered at the *conseil* of Cap François on December 8, 1777, and that of Port au Prince on December 10 (*Loix et constitutions des colonies françoises de l'Amérique sous le vent* [Paris: chez l'auteur, 1784–1790], vol. 5, p. 785). A copy of the law, indicating its registration by the Parlement of Bordeaux, can be found in (A.N., Colonies F¹B 1, fol. 5a).

5. "Registre pour l'enregistrement des actes, édits, déclarations, provisions et receptions d'officiers, passeports et autres enregistremens, Commencé le 7 août 1775" (A.N., Z¹D 42). Official correspondence confirms the law's registration by several Admiralty courts within the Paris jurisdiction in September (B.N., MSS Joly de Fleury, vol. 485, fols. 407, 408).

6. Sartine to Joly de Fleury, August 28, 1777, (B.N., MSS Joly de Fleury, vol. 485, fol. 402).

7. "Lettre commune à MM. les administrateurs des colonies sur la déclaration des noirs," September 1, 1777 (B.N., MSS fonds français 13357, p. 38).

8. Ibid., p. 43.

9. "Lettre circulaire à M. les intendants des colonies, sur la caisse de la consignation des noirs," September 30, 1777 (B.N., MSS fonds français 13357, fol. 47). Sartine's specific instructions to Poncet de la Grave can be found in A.N., Colonies F¹B 4, fols. 39–40. Responses from Brest, Marseilles, Rochefort, and Le Havre, acknowledging the receipt of the *Police des Noirs,* can be found in the same collection, fols. 600–602, 604.

10. "Arrêt du conseil portant que les habitant des colonies qui ont amené pour leur service les gens de couleur, et qui se sont conformés à l'article 9 de la déclaration du mois d'août dernier, auront un nouveau délai de deux mois pour faire repasser ces domestiques dans les colonies; faute par eux de ce faire, les domestiques ne pourront être retenus que par leur consentement au service de leurs maîtres," September 7, 1777, in Isambert, *Recueil,* vol. 25, p. 131. The *arrêt* also had the effect of closing a loophole in the *Police des Noirs* that would have permitted those who registered their blacks in compliance with the law to retain them indefinitely.

11. Twenty-two more registered between the expiration of the July 7 ordinance's grace period on August 8 and the Parlement's registration of the *Police des Noirs* on August 27, bringing the grand total of registered blacks in Paris to 336 from April 16 through September 27, 1777 (A.N., Z¹D 139).

12. Pierre Boulle, "Les gens de couleur à Paris à la veille de la Révolution," in *L'Image de la Révolution française: Communications présentées lors du Congrès Mondial pour le Bicentenaire de la Révolution,* ed. Michel Vovelle (Paris: Pergamon, 1989), p. 159. Professor Boulle's forthcoming study, *Being Black in Eighteenth-Century France: Non-White Residents According to the Census of 1777,* analyzes the declarations for the entirety of France.

13. [Chardon] to Poncet de la Grave, September 6, 1777 (A.N., Colonies F¹B 4, fol. 39ᵛ). Article 3 of the *Police des Noirs* provided for the arrest of any blacks who arrived in France after the publication of the *Police des Noirs.*

14. Summary of Poncet de la Grave's requests of September 9, 1777, to Sartine (A.N.,

Colonies, F¹B 4, fol. 447). The summary appears to have been composed by Chardon in order to brief Sartine or the king. Another letter from Poncet de la Grave to Chardon sought authorization to circumvent Lenoir's permission for arrests (Poncet de la Grave to Chardon, October 1, 1777 [A.N., Colonies F¹B 4, fol. 446]).

15. [Chardon] to Poncet de la Grave, October 3, 1777 (A.N., Colonies F¹B 4, fol. 596). The letter goes on to specify that *ordres du roi* can only be issued by one of the king's ministers or the lieutenant of the police.

16. [Chardon] to Poncet de la Grave, October 3, 1777 (A.N., Colonies F¹B 4, fol. 597).

17. The transcription of the December 12, 1777, interrogation can be found in A.N., Z¹D 135. They were arrested on February 6 and 7, 1777. The interrogation explored the women's origins, their arrival in Paris, their history of prostitution and motherhood, and the names of other blacks (both male and female) with whom they consorted. It is noteworthy that when Fauchonette claimed that her clientele was white, Poncet de la Grave did not question her as to their identities.

18. Poncet de la Grave, "Extrait de l'interrogation de Marie Louise Latour, ditte L'Espere," December 16, 1777 (A.N., Colonies F¹B 4, fol. 199).

19. Poncet de la Grave, "Extrait de l'interrogation de Marie Françoise La Perle, ditte Fauchonette," December 16, 1777 (A.N., Colonies F¹B 4, fol. 201).

20. Poncet de la Grave, "Extrait de l'interrogation d' Espere," fol. 200.

21. Poncet de la Grave to Chardon, December 19, 1777 (A.N., Colonies F¹B 4, fol. 196ᵛ).

22. "[Il] me paraît sujet aux plus grands inconvenients, ainsi qu'au plus grand dangers pour la nation blanche," ibid., fol. 195ᵛ.

23. Another letter from Poncet de la Grave, dated December 24, 1777, articulated in painful detail his own understanding of the extent of his powers vis-à-vis the authority of Lenoir (A.N., Colonies F¹B 4, fol. 460).

24. [Chardon] to Lenoir, December 29, 1777 (A.N., Colonies F¹B 4, fol. 210).

25. [Chardon] to Poncet de la Grave, October 3, 1777 (A.N., Colonies F¹B 4, fol. 596).

26. Chardon to Poncet de la Grave, December 3, 1777 (A.N., Colonies F¹B 4, fol. 452).

27. Poncet de la Grave to Chardon, December 6, 1777 (A.N., Colonies F¹B 4, fol. 455).

28. Ibid. Poncet de la Grave had raised the same issue in one of his earliest letters to Chardon in September 1777. Chardon responded in his October 3 letter that the king would hear none of his complaints on this matter (A.N., Colonies F¹B 4, fol. 598).

29. Le Moyne to Chardon, October 18, 1777 (A.N., Colonies F¹B 4, fol. 450).

30. Letters requesting these tallies from Bourgogne, Brest, Paris, Dunkerque, and Rochefort appear in A.N., Colonies F¹B 4, fols. 614–18, 626.

31. [Le Moyne], "Réflexions" (A.N., Colonies F¹B 4, fol. 409ᵛ).

32. Ibid., fol. 410.

33. "Lettre circulaire [aux] Mrs. les procureurs du roi des amirautés," October 2, 1777 (A.N., Colonies F¹B 4, fol. 378ᵛ).

34. [Chardon] to Poncet de la Grave, December 11, 1777 (A.N., Colonies F¹B 4, fol. 630).

35. Mistral to Chardon, November 9, 1777 (A.N., Colonies F1B 4, fols. 611–12). Marchain informed Chardon of the depot's establishment of Rochefort on December 2, 1777 (ibid., fol. 628).

36. Mistral to Chardon, November 18, 1777 (A.N., Colonies F¹B 4, fols. 619–20).

37. Mistral to Chardon, November 25, 1777 (A.N., Colonies F1B 4, fol. 621).

38. Chardon to Mistral, November 26, 1777 (A.N., Colonies F¹B 4, fol. 622).

39. Mistral to Chardon, December 2, 1777 (A.N., Colonies F¹B 4, fol. 627).

40. Chardon to De Selle, December 29, 1777 (A.N., Colonies F¹B 4, fol. 635).

41. "Ordonnance du Roi, portant défenses aux Capitaines de Navires de laisser débarquer aucun Noir, Mulâtre, ou autre Gens de couleur, avant d'avoir fair leur rapport à l'Amirauté," February 23, 1778, in Moreau de Saint-Méry, *Loix et constitutions,* vol. 5, p. 814. A circular letter of April 12, 1778, advised port authorities of the new ordinance (A.N., Colonies F¹B 4, fol. 643).

42. D'Argout and De Vaivre to Chardon, December 23, 1777 (A.N., Colonies F¹B 4, fols. 631–33). These requests closely parallel the exemptions already suggested by Le Moyne (A.N., Colonies F¹B 4, fols. 401–11).

43. De Vaivre to Chardon, January 12, 1778 (A.N., Colonies F¹B 4, fols. 636ᵛ–37).

44. Unsigned and undated document (A.N., Colonies F¹B 4, fol. 644).

45. "Lettre du Ministre à M. l'Intendant, concernant les Consignations pour les Nègres amenés en France," December 16, 1778, in Moreau de Saint-Méry, *Loix et Constitutions,* vol. 5, p. 848.

46. Poncet de la Grave to Chardon, December 19, 1777 (A.N., Colonies F¹B 4, fols. 458–59).

47. Poncet de la Grave to Chardon, December 19, 1777 (A.N., Colonies F¹B 4, unnumbered folio, inserted between fols. 459 and 460).

48. "Arrêt de conseil qui ordonne à tous noirs, mulâtres ou gens de couleur qui ont été enregistrés conformément à la déclaration du 9 août dernier, de se faire délivrer un certificat contenant leurs noms, âge, signalement, etc., sinon qu'ils seront embarqés pour les colonies," January 11, 1778, in Isambert, *Recueil,* vol. 25, p. 189. A printed copy of the *arrêt* and a blank *cartouche* may be found in A.N., Colonies F¹B 4, fols. 224–26.

49. "Arrêt de conseil portant défense de célébrer mariage entre les blancs, noirs, mulâtres, et autres gens de couleur, et à tous notaires de passer aucun contrat entre eux," April 5, 1778, in Isambert, *Recueil,* vol. 25, pp. 257–58. The text of the law makes it clear that the ban was to apply to marriages between whites and people of darker hues, rather than to marriages amongst blacks. The prescription regulated the actions of priests and notaries, but the punishment applied to those who contracted the marriage: they were to be sent to the colonies.

50. David Avrom Bell has observed that "Much of eighteenth-century political history can be recounted as a series of . . . jurisdictional battles, which each side fought with lengthy, tedious, and tiresome recourse to precedent. Yet for all its tedium, jurisdiction was a deadly serious matter. The extent of one's jurisdiction determined one's rank in an institutional hierarchy, and the loss of rank meant a loss of honor, a quality which, as Montesquieu knew, mattered above all else" ("Lawyers and Politics in Eighteenth-Century Paris (1700–1790)" Ph.D. diss., Princeton Univ., 1991, pp. 21–22).

51. Poncet de la Grave to Sartine, February 3, 1778 (A.N., Colonies F¹B 4, fols. 240–51).

52. Poncet de la Grave to Sartine, February 9, 1778 (A.N., Colonies F¹B 4, fol. 252).

53. Sartine to Poncet de la Grave, February 12, 1778 (A.N., Colonies F¹B 4, fol. 255).

54. Mantel to Sartine, February 13, 1778 (A.N., Colonies F¹B 4, fol. 256), and De la Haye to Sartine, February 16, 1778 (ibid., fol. 293). A lengthy report criticized both the *arrêt de conseil* of January 11, 1778, and the *Déclaration pour la Police des Noirs* in great detail: "Observations pour les officiers de l'amirauté de France au siège général de la Table de Marbre du Palais à Paris, a sujet de l'arrêt de conseil du 11 janvier 1778 concernant les negres," undated and unsigned (A.N., Colonies F¹B 4, fols. 419–30).

55. Sartine to "MM les officiers de l'amirauté de France," March 27, 1778 (A.N., Colonies F¹B 4, fol. 300).

56. Mantel to Sartine, April 11, 1778 (A.N., Colonies F¹B 4, fols. 301–302).

57. Sartine to "MM les officiers de l'amirauté de France," May 19, 1778 (A.N., Colonies F¹B 4, fol. 303).

58. Letter from Crublier de Chandaire to [Sartine], March 5, 1778 (B.N., MSS Joly de Fleury, vol. 485, fol. 459). Crublier de Chandaire wrote to Sartine again on March 30 when his first letter remained unanswered (ibid., fol. 460).

59. "Extrait de la lettre à M. Chardon," undated (B.N., MSS Joly de Fleury, vol. 485, fol. 458).

60. "Lettre circulaire aux evesques," April 5, 1778 (A.N., Colonies F¹B 4, fol. 457).

61. "Extrait de la lettre à M. Chardon," undated (B.N., MSS Joly de Fleury, vol. 485, fol. 458).

62. Rancher, parish priest of Champigny-sur-vende, to [De Castries], April 7, 1786 (B.N., MSS Joly de Fleury, vol. 1027, fol. 245), and response dated April 13, 1786 (ibid., fol. 246).

63. [Chardon] to Poncet de la Grave, September 6, 1777 (A.N., Colonies F¹B 4, fols. 40–40ᵛ).

64. The account of Gotton's life recounted here, except where otherwise noted, is from Poncet de la Grave's "Cause jugée au siège général de l'amirauté de France du palais à Paris le 21 aoust [sic], 1779," May 1, 1779 (A.N., Colonies F¹B 4, fols. 480–83). The case was actually decided on April 21, 1779 (A.N., Z¹D 27 and 135).

65. Poncet de la Grave, "Cause jugée" (A.N., Colonies F¹B 4, fol. 480ᵛ).

66. The court's sentence of October 12, 1775, specifically prohibited the Marquis d'Anache from attempts on her freedom, which suggests that Brion's arrangement for Gotton's hearing was not as disinterested an action as Poncet de la Grave would have us believe.

67. Registration of September 25, 1777 (A.N., Z¹D 139). Gotton would receive a *cartouche* on February 5, 1778.

68. See the registers of October 11, 1777 (A.N., Z¹D 139).

69. According to Poncet de la Grave, D'Anache obtained the order on February 24, 1778.

70. Petition of Margueritte, called Gotton, April 1, 1778 (A.N., Z¹D 135).

71. Sentence of April 21, 1779 (A.N., Z¹D 27).

72. Louis Joseph Azor and Jean Joseph Aza petitioned on July 13 and July 24, 1778, respectively. Preliminary sentences recognized their freedom and put them under the king's protection. Neither man pursued his initial claims to back wages (A.N., Z¹D 135).

73. Jean Alexandre "James" or "Gintz" petitioned for his freedom on June 9, 1779,

and was awarded it by a sentence of July 7, 1779. Achille's petition for freedom is dated June 25, 1779 (A.N., Z¹D 135).

74. [Lafarge Paquot?] to Chardon, September 28, 1780 (A.N., Colonies F¹B 1, fol. 28).

75. The king's orders were issued on September 30, 1780, and again on September 30, 1781 (A.N., Colonies F¹B 1, fols. 24, 25, and 33).

76. Comtesse de Bethune to [De Castries], August 13, 1781 (A.N., Colonies F¹B 1, fol. 21).

77. Petition and Sentence of October 12, 1781 (A.N., Z¹D 135).

78. A September 1781 report entitled "Colonies" discussed the failure of the *Police des Noirs,* specifically citing the cases of Henriette Lucille, Sibilly, and Azov and observations on each (A.N., Colonies F¹B 1, fols. 35–39). Sibilly was a slave in Bordeaux who had stayed beyond the time permitted by law and had "become libertine" ([Poncet de la Grave?] to De Castries, August 3 [1781] [A.N., Colonies F¹B 1, fols. 18–19]). De Castries obtained an order from the king to ship Sibilly back to the colonies (A.N., Colonies F¹B 1, fol. 15).

79. "Arrêt du conseil qui défend à tous curés, notaires, arpentaires et autres officiers publics, de qualifier aucunes gens de couleur du titre de sieur et dame," November 6, 1781, in Isambert, *Recueil,* vol. 27, p. 107.

80. "Avis du comité de legislation sur les deux questions de Monsieur le Marquis de Castries au sujet des noirs et mulâtres qui se trouvent en France," February 23, 1782 (A.N., Colonies F¹B 4, fols. 316–25). The committee included De la Rivière, De Vaivre, Lacoste, Mangrennet (sp?), and Mouracy (sp?).

81. An anonymous report, "Observations sur l'avis du comité relativement aux noirs qui se trouvent actuellement en France," dated March 9, 1782, articulates the positions attributed to Chardon by the legislative committee (A.N., Colonies F¹B 4, fols. 328–32).

82. Ibid.

83. "Arrêt de conseil pour le renouvellement des cartouches des noirs et autres gens de couleur qui sont à Paris," March 23, 1783, in Isambert, *Recueil,* vol. 27, p. 268. See also Moreau de Saint-Méry, *Loix et constitutions,* vol. 6, p. 305.

84. "Lettre du Ministre aux Administrateurs, sur les Négres amenés en France," March 28, 1783, in Moreau de Saint-Méry, *Loix et constitutions,* vol. 6, p. 306.

85. Ibid.

86. Ibid.

Epilogue

1. Most recently, David Geggus has given an insightful overview, "Racial Equality, Slavery, and Colonial Secession during the Constituent Assembly," *American Historical Review* 94, no. 5 (December 1989): 1290–1308. See also Shanti Marie Singham, "Betwixt Cattle and Men: Jews, Blacks, and Women and the *Declaration of the Rights of Man and Citizen,*" in *The Rights of Man: Its Origins,* ed. Dale Van Kley (Palo Alto: Stanford Univ. Press, 1994). For the broader Atlantic context and developments during the nineteenth century, see Robin Blackburn's excellent *The Overthrow of Colonial Slavery* (London: Verso, 1988), pp. 161–264. Earlier works to deal with the Revolution and slavery include Anna Julia Cooper, *Slavery and the French Revolutionists,* trans. Frances Richardson Kelly (Lewiston, N.Y.: Edwin Mellon, 1988); C. L. R. James, *The Black Ja-*

cobins, 2nd rev. ed. (New York: Vintage, 1989); David Brion Davis, *The Problem of Slavery in the Age of Revolution* (Ithaca: Cornell Univ. Press, 1975), pp. 137–48; Valerie Quinney, "Decisions on Slavery, the Slave-Trade and Civil Rights for Negroes in the Early French Revolution," *Journal of Negro History* 55 (1970): 117–30; William B. Cohen, *The French Encounter with Africans: White Response to Blacks, 1530–1880* (Bloomington: Indiana Univ. Press, 1980), pp. 113–20; and David Geggus, *Slavery, War, and Revolution* (Oxford: Oxford Univ. Press, 1982), pp. 52–55. For primary documents on slavery during the Revolution see the collection *La Révolution et l'abolition de l'esclavage,* 8 vols. (Paris: Editions d'histoire sociale, 1968).

2. Buffet, "Amirauté de France" in *Guide des recherches dous les fonds judiciaires de l'ancien régime* (Paris: Imprimerie Nationale, 1958), p. 282.

3. François André Isambert, *Recueil général des anciennes lois françoises depuis l'an 420 jusqu'à la révolution de 1789* (Paris: Belin-Leprieur, 1830), vol. 25, p. 81, n. 1.

4. Blackburn argues that the Constituent Assembly's enactment of emancipation was, in effect, a retroactive approval of the *status quo* because in Saint Domingue, at least, freedom was offered to those slaves who were willing to fight against the British.

5. The *Police des Noirs* was renewed on 16 Pluviôse, an 10 (Isambert, *Recueil,* vol. 25, p. 81, n. 1). An *arrêté* of 13 Thermidor, an 10, renewed earlier royal legislation requiring blacks to carry *cartouches* (ibid., vol. 27, p. 268, n. 1). Lucien Peytraud states that as of 13 Messidor, an 10, people of color were prohibited from entering France, but that the ban was lifted again on August 5, 1818 (*L'Esclavage aux Antilles françaises avant 1789, d'après les documents inédits des archives coloniales* [Paris: Librairie Hachette, 1897], pp. 398–99). The *Œuvres Complètes de Pothier* new ed. (Paris: chez Thomine et Fortic, Librairies, 1821) affirmed that the *Police des Noirs* of August 9, 1777, was still in effect in 1821.

6. Edouard Thureau, *Plaidoyer pour le sieur Furcy indien demeurant à l'Isle de France appelant contre les veuve et héritiers Lory demeurant à l'Isle de Bourbon* (Paris: Imprimerie de J. Delalain, 1844), pp. 28–30.

7. Pierre Etienne Regnaud, *La Journée du Aoust 1792.*

8. Michael P. Fitzsimmons, *The Parisian Order of Barristers and the French Revolution* (Cambridge: Harvard Univ. Press, 1981), p. 120.

9. These include the *Mémoires intéressants pour servir à l'histoire de France, ou Tableau historique, civil, et militaire des maisons royales, châteaux, et parcs des rois de France,* 4 vols. (Paris: chez Nyon l'aîné, 1788–1790) and *Histoire générale des descentes faites tant en Angleterre qu'en France, depuis Jules César, avec des notes historiques, politiques et critiques,* 2 vols. (Paris, 1799).

10. Guillaume Poncet de la Grave, *Considérations sur le célibat relativement à la politique, à la population, et aux bonnes mœurs* (Paris: Moutardier, An IX [1801]).

11. Guillaume Poncet de la Grave, *Défense des considerations sur le célibat . . . en réponse à la critique du célibataire anonyme, insérée dans le journal de Paris du 24 Brumaire, an 10, no. 54, pag. 320 et 321* (Paris: Moutardier, An X [1802]).

12. Pampy registered with the Admiralty of France on June 4, 1777, stating that he resided "chez l'abbé de Serre, rue des postes," and received an indentification card on February 2, 1778 (A.N., Z¹D 139). On May 23, 1783, he returned for new identification papers, in compliance with the new law, stating that he was in the service of one "Mᵉ de Versigny, rue de la Lune."

Bibliography

Manuscript Sources

Archives Nationales (A.N.), Paris. The following series were particularly useful in the preparation of this work:

AD+ 738 and 850	Printed copies of legislation.
X^1A 8436	Registers of the *Conseil secret* of the Parlement of Paris.
Z^1D 24–42	Sentences of audiences and registration of royal acts in the Admiralty of France.
Z^1D 125–137	Judgments and procedural documents of the Admiralty of France.
Colonies B	Ministerial correspondence and king's orders.
Colonies C^{7-10}	Letters to the minister of the marine from the administrators of Guadeloupe, Martinique, Saint Domingue, and other islands of the Antilles.
Colonies F^1B 3–4	Administration of blacks in France.
Colonies F^3 79–90	Collection Moreau de Saint-Méry. This important collection contains a wide range of documents pertaining to blacks in the colonies and in France.
Marine B^3	Ministerial correspondence and letters to the minister of the marine from French provinces.

Bibliothèque Nationale (B.N.), Paris. The Joly de Fleury collection was especially useful for notes on specific cases concerning black slaves in France.

189

Published Sources

Allard, Paul. *Esclaves, serfs et mainmortables.* Rev. ed. Paris: Sanard & Derangeon, 1894.

Almanach Royal. Paris, 1762.

Alpers, Edward. *Ivory and Slaves: Changing Patterns of International Trade in East Central Africa to the Later Nineteenth Century.* Berkeley: Univ. of California Press, 1975.

Anex-Cabanis, Danielle. *Le Servage au Pays de Vaud (XIIIe–XVIe siècle).* Lausanne: Bibliothèque historique vaudoise, 1973.

Antoine, Michel. *Le Gouvernement et l'administration sous Louis XV; dictionnaire biographique.* Paris: Editions du Centre National de la Recherche Scientifique, 1978.

Baker, Keith Michael. *Inventing the French Revolution: Essays on France's Political Culture in the Eighteenth Century.* Cambridge: Cambridge Univ. Press, 1990.

———. "Introduction." In *The Political Culture of the Old Regime,* vol. 1 of *The French Revolution and the Creation of Modern Political Culture* ed. Keith Michael Baker, Colin Lucas, and François Furet. Oxford: Pergamon Press, 1987, pp. xi–xxiv.

Bamford, Paul W. *Fighting Ships and Prisons: The Mediterranean Galleys of France in the Age of Louis XIV.* Minneapolis: Univ. of Minnesota Press, 1973.

Barzun, Jacques. *The French Race: Theories of Its Origin and the Social and Political Implications Prior to the Revolution.* New York: Columbia Univ. Press, 1932.

Bauer, Carol Phillips. "Law, Slavery, and Sommersett's Case in Eighteenth-Century England: A Study of the Legal Status of Freedom." Ph.D. diss., New York University, 1973.

Beaune, Collette. *The Birth of an Ideology: Myths and Symbols of Nation in Late-Medieval France.* Trans. Susan Ross Huston. Ed. Frederic L. Cheyette. Berkeley: Univ. of California Press, 1991.

Bell, David Avrom. *Lawyers and Citizens: The Making of a Political Elite in Old Regime France.* New York: Oxford Univ. Press, 1994.

———. "Lawyers and Politics in Eighteenth-Century Paris (1700–1790)." Ph.D. diss., Princeton Univ., 1991.

Bibliothèque Nationale, Département des Imprimés. *Catalogue général des livres imprimés de la Bibliothèque Nationale: Actes Royaux.* Published under the direction of S. Honoré. Vol. 5: *Louis XV (1715–1755).* Paris: Imprimerie nationale, 1955.

Bisson de Barthélemy, Paul. *Les Joly de Fleury: Procureurs généraux au Parle-*

ment de Paris au XVIIIᵉ siècle. Paris: Société d'édition d'enseignement supérieur, 1964.

Blackburn, Robin. *The Overthrow of Colonial Slavery, 1776–1848.* London:
Verso, 1988.

Blakely, Allison. *Blacks in the Dutch World: The Evolution of Racial Imagery in
a Modern Society.* Bloomington: Indiana Univ. Press, 1993.

Bloch, Marc. *Slavery and Serfdom in the Middle Ages.* Trans. William R. Beer.
Berkeley: Univ. of California Press, 1975.

Bluche, François. *Les Magistrats du parlement de Paris au XVIIIᵉ siècle, 1715–
1771.* Paris: Les Belles Lettres, 1960.

Bodin, Jean. *The Six Bookes of a Commonweale: A Facsimile Reprint of the
English Translation of 1606, Corrected and Supplemented in Light of
a New Comparison with the French and Latin Texts.* Ed. and with
introduction by Kenneth Douglas McRae. Cambridge: Harvard Univ.
Press, 1962.

Bonnassie, Pierre. *From Slavery to Feudalism in South–Western Europe.* Trans.
Jean Birrell. New York: Cambridge Univ. Press, 1991.

Boucher, Philip. *Les Nouvelles Frances: France in America, 1500–1815,
An Imperial Perspective.* Providence: John Carter Brown Library,
1989.

Boulle, Pierre. *Being Black in Eighteenth-Century France: Non-White Residents According to the Census of 1777* (forthcoming).

———. "In Defense of Slavery: Eighteenth-Century Opposition to Abolition
and the Origins of Racist Ideology in France." In *History from Below,*
ed. Frederick Krantz. Oxford: Oxford Univ. Press, 1988, pp. 219–46.

———. "Les Gens de couleur à Paris à la veille de la Révolution." In *L'Image
de la Révolution française: Communications présentées lors du Congrès Mondial pour le Bicentenaire de la Révolution,* ed. Michel
Vovelle. Paris: Pergamon, 1989, pp. 159–68.

———. "La Législation sur les résidents noirs en France au XVIIIᵉ siecle."
Paper presented at the Colloque international de Port-au-Prince, Haiti,
December 4–10, 1989.

Bresc, Henri. "L'Etat, l'église, et les esclaves." In *Normes et pouvoir à la fin
du moyen âge: Actes du colloque en études médiévales au Québec et
en Ontario, May 16–17, 1989,* ed. Marie-Claude Déprez-Masson.
Quebec: CERES, 1989, pp. 37–38.

Buffon, George Louis Leclerc, Count of. *Natural History, General and Particular, by the Count de Buffon.* Trans. William Smellie. 45 vols. London:
T. Cadell and W. Davies, 1812.

Cobban, Alfred. "The Parlements of France in the Eighteenth Century." *History* 35 (1950): 64–80.

Cohen, William B. *The French Encounter with Africans: White Response to Blacks, 1530–1880.* Bloomington: Indiana Univ. Press, 1980.

Church, William Farr. *Constitutional Thought in Sixteenth-Century France: A Study in the Evolution of Ideas.* New York: Octagon, 1979.

Curtin, Philip D. "The French Slave Trade of the Eighteenth Century. In *The Atlantic Slave Trade: A Census.* Madison: Univ. of Wisconsin Press, 1969, pp. 163–203.

———. *The Image of Africa: British Ideals and Action, 1780–1850.* Madison: Univ. of Wisconsin Press, 1964.

Dalperrie de Bayac, Jacques. *Louis VI: La naissance de la France.* Paris: J.C. Lattès, 1983.

Darnton, Robert. *The Business of Enlightenment: A Publishing History of the Encyclopédie, 1775–1800.* Cambridge, Mass.: Belknap, 1979.

Davis, David Brion. *The Problem of Slavery in the Age of Revolution.* Ithaca: Cornell Univ. Press, 1975.

———. *The Problem of Slavery in Western Culture.* Ithaca: Cornell Univ. Press, 1966.

Davis, Natalie Z. *Fiction in the Archives: Pardon Tales and their Tellers in Sixteenth-Century France.* Stanford: Stanford Univ. Press, 1987.

Debbasch, Yvan. *Couleur et liberté: Le jeu du critère ethnique dans un ordre juridique esclavagiste.* Paris: Dalloz, 1967.

Debrunner, Hans Werner. *Presence and Prestige: Africans in Europe: A History of Africans in Europe before 1918.* Basel: Basler Afrika Bibliographien, 1979.

Delesalle, Simone, and Lucette Valensi. "Le Mot 'nègre' dans les dictionnaires français d'ancien régime: Histoire et lexicographie." *Langue française* 15 (1972): 79–104.

Denisart, Jean Baptiste. "Nègres." In *Collection de décisions nouvelles relatives à la jurisprudence actuelle.* New ed. Paris: chez la Veuve Desaint, 1775, vol. 3, pp. 312–13.

Des Essarts, Nicolas Toussaint Le Moyne. "Un Nègre et une négresse qui réclament leur liberté contre un juif." In *Causes célèbres, curieuses et intéressantes de toutes les cours souveraines du royaume avec les jugements qui les ont décidées.* Paris, 1777, vol. 36, pp. 49–110.

Dessalles, Pierre Régis. *Annales du Conseil Souverain de la Martinique.* 2 vols. Bergerac: chez J. B. Puynesge, 1786.

Dockès, Pierre. *Medieval Slavery and Liberation.* Trans. Arthur Goldhammer. London: Methuen, 1982.

Dodds, Muriel. *Les Récits de voyages: Sources de L'Esprit des lois de Montesquieu.* Paris: H. Champion, 1929.

Doyle, William. "The Parlements of France and the Breakdown of the Old Regime, 1771–1788." *French Historical Studies* 6 (1970): 415–58.

Drescher, Seymour. *Capitalism and Antislavery: British Mobilization in Comparative Perspective.* New York: Macmillan, 1986.

———. "The Ending of the Slave Trade and the Evolution of European Scientific Racism." *Social Science History* 14, no. 3 (Fall 1990): 415–50.

———. The Long Goodbye: Dutch Capitalism and Antislavery in Comparative Perspective." *American Historical Review* 99, no. 1 (February 1994): 44–69.

———. "Manumission in a Society without Slave Law: Eighteenth-Century England." *Slavery and Abolition* 10, no. 3 (December 1989): 85–101.

Duchet, Michèle. *Anthropologie et histoire au siècle des lumières.* Paris: François Maspéro, 1971.

———. *Diderot et* l'Histoire des Deux Indes, *ou, l'écriture fragmentaire.* Paris: Nizet, 1978.

Egret, Jean. *Louis XV et l'opposition parlementaire, 1715–1774.* Paris: Armand Colin, 1970.

Elisabeth, Léo. "The French Antilles." In *Neither Slave Nor Free: The Freedmen of African Descent in the Slave Societies of the New World,* ed. David W. Cohen and Jack P. Greene. Baltimore: Johns Hopkins Univ. Press, 1972.

Encyclopédie, ou dictionnaire raisoné des sciences, des arts et des métiers. 17 vols. Paris: Briasson, 1751–1765.

Fairchilds, Cissie. *Domestic Enemies: Servants and Their Masters in Old Regime France.* Baltimore: Johns Hopkins Univ. Press, 1984.

Farge, Arlette. *Vivre dans la rue à Paris au XVIIIᵉ siècle.* Paris: Editions Gallimard/Julliard, 1979.

Fiddes, Edward. "Lord Mansfield and the Sommersett Case." *Law Quarterly Review* 50 (1934): 499–511.

Fields, Barbara J. "Ideology and Race in American History." In *Region, Race and Reconstruction: Essays in Honor of C. Vann Woodward,* ed. J. Morgan Kousser and James M. McPherson. Oxford: Oxford Univ. Press, 1982.

Fitzsimmons, Michael. *The Parisian Order of the Barristers and the French Revolution.* Cambridge: Harvard Univ. Press, 1987.

Flammermont, Jules. *Remonstrances du Parlement de Paris.* 3 vols. Paris: Imprimerie Nationale, 1888–1898.

Fournier, Marcel. *Essai sur les formes et les effets de l'affranchissement dans le droit Gallo-franc.* Paris: F. Vieweg, 1885.

———. "Les Affranchissements du Vᵉ au XIIIᵉ siècle: influence de l'église, de la royauté et des particuliers sur la condition des affranchis." *Revue historique* 21 (1883): 1–58.

Fredrickson, George M. *The Black Image in the White Mind: The Debate on*

Afro-American Character and Destiny, 1817–1914. New York: Harper & Row, 1971.

Fryer, Peter. *Staying Power: The History of Black People in Britain.* London: Pluto Press, 1984.

Garrioch, David. *Neighborhood and Community in Paris, 1740–1790.* Cambridge Studies in Early Modern History. Cambridge: Cambridge Univ. Press, 1986.

Gautier, Arlette. "Les esclaves femmes aux Antilles françaises, 1635–1848." *Historical Reflections* 10 (1983): 418–30.

[Gayot de Pitaval, François]. "Liberté reclamée par un nègre, contre son maître qui l'a amené en France." In *Causes célèbres et intéressantes, avec les jugemens qui les ont décidées.* Paris: Jean de Nully, 1747, vol. 13, pp. 492–586.

Geggus, David. "Racial Equality, Slavery, and Colonial Secession during the Constituent Assembly." *American Historical Review* 94, no. 5 (December 1989): 1290–1308.

———. "Sex Ratio, Age and Ethnicity in the Atlantic Slave Trade: Data from French Shipping and Plantation Records." *Journal of African History* 30 (1989): 20–35.

Gerzina, Gretchen. *Black England: Life Before Emancipation.* London: John Murray, 1995.

Giesey, Ralph E. "The Juristic Basis of Dynastic Right to the French Throne." *Transactions of the American Philosophical Society* 51, no. 5 (1961).

Guide des recherches dans les fonds judiciaires de l'ancien régime. Paris: Imprimerie Nationale, 1958.

Hanley, Sarah. *The Lit de justice of the Kings of France: Constitutional Ideology in Legend, Ritual, and Discourse.* Princeton: Princeton Univ. Press, 1983.

———. "The Monarchic State in Early Modern France: Marital Regime Government and Male Right." In *Politics, Ideology, and the Law in Early Modern Europe,* ed. Adrianna E. Bakos. Rochester: Univ. of Rochester Press, 1994, pp. 107–26.

Hardy, James David. *Judicial Politics in the Old Regime: The Parlement of Paris during the Regency.* Baton Rouge: Louisiana State Univ. Press, 1967.

Harris, Joseph. *The African Presence in Asia: Some Consequences of the East African Slave Trade.* Evanston, Ill.: Northwestern Univ. Press, 1971.

Henrion de Pansey, Pierre Paul Nicolas. "L'Abbé Pluche." *Galerie françoise* 2, no. 8 (1772).

Henrion de Pensey [sic], Pierre Paul Nicolas. *Discours prononcé à la rentrée de la Conférence publique de messieurs les avocats au Parlement de Paris, le 13 janvier 1775.* Lausanne, 1775.

————. *Mémoire pour un nègre qui réclame sa liberté.* N.p.: L'Imprimerie de J. Th. Hérissant, Imprimeur du Cabinet du Roi, 1770.

Henry, J.-F. "Une Mulatresse de pension à Nantes en 1777." *La Revue du Bas Poitou et des provinces de l'ouest* (May–June, 1972): 241–44.

Hoefer, Jean Chrétien Ferdinand, ed. *Nouvelle biographie générale.* Paris: F. Didot frères, 1870.

Howell, Thomas Bayly. *A Complete Collection of State Trials.* London: Hurst, Rees, Orme and Brown, 1814, vol. 20, col. 1–82 and 1369–1386.

Hufton, Olwen. *The Poor of Eighteenth-Century France.* Oxford: Clarendon Press, 1974.

————, and Frank Tallett. "Communities of Women, the Religious Life, and Public Services in Eighteenth-Century France." In *Connecting Spheres: Women in the Western World, 1500 to the Present,* ed. Marilyn J. Boxer and Jean H. Quaetaert. New York: Oxford Univ. Press, 1987.

Ingersoll, Thomas N. "Free Blacks in a Slave Society: New Orleans, 1718–1812." *William and Mary Quarterly* 3rd ser., 48, no. 2 (April 1991): 173–200.

Isambert, François André. *Recueil général des anciennes lois françaises depuis l'an 420 jusqu'à la révolution de 1789.* Paris: Belin-Leprieur, 1830.

Jameson, Russell Parsons. *Montesquieu et l'esclavage: étude sur les origines de l'opinion antiesclavagiste en France au XVIIIᵉ siècle.* Paris: Hachette et cie, 1911.

Joly de Fleury, [Jean Omer?], De la Roue, and [Bon Joseph Antoine?] Collet. *Mémoire signifié pour le nommé Francisque, Indien de Nation, Néophyte de l'Eglise Romaine, Intimé; contre le Sieur Allain-François-Ignace Brignon, se disant Ecuyer, Appellant.* Paris: P. G. Simon, Imprimeur du Parlement, 1759.

Jordon, Winthrop. "American Chiaro-scuro: The Status and Definition of Mulattoes in the British Colonies." In *Slavery in the New World: A Reader in Comparative History,* ed. Laura Foner and Eugene D. Genovese. Englewood Cliffs, N.J.: Prentice-Hall, 1969.

————. *White over Black: American Attitudes toward the Negro, 1550–1812.* Chapel Hill: Univ. of North Carolina Press, 1968.

Kaplan, Steven L. *Bread, Politics, and Political Economy in the Reign of Louis XV.* 2 vols. The Hague: Martinus Nijhoff, 1976.

Krakovitch, Odile. *Arrêts, déclarations, édits et ordonnances concernant les colonies, 1666–1779: Inventaire analytique de la série Colonies A.* Paris: Archives Nationales, 1993.

Labat, Jean Baptiste. *Nouveau voyage du père Labat en Amérique.* Paris: P. F. Giffart, 1722.

————. *Nouvelle relation de l'Afrique occidentale.* Paris, T. Le Gras, 1728.

————. *Voyage aux Iles de l'Amérique (Antilles), 1693–1705.* Ed. baniel Radford. Paris: Seghers, 1979.

Lebeau, Auguste. *De la condition des gens de couleur libres sous l'ancien régime.* Paris: Guillaumin, 1903.

Lemaire, André. *Les lois fondamentales de la monarchie française d'après les théoriciens de l'ancien régime.* Paris, 1907. Reprint. Geneva: Slatkine-Megariotis, 1975.

Loisel, Antoine. *Institutes coutumières.* Paris: Abel l'Angelier, 1608.

————. *Institutes coutumières* . . . Paris: Henry le Gras, 1657.

————. *Institutes coutumières* . . . Paris: Michel Bobin and Nicolas le Gras, 1665.

————. *Institutes coutumières* . . . Notes by Eusèbe de Laurière. 2 vols. Paris: Nicolas Gosselin, 1710.

Lovejoy, Paul E. *Transformations in Slavery: A History of Slavery in Africa.* African Studies Series, no. 36. Cambridge: Cambridge Univ. Press, 1983.

Loysel [sic], Antoine. *Institutes coutumières d'Antoine Loysel ou Manuel de plusieurs et diverses règles, sentences et proverbes, tant anciens que modernes du droit coutumier et plus ordinaire de la France,* new ed., ed. Dupin and Edouard Laboulaye. Paris: Durand, 1846.

Luchaire, Achille. *Louis VI, le gros: Annales de sa vie et son règne, 1081–1137.* Paris: A. Picard, 1890.

Mallet. *Mémoire pour Jean Boucaux, Nègre, Demandeur. Contre le Sieur Verdelin, Défendeur* [Paris]: L'Imprimerie de Claude Simon, Père, 1738.

Mathorez, J. *Les Etrangers en France sous l'Ancien Régime: Histoire de la formation de la population française.* Paris: E. Champion, 1919.

Maupertuis, Pierre-Louis Moreau de. *The Earthly Venus by Pierre-Louis Moreau de Maupertuis, Translated from Venus Physique.* Trans. Simone Brangier Boas. Introduced by George Boas. New York: Johnson Reprint Corporation, 1966.

Maza, Sara. *Servants and Masters in Eighteenth-Century France: The Uses of Loyalty.* Princeton: Princeton Univ. Press, 1983.

————. "Le Tribunal de la nation: Les mémoires judiciaires et l'opinion publique à la fin de l'ancien régime." *Annales: Economies, Sociétés, Civilisations* (January–February 1987): 73–90.

McCloy, Shelby T. *The Negro in France.* Lexington: Univ. of Kentucky Press, 1961.

Meyer, Jean. *Les Européens et les autres de Cortès à Washington.* Paris: A. Colin, 1975.

Michaud, Jean François. *Biographie universelle ancienne et moderne.* Paris, 1818. Reprint. Graz, Austria: Akademische Druck- u. Verlagsanstalt, 1968.

Michel, Jacques. *Du Paris de Louis XV à la marine de Louis XVI: L'Œuvre de Monsieur de Sartine. Vol. 1. La vie de la capitale. Vol. 2: La reconquête de la liberté des mers.* Paris: Les Editions de l'Erudite, 1983–84.

Molinier, A. *Inventaire sommaire de la collection Joly de Fleury.* Paris: Picard, 1881.

Montesquieu, Charles de Secondat, Baronde. *The Spirit of the Laws.* Trans. and ed. by Anne Cohler, Basia Carolyn Miller, and Harold Samuel Stone. Cambridge Texts in the History of Political Thought. Cambridge: Cambridge Univ. Press, 1989.

Moreau de Saint-Méry, Méderic Louis Elie. *Description topographique, physique, civile, politique, et historique de la partie française de l'isle Saint-Domingue.* New ed. Ed. Blanche Maurel and Etienne Taillemite. 3 vols. Paris: Société de l'Histoire des Colonies Françaises, 1958.

———, ed. *Loix et constitutions des colonies françoises de l'Amérique sous le vent.* 6 vols. Paris: chez l'auteur, 1784–1790.

Munford, Clarence J. *The Black Ordeal of Slavery and Slave Trading in the French West Indies, 1625–1715.* Lewiston: Edwin Mellen Press, 1991.

Nadelhaft, Jerome. "The Sommersett Case and Slavery: Myth, Reality, and Reprecussions." *Journal of Negro History* 51 (July 1966): 193–208.

"Nègre." In *Dictionnaire de l'Académie Française.* 5th ed. Paris, 1798–1799, vol. 2, p. 154.

Parain, Charles. *Outils, ethnies et développement historique.* Paris: Editions sociales, 1979.

Petit, Emilien. *Traité sur le gouvernement des esclaves.* 2 vols. Paris: Knapen, 1777.

Peytraud, Lucien. *L'Esclavage aux Antilles françaises avant 1789, d'après des documents inédits des archives coloniales.* Paris: Librairie Hachette, 1897.

Pluchon, Pierre. *Nègres et Juifs au XVIIIe siècle: Le racisme au siècle des lumières.* Paris: Tallandier, 1984.

Poncet de la Grave, Guillaume. *Considérations sur le célibat relativement à la politique, à la population, et aux bonnes mœurs.* Paris: Moutardier, An IX (1801).

———. *Défense des considérations sur le célibat . . . en réponse à la critique du célibataire anonyme, insérée dans le journal de Paris du 24 Brumaire, an 10, no. 54, pag. 320 et 321.* Paris: Moutardier, An X (1802).

Popkin, Richard H. "The Philosophical Basis of Eighteenth–Century Racism." *Studies in Eighteenth–Century Culture* 3 (1973): 245–62.

Prévost, Antoine François, ed. *Histoire générale des voyages.* 21 vols. Paris: Didot, 1746–1770.

Raynal, Guillaume Thomas. *Histoire philosophique et politique des établissemens et du commerce des Européens dans les deux Indes.* 5 vols. Geneva: J. L. Pellet, 1780.

Regnaud, Pierre Etienne. *La Journée du 10 Aoust 1792, avec des réflexions tant sur les événements qui l'ont immédiatement précédé et suivie, que sur la Révolution en général.* Paris: Crapart, 1795.

Richelet, Pierre. *Dictionnaire de la langue française, ancienne et moderne.* 3 vols. Lyon: chez les Bruyset, 1728.

Robin, C. C. *Voyage to Louisiana: An Abridged Translation.* Trans. Stuart O. Landry, Jr. New Orleans: Pelican, 1966.

Roche, Daniel. *The People of Paris: An Essay in Popular Culture in the Eighteenth Century.* Trans. Marie Evans in association with Gwynne Lewis. New York: Berg, 1987.

Rousseau, Jean-Jacques. *Discours sur l'origine et les fondements de l'inégalité parmi les hommes.* Introduced by F. C. Greene. Cambridge: Cambridge Univ. Press, 1941.

———. *On the Social Contract.* Trans. Judith R. Masters. Ed. Roger Masters. New York: St. Martin's Press, 1978.

Rudé, George. "Paris et Londres au XVIIIᵉ siècle: Société et conflits de classes." *Annales Historiques de la Révolution Française* (1973): 476–95.

Sala-Molins, Louis. *Le Code Noir, ou le calvaire de Canaan.* 2nd ed. Paris: Presses Universitaire de France, 1988.

Savary des Bruslons, Jacques. "Nègre." In *Dictionnaire universel de commerce: Contenant tout ce qui concerne le commerce qui se fait dans les quatre parties du monde.* Copenhagen: C. & A. Philibert, 1761, vol. 3, cols. 1095–97.

Seeber, Edward Derbyshire. *Anti-Slavery Opinion in France during the Second Half of the Eighteenth Century.* Johns Hopkins Univ. Press, 1937. Reprint. New York: Greenwood, 1969.

Shennan, J. H. *The Parlement of Paris.* Ithaca: Cornell Univ. Press, 1968.

Shiebinger, Londa. "The Anatomy of Difference: Race and Sex in Eighteenth-Century Science." *Eighteenth-Century Studies* 23 (Summer 1990): 387–405.

Shyllon, F. O. *Black People in Britain, 1555–1833.* London: Pluto Press, 1984.

———. *Black Slaves in Britain.* London: Institute for Race Relations, 1974.

Singham, Shanti Marie. "Betwixt Cattle and Men: Jews, Blacks, and Women and the *Declaration of the Rights of Man and Citizen,*" in *The Rights of Man: Its Origins.* Edited by Dale Van Kley. Palo Alto: Stanford Univ. Press, 1994.

———. "A Conspiracy of Twenty Million Frenchmen: Public Opinion, Patriotism, and the Assault on Absolutism during the Maupeou Years, 1770–1775." Ph.D. diss., Princeton Univ., 1991.

———. "Rehearsal for Revolution: Political Opposition in France during the Maupeou Years." Paper delivered at The Bunting Institute, Radcliffe College, March 17, 1993.

Stein, Robert Louis. *The French Slave Trade in the Eighteenth Century: An Old Regime Business.* Madison: Univ. of Wisconsin Press, 1979.

———. *The French Sugar Business in the Eighteenth Century.* Baton Rouge: Louisiana State Univ. Press, 1988.

Stone, Bailey. *The French Parlements and the Crisis of the Old Regime.* Chapel Hill: Univ. of North Carolina Press, 1986.

Trayer, Paul. *Etude historique de la condition légale des esclaves dans les colonies françaises.* Paris: Guillaumin, 1887.

Van Kley, Dale. *The Damiens Affair and the Unraveling of the Ancien Régime, 1750–1770.* Princeton: Princeton Univ. Press, 1984.

———. *The Jansenists and the Expulsion of the Jesuits from France, 1757–1765.* New Haven: Yale Univ. Press, 1975.

Verlinden, Charles. *L'esclavage dans l'Europe médiévale.* 2 vols. Brugge: De [Tempel, 1955.]

Vulson, . "Commentaire [...] dévolues en France de la succession à la couronne." *Mémoires de l'Académie des sciences, inscriptions, et belles lettres* 34 (1894): 125–[ ]8.

Voltaire, François Marie Arouet de. *Voltaire's Correspondence.* Ed. Theodore Besterman. Geneva: Institut et Musée Voltaire, 1953.

Le Voyageur à Paris. Paris, 1789. Reprint. Leuven, Belgium: Bernard Copens, 1989.

Walvin, James, *Black and White: The Negro and English Society: 1555–1945.* London: Allen Lane, The Penguin Press, 1973.

Watson, Alan. *Slave Law in the Americas.* Athens: Univ. of Georgia Press, 1989.

Wiecek, William. "Somerset: Lord Mansfield and the Legitimacy of Slavery in the Anglo-American World." *University of Chicago Law Review* 42 (Fall 1974): 86–146.

Williams, Alan. *The Police in Paris, 1718–1789.* Baton Rouge: Louisiana State Univ. Press, 1979.

Winks, Robin. *The Blacks in Canada: A History.* New Haven: Yale Univ. Press, 1971.

Zysberg, André. *Les Galériens: Vies et destins de 60,000 forçats sur les galères de France, 1680–1748.* Paris: Seuil, 1987.

Index

Abolitionism, 19, 101, 104, 105.
See also Antislavery sentiment
Admiralty, 58, 109; and enforcement
of Ordinance of February 23,
1778, 127; jurisdiction, 131; officers, 130; registration of blacks,
4, 52, 69, 74–75, 117, 118, 125;
registration of slaves, 17, 39, 50–
51, 54, 58, 72, 88; and struggle
with Lenoir, 123–124, 129–130,
132
Admiralty Court of France (Paris),
6–7; cases heard, 23, 25, 53–54,
58–59, 73, 91, 106–111, 114,
132, 134, 151n. 12; decisions, 36,
40, 51–52, 55, 103, 109, 110,
151n. 12; dismantling of, 138; enforcement of legislation, 23, 50–
51, 130–131; and Freedom Principle, 89; jurisdiction, 48–49, 156n.
21; and manumission, 52–53, 55,
91–92, 93, 115, 135; and
Maupeou, 9, 105, 178n. 1; registration of legislation, 115, 122.

See also Admiralty courts; Law-
suits for freedom
Admiralty courts, 5, 15; La
Rochelle, 98; Nantes, 15, 41, 44,
46–48
Admiralty Ordinance of April 5,
1762, 73, 79, 81, 82
Admiralty Ordinance of April 16,
1777, 118, 122–123
Admiralty Ordinance of July 7,
1777, 122–123
Affranchis, 14, 145n. 14. *See also*
Blacks
Affranchissement. See Manumission
Africa, 61–66
Aigullon, Duc d', 95
Amis des Noirs, 104, 109, 138
Anache, Marquis d' (slaveowner),
133
Anti-Semitism, 178n. 4, 179n. 24
Antislavery sentiment, 12, 29, 96–
97, 101–103, 109. *See also* Abo-
litionism
Apprenticeship, slaves', 82–83